OFFSTAGE AND BACKSTAGE

When they're away from the public, alone with their own private concerns—celebrated female performers face the same obstacles we all do.

Share with them their triumphs and heartbreaks, their fears and fantasies, the nightmarish storms they've endured, and the dreams they hold that carry them through it all.

Collected here for the first time is Alan Ebert's highly regarded series of celebrity interviews.

INTIMACIES

Stars Share Their Confidences and Feelings

Alan Ebert

A DELL BOOK

Published by
Dell Publishing Co., Inc.
1 Dag Hammarskjold Plaza
New York, New York 10017

The pieces with Lena Horne, Sarah Vaughan, Diahann
Carroll, Eartha Kitt, Leontyne Price, Labelle, Aretha
Franklin, Leslie Uggams, Diana Ross, Roberta Flack, Cleo
Laine, and Joyce Bryant first appeared in *Essence;* with
Dyan Cannon, Ann-Margret, Katharine Hepburn (Chap-
ter 7 in this book), Beverly Sills, Cloris Leachman, and
Jessica Lange in *Sunday Woman;* with Rosemary Clooney,
Faye Dunaway, and Carol Burnett in *Ladies' Home Jour-
nal;* with Elizabeth Taylor, Goldie Hawn, Loretta Lynn,
Ann Landers, and Brooke Shields in *Us;* with Joanne
Woodward in *Good Housekeeping;* with Cindy Williams
in *New Dawn;* and with Nancy Walker in *Family Circle.*

Dell ® TM 681510, Dell Publishing Co., Inc.

ISBN: 0-440-13653-9

Printed in the United States of America
First printing—December 1980

For my mother, who believed in dreams,
For my father, whose reality made dreaming possible,
And Lou Anzolut, who helped me achieve them.

CONTENTS

INTIMACIES

Stars Share Their Confidences and Feelings

INTRODUCTION

So what's Elizabeth Taylor *really* like?

When I returned from my day's journey to Washington, D.C., to interview Mrs. John Warner, that question followed me around town for several months. It amazes me how people are always hungry for any detail about the stars I write about. It also amazed me that many who asked the question were not necessarily as interested in an answer as in giving their own interpretation of the superstar's psyche. What people think Elizabeth Taylor is *really* like is an article—no, a book!—in itself.

The funniest question ever asked of me, though it was asked in all seriousness, was "Is that really Barbra Streisand's nose or a prop from wardrobe?"

It seems we all have a preoccupation with "the stars." I leave the whys to the psychologists among us. I myself am motivated in my work to discover . . . what So-and-So is *really* like. I go for the core rather than the throat of a person. It is no longer surprising to me when I discover that So-and-So, who has been elevated to superhuman and mythical proportions by the press and public, has feelings similar to my own and to most everybody's.

My work as a celebrity profiler is an outgrowth of many years of work in the entertainment industry. When I was in college, nepotism gained me nightclub reviewer status for a small but influential New York entertainment guide. For many years I saw the best— from Garland and Sinatra to Sammy and Streisand.

Later, full-time employment would take me from a short "season" at CBS to a long run at NBC. At the **television networks my knowledge of the entertain**ment industry was increased. On my days off I would train out to the Brooklyn color studio to watch Perry Como rehearse or Bell Telephone put together its hour-long show. I watched performers behind the scenes, learned of temperament and talent—frequently one package.

My four years in public relations, eventually as an executive vice-president, I consider to be my postgraduate work in show business. Press agents are the unsung heros—the behind-the-scenes adventurers—in the entertainment industry. They, probably more so than anyone else, know, *really know*, what So-and-So is *really* like. Among the so-and-sos I represented were Rod Steiger, Anthony Quinn, Julie Andrews, Carol Burnett, Dyan Cannon, Ann-Margret, Godfrey Cambridge, David Niven, Lana Turner, Dick Chamberlain, Lee Remick, and . . . Anita Bryant. It was Lana—or "L.T." as Miss T. refers to her professional self—who unwittingly motivated my career change.

Lana had come to New York to star in *Forty Carats*. My West Coast office called Lana "madam" in deference to her stature. They had flown me to L.A. to meet "madam" in the hopes that "madam" would approve of me and not make too many waves when in New York. "Madam" arrived late to the Polo Lounge. Her "star" entrance earned the oohs and aahs she desired. When she seated herself, I caught her eye and saw to my delight a twinkle. That's right! A twinkle. A goddamn merry ole twinkle that was making very definite announcements *if* you were listening.

"Madam" came to New York and not a wave did she make because to me she was Lana, period. And if you want to know what L.T. is *really* like, I can tell you. She's terrific! She's a funny, ballsy, savvy, witty lady who responds to strength and honesty.

The Lana I came to know, and love, was not the

Lana the press lionized. When writing of her, even after protracted interviews, they wrote of the myth, the legend, the Oracle of Culver City. Nowhere did the woman's humor and humanness emerge. Not one writer came close to telling what Lana Turner was really like. And you know why? They didn't care. They were buying and then selling the image and not the person.

When I decided to leave public relations, part of my reason was about writing. I felt if I were profiling Lana Turner, I could do a helluva lot better than those who had previously tried. Alas, eight years have passed since the day I closed the door on one career and walked hesitantly through the doors of another, and I've yet to write one word about Lana. Perhaps it's just as well. Perhaps after saying how much I really like the lady, I've said it all.

My second career has been a second chance . . . a second life. And what a life! In the past years I have been privileged not only to have entered the homes of the famous, but their lives. They have allowed me to share their experiences and their feelings. In listening to and evaluating their thoughts and opinions, I have defined mine. In probing their emotions, I have felt my own. In truth, I have had an experience few in this world have realized. And I've loved it. My work is my fun . . . my pleasure.

From the beginning I have held certain attitudes about my work. First I believe a writer is secondary to the subject. Too often writers make themselves the foreground rather than the background of an article. They emerge as the "star." It's a valid technique for attaining a "stardom" of sorts, but it is invalid, in my opinion, as a professional procedure. The public is interested in the star—not the writer. So stand clear, writer, and let the personality speak.

I also believe the public is entitled to as much of the personality as the personality will share. I resist the so-called "sharply angled feature" that concentrates on one particular aspect of a person's life. It's the whole person who interests me: the sum of the parts and not the parts in themselves. But mainly what I care about is the *person*, and that to me means the intellect and the feelings. Although I have studied all aspects of the entertainment industry, I am not interested in writing about "technique"—be it on stage or on film or television.

It wasn't until I started writing for *Essence* magazine that what I wanted to do as a celebrity profiler, and what the publisher allowed, coalesced.

Marcia Ann Gillespie, then editor-in-chief of *Essence* magazine, not only understood my professional needs but saw, rightfully, that they were the needs of her readers. She felt the black women who read *Essence* needed to know about black celebrities as *people*. It was Marcia, endorsed by *Essence* publisher Ed Lewis, who cared enough to allow me to ask such a simple question of not-so-simple celebrities: "How do you feel?" The answers were often painful and always honest. And *Essence* readers reacted. I know because I saw the mail. What was so wonderful was that as people learned about Lena and Aretha, they learned about themselves. They drew comparisons and saw . . . felt . . . a common bond . . . a common reality.

Eventually my work for *Essence* brought me to other major magazines—most notably *Ladies' Home Journal.* It was Mary Fiore's faith (she was then *LHJ*'s articles editor and is now *Good Housekeeping*'s managing editor) in my ability to bring Rosemary Clooney's story into focus on paper that moved my career to higher ground (financially, that is). To this day I consider the Clooney piece, of which I will speak more later, to be the most significant contribution I have made to magazines. It reached and touched millions, which had more to do with Rosemary's honesty than with my talents.

The Clooney article and Mary Fiore opened the door to a series of most gratifying articles for *LHJ* and Dick Kaplan, then the magazine's executive director and till recently the editor-in-chief of *Sunday Woman*. The Faye Dunaway feature—again one of my favorites—speaks to many issues confronting the modern woman. Dick Kaplan stayed with me all the way on that piece. "All the way" refers to the many months before I could "nail" Dunaway to a time and place. At his *Sunday Woman*, Kaplan has provided me with an outlet similar to *Essence*. I'm proud of my Ann-Margret, Dyan Cannon, and Cloris Leachman features for *SW*. The women are real. It was Kaplan, reacting to Leachman's reality, who suggested this book be done. Sooo, depending on your point of view, send letters of commendation or castigation directly to him. Ditto, Peter Travers, formerly of *Us* magazine, who has always been both supportive of and understanding about my work. My Elizabeth Taylor feature for Peter remains among my favorites. Peter never dictates what he wants from an interview but tells his writers—or this one anyway: go out and do your thing.

My "thing" has been strongly influenced by many. In growing up, I teethed on profiles by Richard Gehman and Bill Davidson. But the greatest influence in my professional writing life has been Rex Reed from the days when he was turning out Rembrandt/Van Gogh-like portraits of such stars as Bette Davis, Ava Gardner, and Marlene Dietrich. They were so brilliant, so vividly drawn, that I can still remember chunks of them these many years later. To me, Rex Reed legitimized the celebrity profile . . . made it an art. His subjects all emerged as people rather than legends or myths.

Writers are my true heroes. I think Joan Barthel is brilliant. Ditto, Tommy Thompson. Guy Flatley, Judy Klemensrud, and Claire Safran are only terrific. Aljean Harmetz is super, as is Barbara G. Harrison.

Not all of our current crop of celebrity profilers are good or responsible. One of our best known boasts to me frequently of the sexual gymnastics in which he engages with most of the women he interviews. I hope he is better in the sack than he is on paper.

I do not subscribe to the theory held by some that all interviews are like a game of sexual tennis. For me, when sex enters the interviewing arena, confidentiality—the ability to express oneself freely and honestly—exits. That does not mean one is oblivious to the attraction one feels when in the company of gorgeous people. It's pretty difficult to sit opposite a Diana Ross or a Peter Frampton, a Warren Beatty or a Dyan Cannon, and not be aware of that person's attractiveness and sexual appeal. But to act on that awareness is, I believe, a foolproof way of destroying the intimacy so necessary to a successful interview.

People have often asked me: how did you ever get So-and-So to say such-a-thing? I'm never certain. I research all my interviews. I prepare myriad questions. But once in the room with the subject I strive to hold a conversation rather than an interview. And that means . . . give-and-take. Although I try to stay out of the article itself, within the interview process I'm all there—body and soul and pencil. I also listen to what's said and . . . to what isn't. Often the latter is even more interesting (and revealing) than the former. And I never stop observing the face and body language of the subject. I also react to what's said. To keep it at a conversational level, if I think something is off the wall, I'll say it. I'll never challenge a person's feelings but I'll react to them visibly and vocally.

So much for "technique." Onto sexual preference.

I do prefer to interview women and my best work, with exceptions, is about women. The reason for this is fairly obvious to me. I work mainly on a feeling level and most men are threatened by this process. Men do not like to admit to, let alone share their feelings, particularly with another man. Competition—the "macho factor"—interferes. There is much posturing . . . strutting and vying for position when two men meet in an interview process. The exceptions are rare. In my career I would say only the late Godfrey Cambridge, Paul Winfield, and Richard Pryor were "open"—actually near naked. Warren Beatty tried to be, but Warren, one of the brightest persons I've ever worked with, keeps a stranglehold on his feelings. As does Roy Scheider. Men don't let down generally, and when they do, they are more comfortable doing it with a woman.

Talking about "letting down" and "letting go" or "letting it all hang out" brings to mind certain women who did all three. No one turned my head around faster than Lena Horne. It was early in my career as a writer that Lena stood in my living room, shaking her finger at me and saying clearly—loudly— that I, as a white man, was the "enemy" and that I, as a white man, no matter how long or loud I ran-that-rap about how all persons' feelings on the deepest level are the same, would never but ever understand *on a feeling level* what it means to be black in America. She was right, of course. I didn't want to know that then but that afternoon Lena gave me a long, hard look at reality for blacks in America. Her rage was forty years thick. I listened. I observed. I felt her.

These many years later I still feel a special attachment to Lena. I remember that when our series of interviews ended, it was difficult for me to leave. I felt "bonded" to her. I had come to love her. I still do. And I'm still grateful to her for turning my head around and putting me in the right direction.

Funny, but it wasn't until I began compiling this book that I reread previous articles and certain dangling "thoughts" fell into place. Shortly after reliving my experience with Lena, I turned my attention to Aretha Franklin. Talk about opposites. Lena put it all out front. Aretha, also in my living room, sat like the Sphinx. I never understood my discomfort with

Aretha until rereading my own article. There, on paper, is her sister, Carolyn, stating: "she (Aretha) had a way of beng angry that was terrifying." Then the dots connected. It was Aretha's unspoken rage, bottled and distilled, that made our interview difficult. It took the surrounding members of her family to bring the piece to life. I'm very proud of the Aretha Franklin piece because it proves a successful profile can be written about a personality without the personality's total cooperation.

As previously mentioned there is no article of which I'm prouder than the Rosemary Clooney feature. And it happened by chance, or fate. Since I enjoy Merv Griffin immensely as an interviewer, I tend when home to watch his show more than network offerings. One particular evening he was doing a Griffin rarity: a show with talent but without audience. Rosie, who had done a disappearing act from the business, was a guest. She sang "I Won't Last a Day Without You" and she made me listen. I grew up listening to Rosie Clooney. But she was never like this. From the way she approached the lyric, the way she presented the music, I *felt* Rosie had been through changes. In short: she was wonderful.

Since there was no "panel" that night, the only conversation between Rosie and Griffin consisted of Merv saying: "You've had some bad years, haven't you?" and Rosie responding: "Rotten, really rotten." End of Clooney segment. Fade to Ronzoni commercial.

Through another assignment (a tribute to Duke Ellington) shortly thereafter, I was speaking on the phone with Rosie and boldly asking her about her "rotten years." She said simply, "I had a breakdown," which is exactly what I had intuited. I asked what kind and she again responded evenly and honestly, "a psychotic episode." I asked if she would be willing to talk about it for print, and a few days later, after "thinking about it," she decided she would.

Two months later I was sitting with Rosie in her kitchen. Her story began at 10:00 A.M. and concluded somewhere near 3:00 P.M. Never before have I felt such terror . . . anguish . . . horror. At several points I wanted to say: "Stop!" I distinctly remember wanting to run out of that house. Yet I was riveted to the story-telling. And just when it looked like we had reached an ending, the phone rang announcing death had claimed the very person Rosemary had just been talking about: her father.

I remember Rosie's grief and I remember holding her as she poured it out. I remember the closeness between us. I remember Rosie. I have not seen her since—although we have corresponded—but to this minute the feelings I felt for Rosie—of caring and love—remain. Never before in an interview, and not since, have I ever felt so close to a subject. It's good to see Rosie's life and career chugging right along these days. She deserves the best.

The same is true of Dyan Cannon. She deserves the best. If there is anyone who ever worked at her life— personally and professionally—it's Dyan. What an amazing, courageous woman! But don't ever get on a volleyball court with her. She's a killer. My favorite Cannon caper took place a few years ago on a Sunday outside her back door on the Malibu beach. Dyan had assembled an all-star volleyball game. Her team, mainly composed of women, were losing. Until at a pivotal point in the game, Dyan flashed. That's right, flashed! She lifted her skirt and gave her all to the game. It totally wrecked the opposition, which included me. We were never able to reassemble after that. We lost the game. Our team, instead of keeping their eyes on the ball, focused on Dyan, hoping for an instant replay. This is Dyan Cannon. If she can't win at life in one way, she'll find another.

When you talk to Ann-Margret, you hold her feelings in your hand the way you would a baby bird. This has always been such a lovely, delicate lady.

There are certain people you meet who are just genuinely nice, good people. That's Ann-Margret. She,
too, by necessity, has had to work at her life. The
results of her work are obvious.

Ditto, Diahann Carroll. Underneath that gorgeous,
glamorous exterior is one of the most endearing,
funny, and totally terrific persons I've ever met. And
we almost missed one another. At the time I was as-
signed to the Carroll article, she was controversial.
She had been shunning the press and was generally
unavailable and uncooperative. Then the call came
from her West Coast office saying she would see me
after all. The next day I was L.A. bound and that
same night I was informed Ms. Carroll had changed
her mind. Her press agent, then Lee Solters, one of
the industry's most professional and savvy PR men,
worked his magic and managed to change Diahann's
mind again. I not only gained an interview because
of Lee, but a friend.

Friend . . . the word brings to mind Carol Burnett, whom I have known since way back in 1961. I
was enamored of Carol. Actually I had this terrific
crush on her. Somehow I managed to persuade her to
have dinner with me one night. In the middle of it
Carol looked me square in the eye and said: "Now I
want you to realize this is *not* a date. This is strictly
two friends having dinner." I've been meaning to
speak to Carol about that ever since. Talk about rejection!

There is this "myth" about Carol in the magazine
industry—that she is bland, uninteresting, bordering
on dull. Forget it! Carol, perhaps more so than any
other person I have met in the entertainment industry, understands fame, the public, and "the business."
Having been burnt, she plays the game by her rules.
Someday, if she chooses, Carol will write a book that
will reveal just how *un*bland and *non*dull she is.

No one ever quite so tried my patience as much as
Faye Dunaway. Was she worth the endless procras-

tination and postponements? You better believe it! When her guard is down, Faye Dunaway is gorgeous. **Just gorgeous. Unfortunately her guard is not down** often and when it is, it tends to reescalate almost immediately. But Faye is a bona fide beauty. In all ways! To many she seems tough, callous, even mean. I don't believe she is any of those things. At her worst I think Faye is mainly scared. At her best she is bright, caring, and utterly feminine. I was quite smitten with Dunaway. I'm still quite smitten with her.

As I was with Elizabeth Taylor, only I didn't feel "romantic" toward Elizabeth, just amused and delighted. What a no-nonsense lady! Ask her a question and the answer is right there. Out front and unpremeditated. Elizabeth Taylor made me laugh. Repeatedly. Whoever thinks of gorgeous Liz as being funny? But she is. The interview began with Liz there but not there. After a few thousand interviews this is understandable. The questions must all seem alike to her at this point. It was one of my "on" days. My questions were different. I knew I had Elizabeth when she looked up and out of her doldrums to evaluate this "person-with-paper-and-pencil" sitting opposite her. She gave me but one hour and one hour-to-the-dot only. But what an hour! What's Elizabeth Taylor *really* like? I don't know, but I think, based on my article for *Us*, that I'm on the way to finding out.

This book was made possible by the Elizabeth Taylors and Katharine Hepburns who gave so much of themselves to me and thus to readers everywhere. Each woman in this book has special meaning for me. Each has touched my life in a very special way. I thank them for that.

CHAPTER ONE

ROSEMARY CLOONEY

"Come on-a my house," she sang, promising "to give-a you candy. Come on-a my house, my house. I'm-a gonna give you everything."

From appearances it had seemed Rosemary Clooney could give everything because she was the girl who had it all to give. Young, pretty in a blond, blue-eyed, all-American fashion, she emerged from obscurity to become one of the most popular singers of the 1950's; a Cinderella at the ball, marrying her prince, José Ferrer, and producing five children in yearly succession during their eleven-year marriage. She was the star of such motion pictures as *White Christmas* and *Here Come the Girls* and as recently as 1958 the hostess of her own network television show.

Ten years later, in 1968, a hallucinating Rosemary Clooney pounded at the walls of her cell in isolation in the psychiatric ward of St. John's Hospital in Los Angeles. "Be a good girl, Rosemary," intoned the nurses in voices reminiscent of the past. She hated those voices. She didn't want to be a good girl. "I'm tired of being a good girl," she would scream. "Rosemary, don't excite yourself, dear," the voices-in-white would cajole. But Rosemary was excited because she *knew* it was a "plot"; knew she must escape; knew she must fix it for Rosemary just as she had always fixed it for Rosemary since childhood.

*   *   *

Lay people would define Rosemary Clooney's illness as a nervous breakdown. According to psychiatrist Dr. J. Victor Monke, who treated Rosemary for six years, she had suffered a "psychotic reaction with severe depressive and paranoid features. Her symptoms included hallucinations, fear, depression, violently aggressive behavior, and an inability to distinguish between the real and the unreal."

The question becomes, how does an attractive and an accomplished young woman who promises to give the world candy become a psychotic? And how does that same woman fight her way back from what most would call insanity but which doctors refer to as "psychic illness" or "emotional decompensation" to a productive, meaningful life?

Rosemary Clooney and clan live in a big, rambling house which despite its plush Beverly Hills surroundings, spacious grounds, and swimming pool, is near shabby in its need for renovations. Its owner seemingly could not care less. Her home rocks with the clatter and clutter of young people—her children, Miguel, Maria, Gabriel, Monsita, and Rafael Ferrer—ages nineteen through fourteen—their friends, her friends, and four dogs. The house, in the words of Miguel, has "good vibes." So does its mistress.

Although still needing to lose twenty of the eighty pounds she gained during her ordeal, at forty-six Rosemary Clooney is beautiful. There is a softness to her once angular face, a repose that shines from her clear blue eyes. She wears no hint of the tragic. She neither pities herself nor seeks the pity of others for what was. On the contrary. In her analysis she opened the closet doors of her inner self, searched their recesses, rattled the skeletons of times past but still living in the present, and then, after facing the terror and the pain, closed the doors firmly and forever. She knows mental illness can be cured and that is why she wishes to share her experience.

"Many people live in mental anguish but refuse to seek help because of the stigma attached," says Rosemary. "People shouldn't and needn't be alone in their pain. They can be helped. Perhaps my speaking of my experience can help them."

Sitting in a straight-backed chair, a diet un-cola grasped in her hand, Rosemary Clooney plunges into 1968 and the events that led to her insanity. She was "running, forever running without knowing why," she remembers. February found her performing throughout the Far East and "the constantly changing cultures confused me. I never seemed to catch up with myself." At Clark Air Force Base she visited GIs in the hospital. Always "the strong one," she "smiled pretty" for the quadruple amputees and the faceless, "wanting to scream, to cry, but unable to do anything other than what I knew to do—sing." She was working first in Germany and then England when Martin Luther King was assassinated. She took his death and the European anti-American sentiment "as a personal attack. I broke down and cried on a British TV talk show when a heated discussion of the assassination took place. That was my warning signal, but instead of listening I ran to Brazil to still more work." Surrounded by beauty, she was in "constant ecstasy." Weeks later it was "constant fear as I cowered in the corner of my New York hotel room unable to crawl off the floor and into the world outside."

So she would honor her performing contracts in Canada, her lawyer flew in from L.A. to personally board her on a chartered plane. "Just tired," she explained. "Just tired," he agreed, both needing to believe the lie.

For her fortieth birthday May 23, Rosemary gathered together "all the important people in my life. I know now I wanted a present from them, the words: 'Don't work so hard, Rosie. We'll love you whether you sing or not.'" But the words were never spoken, so she ran next to Hawaii, performing en route at a Robert F. Kennedy-for-president rally in Oakland. Upon her return from the islands she flew to San Diego for yet another rally for the man who was her friend and whom she believed would be "the salvation of both this country and myself." She flew back to L.A. with the Kennedys in their private plane, forgetting she had left a closetful of clothes in her San Diego hotel room. The following evening, "bursting with excitement," she attended the final RFK rally at the Ambassador Hotel. She heard Kennedy's speech, heard the applause, but did not hear the shot. "Just the screams. I kept telling myself nothing was wrong." The sight of a woman covered with blood convinced her otherwise. "I began babbling, clutching at my rosary, and was pushed into the street just as Bobby's body was placed in an ambulance. Somehow, I found myself early that morning in church, bargaining that if He spared Bobby, I'd return to Catholicism. I left convinced I had been heard."

RFK died June 5, and on that day Rosemary Clooney's hallucinations began. She rejected the idea of Kennedy's death, telling people it was "a plot to scare us all." Concerned friends brought her to both a hospital and a psychiatrist. The first she talked her way out of; the second she talked into prescribing sleeping pills, using the lack of sleep to explain her overwrought state.

An engagement in Reno followed, and during its rehearsals singer Jerry Vale produced an issue of *Life* magazine with RFK on the cover, his death very evident. Rosemary looked and whooped, "Isn't that a joke!" When no one laughed, "I *knew* the plot was even wider spread than I had thought. I even refused to speak in my dressing room, convinced it was bugged and that 'they' were listening to my every word."

Her performances became as erratic as her thinking. Frequently she would swear at her audiences or walk offstage in the middle of her act. "Both were cries for help," she explains. " 'Love me! Help me! Love me! Help me!' I was really screaming and when no one heard, I decided to punish people by announcing my retirement." At a press conference she explained, "I don't want to sing for people who kill."

In what was to be her last performance, Rosemary belligerently told her audience, "You can't imagine the price I've paid to be here to sing a bunch of dumb songs for you." The declaration brought an alarmed nightclub owner to her dressing room with a doctor who had been in the audience. Smelling the alcohol on the doctor's breath, Rosemary panicked. "He's part of the plot. He's going to put me away." Screaming, she fled from the room, running up the down escalator to the street, where a cab took her to her nearby motel where during the course of the night she demolished the room. At dawn, "convinced no harm could come to me," she raced her car up a curving mountain highway, speeding continuously on the wrong side of the road, until she reached her apartment in Lake Tahoe. There, doctors who had been alerted to her condition had her forcibly restrained and taken by ambulance to the local hospital. Crying of "the plot," she threw personal belongings from the ambulance "in order to leave a trail so I might be rescued." When tranquilizers failed to calm her and she became increasingly violent, she was flown from Tahoe by ambulance plane to the cell in isolation in St. John's Hospital. Within days, by using the cunning many of the mentally ill possess, she talked her way out of St. John's. Weeks later, when her hallucinations increased and "the plot thickened," Rosemary sensed this was the one time she could not "fix it" for herself. She allowed that part of her that was still rational to hear her priest when he said, "Rosemary, God wants you to go for help," and checked herself into the psychiatric division of Mt. Sinai Hospital, where Dr. J. Victor Monke was director of Inpatient Services.

It has taken Rosemary more than an hour to detail 1968. She looks relieved. "Hey!" she says in greeting to a suddenly appearing Miguel. "Guess what? I just ran down *that year* for the first time."

"How about that! How'd it go?" her nineteen-year-old responds.

"Okay," she beams.

Miguel, it is learned, was with her in Reno and Tahoe. He remembers his mother as "uncontrollable, crazy. Once, she told a cabdriver she had a gun and would kill him. When I started to cry, she shoved her rosary in my hands and told me to pray for him." Miguel shakes his head at that and other memories, which he says "made it impossible for me to relate to my mother for several years. I was afraid she'd freak out again. Even after she was obviously okay, I didn't want to forgive her."

For the first time the former pain of Rosemary's life is etched clearly on her face. "It was very hard on him," she says softly, understating what must have been agony. "It took us many years to achieve our current relationship. And without therapy I don't know where we or I would be. If anyplace."

Dr. Monke describes Rosemary when he first attended her at Mt. Sinai as "elusive, evasive, distrustful, and totally undone by what she felt were the inexplicable things that had happened to her. Before any therapy could be given, her sense of safety had to be restored. Medication gave her much needed rest and as her anxiety lessened, her hallucinations stopped, which made contact possible. Then, she could begin to examine the causes of her psychotic episode."

Why 1968 was the year in which Rosemary was to break down is attributed by Dr. Monke to "her turning forty and the onset of menopause, facts of life which unconsciously disturbed her. Additionally, she had unconscious feelings of dependency on others which were unacceptable to her, as neither her mothering nor her fathering experiences had been fulfilling. By necessity Rosemary had learned to be a self-made, stand-on-my-own-two-feet person. To do so her personality structure had developed with considerable rigidity. As an adult Rosemary was inflexible and without any acceptance of her inner self and her conflicting emotional needs. Because she had never learned honest, open exchanges between people were possible, she talked to few people. Because she had never learned all human feelings are acceptable, she censored those which she thought made her 'bad.' In 1968 everything that had been seething, repressed, exploded."

At Mt. Sinai, Rosemary learned to feel "freely." She was "touched" when Bing Crosby wrote her from Europe offering his prayers and his love. She wept when Bob Hope, one of few to know the true facts of her illness, sent a huge basket of flowers with a card that simply read, "Hope it's a boy. Love, Bob." But it was the therapeutic community that truly reached her. Although only there twenty days she thinks of it as a lifetime, but not unhappily so. As part of the treatment she shared a room with three others and such "household" responsibilities as making beds and scrubbing floors—anything that would make the patient function. In group discussions, although she was mainly an observer, when she did speak, "They listened. To me! Other than when I was singing, no one had *ever* listened to me before. And they made me laugh—at them, at the world, at me. When I could do that, laugh at crazy ole Rosemary, I was ready to deal with reality."

Reality confronted her upon her discharge. Her mother, by necessity, was running her household while Rosemary had been in the hospital. Upon her return, Rosemary found, "My mother tried to give me emotional support but couldn't. She never understood I was getting better. She had so taken over the running of my life that any strength I showed threatened her. She resented it; felt I was replacing her. And this was in my own home."

In speaking of her mother in her thrice-a-week sessions with Dr. Monke, Rosemary mainly remembered her *in absentia*. Married unhappily to an alcoholic, she would often deposit Rosemary and her baby sister, Betty, with relatives and disappear, telling her eldest, "Take care of yourself and Betty. You can do it. You're the strong one. You can fix things for yourself." Rosemary's way to "fix things" was to do exactly what her cousins did whether she wished to or not. "Be a good girl, Rosemary," she was told. And she was, for in "being good" she found acceptance and safety. She never made trouble and remained to herself throughout her adolescence, having but one date in high school.

When Rosemary was thirteen, her mother remarried. "She wanted to be with her new husband so she sent Betty and I to live with our father, a man we barely knew and whom my mother had depicted as not worth knowing." Three years later he abandoned the girls in Cincinnati. When down to their last twenty cents, they used ten of it to bus to station WLW, where they auditioned for a local radio show. Hired at twenty dollars a week, one dollar was paid in advance so that the Clooney Sisters, as they were billed, could eat.

"I never thought about being lonely as a child," says Rosemary. "Just scared. Somehow I thought people kept leaving me because I wasn't worth having around. I always felt inadequate, stupid, that I had nothing of interest to say. I didn't think much of myself so I didn't think I deserved very much."

These, she discovered, were the attitudes she brought to her marriage. When she met José Ferrer, she was twenty-two and he was "everything I admired. He was brilliant and sophisticated." They were married in 1953 and divorced in '64. That the marriage lasted eleven years she now thinks a miracle. "I role-played throughout, became the woman I thought would please Joe. I placed his life and his career before mine. Not because he asked me to but because I insisted. After all, he was everything and what was I? Nothing!"

After the birth of her third child, Rosemary began taking pills, mainly Seconal but also tranquilizers. Her "storybook marriage" was disintegrating. There was no communication. Fights were left unresolved. She withdrew gradually into drugs because they were "a lovely escape and gave me a delicious sense of well-being." The cause of the marriage's death is best described in one anecdote. Ferrer, alarmed by Rosemary's increasing usage of pills, told his lawyer who told her lawyer who told her manager who told her doctor who told Rosemary who thought, "How foolish. Why doesn't Joe talk to me?"

When the marriage ended, Rosemary felt "an enormous sense of failure" and in listening to her today, she still assumes the bulk of the responsibility. If she bears any animosity toward Ferrer, if she for one moment believes he may have contributed to a faulty marriage, she keeps it well hidden. It is likely she does so for the children. She is seemingly determined not to turn them against their father as her mother turned her against her own.

The telephone intercom buzzes. Miguel needs to see his mother. She excuses herself and when she returns, she has "fixed it" for one of Miguel's friends: arranged a doctor's appointment so the boy may be treated for gonorrhea, something he most insistently does not want his Hollywood-pure-of-image parents to know. Miguel pops in to thank her. Between them is an ease usually associated with friends rather than

mother-son relationships. Miguel credits it to Rosemary's therapy. "She learned to speak *to* and not *at*
us."

"It began when I told the kids, 'Look, I've got this
problem. I'm getting help but I need yours, too,'"
says Rosemary.

"It took us kids a while to adjust to Mom's
changes; to the person she insisted on being treated
as, rather than the mother we would have her be,"
says Miguel.

"There were times when I hated the role of
'Mama,'" says Rosemary, "but I couldn't admit that
to myself. Today, on those mornings when I wake up
and realize I don't feel like being 'Mama,' I yell down
the hall, 'Hey kids! Your ma is checking out and
Rosemary is checking in and she expects to be treated
like a guest.' I've learned it's okay to be a person first."

"Funny," says Miguel with a smile. "One year your
mother's a nut and the next she is one hellavan understanding chick. I hope the guy she is dating now
realizes how lucky he is. My mother *has* to be the
straightest, and believe it—the most together person I
know."

The "guy" is Dante DiPaulo, whom she first met
and dated when both worked at Paramount Pictures
twenty-one years ago. "He was my belated high school
beau. We had such young, good times. But I was engaged to Joe, who was my fantasy and who meant
safety, and nothing could change that." DiPaulo reen-
tered her life while both waited for a traffic light to
change from red to green. "Hey, Rosella!" she heard
yelled from the car next to her, "and since no one but
Dante had ever called me by that name, I knew it
was him." The relationship is as it was: "We have
fun but marriage is not of interest to me. I'm a lady
without that need today."

For Rosemary to be open to a male-female relationship two things had to happen: her ego increase and
her weight decrease. She had ballooned to a near two

hundred pounds upon returning to work one month after her discharge from Mt. Sinai. "I really didn't want to perform. Neither my heart nor my voice were in it. But I needed the money. I solved my conflict by eating. I literally ate my way out of show business and into the retirement I had previously announced. I also retired into that fat person. She was safe. She didn't have to compete—either as a performer or as a woman. I just turned myself off."

The six-year job of turning herself back on followed. She grew from "a woman of little self-esteem, of little understanding and acceptance of her self and her feelings," as diagnosed by Dr. Monke, to where he now describes Rosemary as "a functioning human being who has made significant changes in her character structure. Her cruel inner critic of many of her feelings has been replaced by an understanding, accepting, and caring sense of self-esteem. She can now share her warmth with others. Thus, she was terminated from individual work in psychotherapy in January 1974."

There was no magical, overnight cure. Initially Rosemary felt "nothing was happening." But as she "talked and talked" in the therapeutic process with Dr. Monke, she began "listening to my own words and hearing the distortions about myself and my capabilities." She questioned their derivation and as she probed, she discovered why and how she had come to a 1968—had broken down into assorted and unrecognizable pieces. In doing so she was then able to pick up the pieces of herself and her life and place them together firmly in their proper perspective.

Her emotional pain was intense. "You sometimes think you will never stop crying, that there will always be pain. But it goes and in its place comes growth, strength, a you who finds she is not about to fall apart but is able to deal with most anything."

In dealing with "most anything," Rosemary saw how her needs for recognition and approval were her

motivating forces in becoming the public Rosemary
Clooney. "The only times I can remember my parents
looking at me was when they would ask me to sing.
Immediately afterward I'd be dismissed, ignored. My
mother never gave me any attention. My father
. . . he was a stranger, some man who floated into
my life occasionally. If you've never had attention,
applause can be a wonderful substitute. Except there
is never enough applause. Never! The public could
never give me enough love. My whole worth was
wrapped up in some dumb hit record."

She pauses, near tears, anger flashing across her
face. "How hurt that little girl was," she says, speaking of herself. "But she couldn't cry out, couldn't
express what she felt. Instead, she bottled it within."
Her voice breaks and tears gather like storm clouds in
her eyes. And when it rains, it pours. "How dare they
have asked me to sing and then pushed me off as
though I was nothing! How dare they have ignored
me as though I were something to be ashamed of! I
was a child with *more* than a voice. I had feelings. I
needed to be touched, to be spoken to, and to be
heard."

During her analysis Dr. Monke introduced Rosemary to group therapy "in the hope that the group
setting, actually a re-creation of family, would teach
Rosemary to be free with her feelings before others."
When three sessions elapsed during which she remained silent, "terrified of unzipping myself before
strangers," Dr. Monke asked her "if you would like to
tell the group about 1968?" She would not like. She
refused. How dare he ask her to . . . "Sing, Rosemary!"

Eventually Rosemary told her group about her
breakdown. "No one laughed. A few did cry. My pain
was understood because each person there was learning to deal with his or her own."

One in particular helped Rosemary find another
piece to her puzzle. When Rosemary explained how

she never looked directly at her audiences when she sang, but over their heads, she was asked, "Why? Who are you afraid won't be there?"

The answer was the person who was never there—her mother—and when she could admit it, "I sobbed uncontrollably. It was so painful to admit how much I had wanted my mother to love me, so painful to feel how much her love, and her not loving, had meant to that little girl who had been such a 'good little girl' in the hopes her mama would love her."

Although Rosemary was never able to resolve her relationship with her mother, "I forgave her when I realized she could not love me because she did not know how to love. It was never me. I was never unlovable. In realizing that, my feelings of inadequacy dissipated and I began to like me. Relationships became more comfortable because I was now giving myself the approval that I had sought from others. Today I am the public Rosemary Clooney because I love to sing and because I have something to share through music—me. My life is pretty darn good, although it is not problemless. Conflicts still arise but I can deal with them. Some people will read this and say that Rosemary Clooney has been through hell. They are right! She has. But without that hell, she would not know joy and that is what I often feel today."

The phone rings persistently. She answers it, and after listening briefly, she hangs up. Her face is ashen as she rises slowly and faces a wall upon which hangs the sole memento of her once great fame—a laminated copy of *Time* magazine with her face on its cover.

"My father just died," she says, her voice barely audible. "My mother last December and now him." She sits heavily, hooking her legs under her as she does. Her thumb is in her mouth and she bites its nail. Tears dribble down a face that is of a little girl in pain. "Funny ole guy," she whispers. And then sobs,

"Oh, damn, how it hurts! Another door shut. We never knew one another . . . never had the chance." Her words kick at her. "Never had the chance? He never gave it to me!" Angry, she jerks to her feet, the woman emerging as the hurt child disappears. She cries as an adult. When her pain subsides, Rosemary Clooney, who had always to fix it for herself, does so once again. She collects her thoughts, gathers her emotions, and then quickly telephones her sister Betty to "fix it for her."

CHAPTER TWO

DYAN CANNON

"People thought I was such a tough broad when I was actually such a chicken; such a frightened child/woman who acted tough because she was terrified of . . . life, living, and who she really was. But that's all changed. Today, in knowing who Dyan Cannon is, I'm not afraid anymore. Not of anything. So it was worth the march through hell—every agonizing step of it—to reach this point in my life."

One of her not-so-long ago agonizing steps took Dyan Cannon to a Los Angeles hospital, where she briefly filled space as a catatonic until doctors could bring her out of her drug-abused state. When discharged, despite her continuing presence in film, "there were days, weeks, when I could barely stay alive. I had to fight like hell not to self-destruct. A lot of times I lost the battle."

But she won the war—*her* war, the one she waged upon herself. Today she is living higher than ever, and without drugs. It is predicted she will within the same year be nominated both for an Oscar and an Emmy; the former for her supporting role in *Heaven Can Wait*, and the latter for her bravura performance as a San Francisco madame who goes straight ("If going into politics is going straight") in *Lady of the House*. If Dyan should win either or both of the awards, the applause from peers and public will be for far more than her professionalism. She has reached a new pinnacle in her life because "I am a

survivor. I won't stay down when knocked down. And
I sure knocked myself down plenty times. Nobody
could tell me anything. I was a hard-head, a lady who
had to make her own mistakes. And I made them.
Did I ever!"

Dyan Cannon was in the process of rectifying one
of her mistakes—her marriage to Cary Grant—when
we first met eleven years ago. People were scandalized, outraged, that the former Dyan Freisen (her
real name) of Tacoma, Washington, was leaving
America's then prince of filmdom. What they had sus-
pected prior to the marriage was now confirmed
. . . in *their* minds. Dyan had married for money,
power, position—anything but love—and was now
about to take Grant to the cleaners. Unknown or forgotten was the fact that it was Grant who sought out
Dyan after viewing her on one of the scores of tele-
plays in which she appeared prior to their meeting.
Also forgotten was the five-year courtship, which often resembled marriage, prior to their exchanging of
legal vows in July of '65. In other words: neither
Dyan nor Cary rushed into their marriage, although
they seemingly were in a helluva rush to get out of it.
Shortly after their daughter, Jennifer, was born in
'66, the couple separated . . . at least in legal
residence. Emotionally, long after their divorce in '68,
Dyan and Cary were in the courts, replaying their
mutual hostilities. It was years before a truce and a
real separation—an ability to just let the other person
be—occurred.

In those years Dyan Cannon had all the softness of
a Brillo pad. There was no hint of the now famous
Cannon-roar, a laugh as infectious as the Goldie
(Hawn) giggle. But then, Dyan didn't have much to
laugh about. She smoked compulsively and she was
given to excessive eating binges. It was not unusual
for her to gain five pounds over a weekend of self-indulgence. She was fighting then for recognition—to be
known as something other than . . . the ex—Mrs.

Cary Grant. Dyan Cannon, actress, had disappeared
from public view and no one was opening any doors
for her out of the goodness of their hearts. Eventually, through sheer persistence, she won the lead in a
Broadway bomb titled *The 90-Day Mistress* and reviews that almost begrudgingly admitted she could
act. The positive notices gave her the courage to refuse a firm film offer, and at decent money, to pursue
a role she desperately wanted. She paid her own way
to Hollywood, screen-tested, and not only won the
part but her first Oscar nomination for her work in
Bob & Carol and Ted & Alice.

Was she happy? Hardly. *Bob & Carol* did more
than introduce Dyan to filmgoers and instant
stardom. In researching her role for the film, Dyan
was introduced to the Esalen Institute, which was
then a new experimental center for therapy. At its
sensitivity, encounter, and marathon group sessions,
Dyan was encouraged to "get in touch" with her
feelings. She did and the result was not pleasant. She
became one of the walking wounded. Rage and hurt
poured out of her. Since she was not in formal
therapy of any kind, Dyan had no follow-up with a
trained therapist to heal her wounds. She never
learned to accept or integrate her feelings. Thus she
walked about smiling, being the public Dyan Cannon, while internally, "I felt like I was constantly
hemorrhaging." She was easy picking for anyone who
offered relief from her pain. Thus when a splinter
group, not associated with Esalen, introduced her to
"mind-expanding" drugs, she partook. "I was in such
emotional disarray," she explains, "that I would have
tried anything to ease the turmoil."

Including men. Her first involvement was with a
writer. He had published one acclaimed novel in the
past but had written nothing of note since. He
seemed, when he accompanied her to New York for
her acceptance of Best Supporting Actress honors

from the New York film critics, to be her guru. He was a strong but hardly silent type, as far removed from the eloquent and elegant Grant as one could get. He was sixties macho—meaning: in the name of talking "straight," he was crude, coarse, and overbearing, particularly in his dealings with Dyan. His existence in her life, however, was short lived and he was soon replaced by a series of men—always one at a time and for extended periods of time—none of whom treated her any better.

Dyan's drug usage accelerated almost in exact proportion to her career. The greater her name became, the greater her unhappiness and her usage of dope. It wasn't until her dependency, particularly on pot, began to "wreck" her head in the morning, as well as at night, that she began experiencing career difficulties. She became disoriented and could not remember lines. Although the press release read that she had been removed from *The Traveling Executioner* for "artistic" reasons, most in Hollywood knew Dyan Cannon was having "bad trips." Not long afterward, Dyan disappeared from her home in the late night only to be found the following day, wandering in the Hollywood Hills. Although she worked with a psychiatrist, Dyan, after her discharge from a local hospital, refused to continue seeing him. "I was not yet ready to accept I was falling apart," she explains.

Had she not filmed *Such Good Friends* for Otto Preminger, Dyan Cannon might never have sought professional help. From day one of filming, Preminger terrified Dyan. Not into "sensitivity training," Preminger directed Dyan in his usual dictatorial style, one which had caused many a collapse in his actors. Often Dyan was reduced to rubble on the set. Once when I went to intervene, Preminger had me bodily removed. Dyan's way of coping with her rage and her fear was to gain twenty pounds during *Such Good Friends* production. Despite her ill feelings toward

Preminger, she owes him. He was the final straw that broke the back of Dyan's remaining resistance to receiving professional psychological help. She wrote to Dr. Arthur Janoff and, upon acceptance into his program, committed herself totally to his Primal Therapy. "I have stopped running," she wrote me from Los Angeles. "I am determined to face my demons."

Today, searching the face of the glorious-looking woman who has just returned from the European premiere of her latest film, *The Revenge of the Pink Panther,* it is hard to imagine she ever had demons to exorcise from her psyche. Slim and sunny, Dyan Cannon repeatedly bursts into laughter and manages between spasms to choke out: "Do you believe it? Do you *really* believe it!" She is referring to her personal reviews for *Heaven Can Wait*—some of which equated her with Chaplin and W. C. Fields. Hail the Conquering Hero indeed! *Heaven* is Dyan's first film in nearly five years. Her last, *Child Under a Leaf,* was never nationally released.

Suntanned and sun-bleached, she makes no effort to disguise her age, which has undergone as many changes over the years as she has. Even I, who once knew, am no longer sure. She is about forty. "But at least twice that in personal experience," she says. She would rather not discuss her past—"too negative," she explains—and would rather speak of her future, which includes *directing* her first major motion picture for Fox, and a non-ghost-written autobiography.

Surprisingly she is not overly grateful to Janoff or his Primal Therapy. Initially she was a total devotee. She installed a Primal Room in her home and took to its womblike interior whenever she felt the need to scream, kick, or punch. She also had a portable Primal Room that came with her on location shootings. "I kicked the drug dependency but substituted another," she now says. "I was hooked on Primal." She

unhooked herself after "three long torturous years."
Her romance with Primal soured abruptly and I
remember the day an *unmade-up*, *hair-in-rollers* Dyan
Cannon greeted me at her Malibu beachfront door
with a "Hey, friend, you wanna buy a Primal Room
cheap?" It was the first time in our relationship that
Dyan had permitted me, a friend, to see her without
paint-and-polish. She looked terrific and one didn't
have to be a shrink or a doctor to know that her so-
called march through hell was at an end. The year
was approaching 1974.

She does credit Primal for "breaking me of my self-
destructiveness. But one day I suddenly looked at
those of us in Primal and I realized we were getting
off on our pain. It was then I said: 'Enough!' Pain be-
gets pain. Almost at the same time, I woke up one
morning and instead of the usual anxieties I began
counting my pluses instead of adding my minuses. I
know it wasn't *one* morning but that many mornings
had to have passed before this particular *one* morning but . . . that day I discovered I liked myself,
that I was a good person, a nice person. That same
morning, for the first time in years, instead of avoiding the mirror, I looked into it. I had been so afraid
of not seeing a perfect beauty. But this day I looked.
And then I laughed. So I wasn't perfect physically.
Big deal."

Still, Dyan did not live "happily ever after" that
day. She found she had been so used to living with
pain that she was "lonely, literally, without it. Pain
had become my best friend, my crutch. I didn't know
how to live without it. I had never learned how to
live freely . . . how to just let myself be. I was always downgrading myself for all that I wasn't and
thought I should be. I had never come to grips with
who Dyan Cannon was. I lived by other people's definitions. I thought if I wasn't glamorous, I was nothing. I thought if I was not a star, I was nothing. I
thought if I was without a man, I was nothing. I dis-

covered that from childhood I had allowed others to define not only who and what I was but what I should be. Like many people couldn't understand why I wasn't happy when I married the prince [Grant]. They couldn't recognize that the slipper never quite fit Cinderella's foot. Nor did my film career make me happy because I projected a sexy image 'they' told me would sell. As if I alone, as *me*, would not. I could never enjoy my fame because I never felt it belonged to me but to some other Dyan Cannon.

"It goes on and on," she says almost impatiently. "My environment dictated that a mother stays home with her child. *My* mother did. But I was an actress who was also a mother. But because I acted, I felt I was a lousy mother. And because I was a mother, I felt I was a lousy actress. And how could I ever be a woman to some man if I was already a mother and an actress. I was so totally and unnecessarily conflicted. It didn't change until I had the strength to say 'Hey, I can be all these persons, wear all those hats, because I *am* all those persons.' I guess I had to come full circle—make all the trips, including the bum ones, to claim all of me . . . to be able to look in a mirror and say, 'Hey girl, I like you.' "

Which is why shortly after she quit Primal, Dyan quit films. "I couldn't play one more lady who was good for a laugh-and-a-lay. Those roles were hurting me *personally*. I never felt they were real women or that the real me was involved in my work. I knew if I were to hold on to me, I had to let go of my career—that I had to wait until I was offered work that either had meaning or was constructive rather than destructive."

She waited a long, long time. Often the wolf was at the door. Contrary to what many thought, her divorce from Grant did not net her one personal penny. Child support was, and is, all Grant pays. On one Saturday but three years ago, Dyan's local grocery refused to deliver an order until she had cleared up past debts. Still she refused to succumb. In '75, rather than vegetate, she applied for entrance and was accepted into the Women's Division of the American Film Institute. She determined: "If Hollywood wasn't about to write or film for women, then I would learn to do both." As part of her education, she was staked to $1,000 by the institute and told . . . "Go make a film!"

Two years later Dyan Cannon's first effort as a producer, director, and writer, *Number One*, came within an eyelash of winning the Academy Award in the field of Best Short Subject. It was a stunning little film about the loss of childhood innocence, and the fact that Dyan conceived and created all its parts stunned many a reviewer. "If you have a body, many people think you can't have a brain. I was known as 'a body.' But *Number One* changed all that."

What it didn't change was her perilous financial condition. By the time her film was complete, she was "up to my *tuchis* in debt"—$65,000 worth to be exact. She was in danger of losing her home. She did lose many friends among those who had staked her to a few hundred here and a few thousand there. Only today is she making final payments on past loans. "I'm sorry I lost those few friends who couldn't wait for me to take work which I could be proud of but . . . better to lose them than to lose me. I simply cannot sacrifice one part of me anymore, ever again, just to please others. This is me. Take it or leave it."

Plenty are taking, or would be if Dyan permitted. Scripts pile up at her door daily, and somewhat similarly, so do men. "And I can remember when most men found me a threatening woman. Well . . . I was. A real killer who attracted killers. No more. My angers toward men have been resolved."

Including her anger toward Cary Grant. Today she speaks of her former husband and sparring partner with both admiration and affection. Of their marriage she says: "We were simply wrong for one another. A part of me knew that always or why else would I have had a crying jag just before the ceremony started? I didn't regret my marriage at all, but I certainly wouldn't want to repeat the experience. Not that I could. I could never again let any man dictate what I should wear; where I should wear it to; who I should see; how I should act. My marriage taught me never to let any man be my God. But Cary and I must have done something right. We share an absolutely gorgeous child . . . an extraordinary twelve-year-old. Despite my having been thought of as the 'Malibu *Meshuggeneh*' (crazy person), Jennifer had a protected childhood. Not that she wasn't aware of what was happening. I have never lied to her. But Jennifer, no matter where Cary or I were at with one another or with ourselves, had the knowledge that both her parents loved her. Cary dotes on Jen. She adores him. Cary has been the kind of father to Jen that all children should have. With that kind of love as a foundation, with respect for her personhood, Jennifer is her own little person. She will never have to fight for her identity. She has it now. I saw to that. Mama here may have had her problems but Jennifer was never one of them. In my worst moments I'd look at this child and thank God for the one thing in my life that made sense. I still thank God daily. Strange as this may sound to some, Jennifer is my best friend."

Mother and daughter live a rather sequestered life in their beach front home. Generally Dyan skips the party and the disco scene she once thought "so very long ago" was vital to her career. Mornings find Dyan jogging for an hour along the Malibu sands. Another hour is spent during the day meditating. "I'm never going to lose touch with myself again," she explains. She is dating for the first time in two years, an actor twelve years her junior. She will not discuss the merits or drawbacks of a younger man–older woman relationship because "I date the person; not his age." All she will say of the new coupling is "We treat each other with respect and caring." She had been celibate prior to meeting him for several years because, as she explains, "The need I once had to be held by a man—any man—disappeared with my desperation. I'm no longer one of America's Hundred Most Needy Cases. I can hold myself today just fine, thank you. Which is why, incidentally, men feel easy with me. They sense I no longer throw the burden on them to make me feel whole or happy or fulfilled."

Where once antimarriage, Dyan is softer on the subject today. "The act, itself, is still meaningless to me but the idea is not. The ultimate so obviously is two people sharing their uniqueness in a form of oneness. I would like that kind of relationship. And I think it will happen. Corny as this will sound, I nonetheless feel that my life, like a big bud, is first unfolding. The best is yet to come. I've done my time in hell. Now I want to make my heaven on earth."

CHAPTER THREE

ELIZABETH TAYLOR

"I've made it through nineteen major operations and what must seem to some to be as many marriages and all because I've got a gut sense of survival," says Elizabeth Taylor, which also explains why she never reads her reviews, including those for the current *A Little Night Music*. At forty-six, the actress who has not made a successful film in years remains a legend. "The hell I am!" she contradicts. "Legends have to be dead and I refuse to be that." She also refuses to be "*that* Elizabeth Taylor. I am me, just me. And me today is Elizabeth Taylor Warner . . . *Mrs. John Warner,* if you please."

It is Mrs. Warner who is sitting in her Georgetown living room looking nothing like the legendary Elizabeth Taylor. Mrs. Warner has but hours ago stepped off a plane and a campaign trail she and her current husband have traveled in the quest to obtain a nomination for senator from the state of Virginia, and looks decidedly the worse for the wear. With her hair and makeup askew, her red pants suit rumpled, Mrs. Warner is frowsy. She is also . . . er . . . plump. But she is also happy. In fact, she glows. With her feet up on a coffee table, she swills beer with gusto and laughs at *that* Elizabeth Taylor with bawdy good humor. Frankly, whereas Elizabeth Taylor often seemed unapproachable, Mrs. Warner is a hoot!

She never reads a word about *that* Elizabeth Taylor, she reveals. And although appreciative, she is not impressed, but at all, by the idol-worshipers who tear down barricades and bodyguards to gaze upon what must be the world's most photographed face. And when asked what she thinks these people are looking for so intently, she responds: "Wrinkles and pimples. And I don't disappoint them, do I?" she giggles. "This face has been around a lot of years. People want to see if my eyes really are violet or bloodshot or both. Once they check me out, they can go home and say: 'I saw Liz Taylor and you know what? She ain't so hot!' And you know what? They're right!"

Elizabeth Taylor Warner laughs, sounding like Vincent Price at his most evil and Phyllis Diller at her merriest-and-maddest. Obviously, under our very eyes, somewhere between Hilton-Wilding-Todd-Fisher-Burton-Warner, Elizabeth Taylor has gone from a great beauty to a great broad. Maybe she was always that. Certainly she claims never to have thought of herself as screen goddess or sex symbol. In fact, she is actually stunned when it is suggested she was the brunette equivalent of Marilyn Monroe, whom she knew but slightly.

"Not so!" says Elizabeth, almost aghast. "I never did cheesecake. I was never in love with the camera. I actually hate having my picture taken and to be a sex goddess you must feel the camera is your lover. Which is pretty damn dull lovemaking if you ask me," she giggles. "And a sex symbol always worries about how she looks. That, too, was never me. I never felt I had to be beautiful. But then, I never felt I had to be *that* Elizabeth Taylor. Frankly, from what little I have read about *her*, she always seemed somewhat ridiculous to me. Thank god I've always had a sense of humor about who she was to some and who she really is."

Another "tool" in her survival kit was her ability to say no to studio pressures. "Marilyn allowed herself to wear the very heavy burden of sex symbol. I watched Monty [Clift] . . . born a free spirit, allow his wings to be clipped, just because of studio pressures and the heaviness they bring. Not me. I refused to wear any sense of responsibility to anything or anyone other than me. The business controlled both Monty and Marilyn. Then as now, *I* controlled me. I lived and live my life as I see fit. No one dictates to me how I should live. I am not and never have been a conformist. I live in an unpredictable fashion and people have either damned or praised my nonconformity. In my time I've been down . . . way down with the public and I've been up. But then sometimes they've resented my freeness and other times they've applauded it. Right now, touch wood," she adds superstitiously, "I'm up."

These days, the "up" Elizabeth Taylor is devoting her energies to helping her husband John secure the Republican nomination for senator. She has acted the dutiful, political wife, smiling and shaking thousands of hands as the couple stump through the Virginia countryside. "I'm carrying my own weight," quips Elizabeth Taylor. She is not sensitive about her poundage—as the beer in front of her attests—and she is truly puzzled why the world is. More is written about her weight gains and losses than the fund-raising she is doing for the Salvation Army, the Gallery of Art, and the Wolftrap Music and Arts Festival—all part of the new Mrs. John Warner image. She is very intent on being "the little woman," so to speak, and in particular Warner's little woman.

Contrary to any current talk and rumors—and about Elizabeth Taylor there is always talk and rumors—she looks and acts like a woman very much in love with her husband. "John is a very caring man," she explains, "not just of me but of people in general. He is really devoted to public service. It matters to him that he work toward making the world a better place. I admire and respect him for this. The difference in this marriage," she continues, "is the extra effort we both put in. It is not a fifty-fifty proposition but a fifty-one-fifty-one. And . . . John is his own man . . . secure in his shoes, confident but not smug. He is not threatened by my image—whatever it might be on any given day."

When asked, considering her image, if it is therefore difficult for a man to be married to Elizabeth Taylor, Mrs. Warner breaks up, laughing and cackling, and nearly drowning in beer bubbles. "Dearie, I'll give you a list of references who will attest to that fact." Including Richard Burton? The laughter stops. "Richard and I had a wonderful marriage," she says. "And we both came away the better for it. We both learned from it." And what was it they learned? "That we could give warmth and love to others," she says calmly. "Richard and Suzy are very happy and that, believe it or not, makes me happy."

There is much that makes Mrs. John Warner happy today. Her children, often not associated with *that* Elizabeth Taylor, are, she says, a constant source of happiness despite their being scattered about the world. "Michael is in London; Maria, in Germany. Lisa lives in California while Chris is here . . . or someplace about," she explains. "The kids know they are always welcome and that John and I leave the door open for them to come and go as they choose. But then," she says softly, "I've always held the apron strings open. Little birds tend to fly back to the nest more readily when they feel free to do so. I kept my children with me until the age when I felt it important that they be at school with peers. But we were never distant. There were . . . and are . . . the holidays *always* spent together. And the phone calls (the Taylor phone bill has been known to top an astronomical $10,000 per month!) keep us a very close family. My children often come home . . . without invitation and without warning. And frankly there is no greater joy to a mother—at least to this mother— than having her children come home because they want to and not because they are asked. And when one volunteers an 'I love you' on the telephone, well . . ."

She does not complete her sentence but her expression says it all. "My life is very content," she states with feeling.

So content that she might not work again? Elizabeth Taylor Warner considers the question. "The truth is, my teeth don't ache to act again. I'm not climbing a wall, itching to be back on screen. My life has passed into another phase and I find it hard to think about acting. My energies are devoted to my marriage . . . to John. Not that he has asked me not to work. Quite the contrary. John is quite proud of what I've accomplished. It is I who do not wish to leave him to make a film. I was considering *The Mudlark* but that's been shelved. There is another TV property that looks interesting but it would have to be filmed in the East for me to consider it. The fact is, I'm just not dying to do that 'Elizabeth Taylor *thing*' at this moment in my life."

It is as if Mrs. John Warner has established her priorities and being yours or anyone's vision of Elizabeth Taylor is not among them. "The minute you do what *they* want of you rather than do what you want, and the moment you believe you are who *they* say you are, you're in trouble," she says. "As I stated, I'm me. I live as I choose. I am not retired but work is not a priority now. I'm too busy living this new life as Mrs. John Warner. I have learned and so grown from my past experiences," she says as if to explain why she feels she can make this soon-to-be two-year-old marriage work. "All of life is a learning process. Even those experiences which were horrendous and whose meaning seemed unfathomable at the time. Let me tell you," says Elizabeth Taylor Warner as she shakes her glass of beer in your direction for emphasis. "Although I am sorry if I ever hurt anybody, when I look back on my life, there is nothing I would change . . . nothing that I regret. Life is to be faced . . . head on . . . and lived. I've done that!"

CHAPTER FOUR

LENA HORNE

She claims to be fifty-five years old, but then most women lie about their age. And it *is* an obvious lie. She is thirty-five if she is a day, at the most forty. She says of herself: "I'm medium tall and slender," thinks a bit, then adds, "Emotional, jealous and possessive—a real Cancer. . . . Sometimes sunshine, most times storm.

"I'm also talky as hell and I'm told I ramble. What I say is perfectly clear to me, but others seem to have trouble following my train of thought. The truth is, I'm strictly nonintellectual and . . . sloppy. I either have to clean my apartment one of these days or move."

The legendary Lena Horne, a superstar and the first black woman to achieve that status. Her career has spanned nearly four decades, and during that time she has traveled from Harlem to Hollywood, from Europe to Broadway. She has been, and is, a film and television star, a recording artist, and—if you've ever seen her you know—*the* cabaret/nightclub performer of our time. She opened many a door for blacks and she is "owed."

She does not see herself as legendary. "Billie [Holiday], sure. Aretha, definitely. But me . . ." And her voice trails off. False humility is expected until she adds somewhat softly, "I'm realizing now that I matter to people and may have mattered for many years. I don't see myself as legendary, however. Longevity is more comfortable. I'm proud of that. I've moved with the times. I'm happier today than I have ever been."

Born in Brooklyn, she now resides on Manhattan's Upper West Side and spends much of her time at the Sidney Lumets'. He is her white son-in-law, a noted director married to her daughter Gail. She likes Sidney. "He is one of the few white men I can argue with, reason with, listen to, and learn from." The mention of Gail makes Lena's face soften. But her "starring role" at the Lumets' is as grandmother.

"This world," she says, meaning the Lumets', "is safe . . . complete . . . real. For as long as I can remember, I wanted a family—to be in its nest, in its circle. Finally, I am."

In recent years Lena Horne has been taken to the larger bosom of the black family at large. She has come out of hiding, and the image on stage which was devastating ain't nothing compared to the flesh-and-blood woman who decided to make her voice, the nonsinging one, heard. As a result she is beginning to accept the position she holds with both black and white America and the affection they feel for her.

She is aware there has been a dramatic change in her life. "I was never one to be frank, particularly when meeting people who had a certain image of Lena Horne. Hell! They didn't know who I was and they didn't want to know. They wanted me to be what they fantasized. So I was. I figured, 'Why bother with anything else?' So the world never knew me. I denied my existence. But all of that has changed and there are no more lies, no more bullshit. No more three separate Lenas; one for white America, one for black, and one for herself."

She recalls having had to be "nothing and yet everything" over the course of her career. "My reactions as a black woman were not allowed, only those as Lena, and Lena was seldom me. She was 'respresentative' and 'useful' and she had to be so careful not to hurt the Cause, not to hurt the white hand that fed her, and lastly not to hurt the box office. There were times in my life when I wanted to scream, 'To hell with being representative, what about me?' But I didn't. I was certain people would look at me and snidely say, 'So what about you, girl?' It's awful stumbling through the years thinking people don't give a damn about the real you."

Part of her pain, she says, was from being a light-skinned black woman. "A lot of whites and a lot of blacks never realized I was a black woman. My light skin was a trapping, and few ever looked beneath the outer layer to see what was there. Whites didn't want to. The reason so few white writers—if any—have ever caught me in print is because they really thought I was white only pretending to be black." Her own people gave her hard times too. "Many put me down because I hadn't been born deep black." In Hollywood back in the forties, blacks forced by the industry to play servants and dolts resented her "grandeur" and her absolute refusal to play those roles. "My thing was hurting theirs," she says of their reaction, but without bitterness. But she was hurt and it was small comfort when black actress Hattie McDaniel told her "Darling, don't let them break your heart. We just haven't learned yet how to stick together." Her mentor and idol, Paul Robeson, helped more when he said: "I promise you, honey, one day a lot of black people are going to know and love you. We are family and many of us will always be there for you."

And they were, but she found also that she was there for herself in that special way that she feels is indigenous to the black woman. "I am a strong woman and that *is* a trait of the black woman. Our pride cannot be killed. That, more than anything, has kept us out of the toilet. It is not in the black woman's nature to be flushed away. Nor will she be spat upon. These are her dividends from years of oppression."

* * *

Lena Horne's parents separated when she was three. Since her mother was an actress touring with black tent shows, Lena was sent to live with foster families in the South. She describes them as "middle-class" but only because "that's how they saw themselves." She knew want but not poverty. She also knew "not to get too comfortable or too attached to anything or anyone in those foster homes. You learn that after the first few wrenches; you learn it's 'hello-and-good-bye,' and to expect anything else is crazy."

Her grandmother was a major influence in her life then. She was a graduate of Atlanta University, an educator and emancipator; a woman of enormous power but "she lacked an affectionate nature and thought softness was a weakness." Her father "did what he had to do to earn a buck. He was a hustler."

At age sixteen Lena was back in New York. Her mother, upon marrying "a nice white man," promised that at long last they would be a family. "But it was too late. I was no longer a child. I was working in the line at the Cotton Club in Harlem and that kind of life grows you up fast." She was neither singer nor dancer, "only youthful exuberance." She remembers the brown ladies of the uptown club "coming on like a bunch of light-skinned, downtown ladies on Broadway. If you had soul then, you hid it. You sang white or you didn't sing at all. Our audience was composed mainly of rich white folk who arrived in chauffeured limousines—the proverbial ermine and pearls.

"You should have seen the girls at the club. Now *they* were beautiful!" she says, implying that if you had seen them, you would know she was not. "I was nothing more than average and in later years when people insisted on calling me 'the beautiful Lena Horne,' I mistrusted and hated it. I saw the *benefits* of beauty but I also saw girl after girl misuse it or be misused for it. Black beauty has always been debased.

"It was horrible to watch," she recalls with a shudder. "So many girls were destroyed because they were beautiful. I fought that tag all of my life. I studied acting, singing, anything that would remove me from just being beautiful. I wanted an identity that had nothing to do with the light color of my skin and my features, which prompted many a person to suggest that I 'pass.' My so-called beauty agonized me at times. I was both adored and hated for it."

While in her teens she ran away from that beauty-trap to marry a college-educated man, the son of a Baptist minister who was "very handsome and very black. I was very young. I knew nothing of cleaning or of how to be a black man's wife. At his job he would get battered and spat on by a hostile white world and he would bring this home to me. He gave me his hurt when I wanted his love. But he had none to give. They had taken it from him."

Before its dissolution the marriage produced two children. Lena's son "was taken from me—the price I paid for my freedom, the only way he would give me a divorce. What else is there to say?" she asks, her eyes revealing the pain still, that she will not focus into words. On her return to New York from Philadelphia, where she had been living, she sought work unsuccessfully until white bandleader Charlie Barnett offered her a job as his band vocalist. The NAACP was adamant she refuse it, raising questions about a black woman's role with a white man's band. It was Billie Holiday who solved the question with one of her own. "Honey, you gotta feed your kid, don't you?" Lena sang with Barnett.

There were always the critics, those who told her she should do this and be that because she was "representative." Then, too, there were those who reviled her no matter what she did. When she married Lennie Heyton, whom she had met when both were under contract at MGM, the hate mail poured in. A black woman married to a white man was big news back in the forties. Big news and bad news. The abuse resulted in a move to Europe, but there, "anti-American sentiment caused me to come home. And home is exactly how I felt about this country despite all that existed then for a black person." Part of that "all" found her reacting to a racial slur flung at her in a Beverly Hills nightclub by flinging an ashtray at the racist's head. That made front-page headlines.

"Paul [Robeson] had taught me about being black and gave me a sense of my own history. He added a dimension to me. Today it is called black pride. When I threw that ashtray, it marked the first time in my life I had spoken as a black woman . . . acted as I felt—angry."

Today she recognizes anger has been her life's companion. When performing in nightclubs, earning her standing ovations, it was anger that motivated her performances. The paying customers never knew it, "never knew what I was thnking when I was singing. Everyone thought that Lena was sending out 'let's ball' weather reports, which amazed me, as sex was the *furthest* thing from my mind. I'm just not one of those dames who is into a group sex performance. I believe only one man can love me at a time. And one man at a time is all I can love or wish to love. All that sex people thought I was giving off, that so-called smoldering passion, was smoldering rage. Black rage.

"When performing, my mind would wander to the back exits my black musicians had to use and to room service which never delivered what they had ordered *if* they delivered at all. Anger! Anger! Anger! I look back on that sadly and with regret. All those years of nightclub appearances, those thousands of people, and never once did I feel the joy of performing, of entertaining. I conquered my audiences and that's a whole other trip from entertaining."

But audiences loved her. "If that's true, it was from afar and I didn't feel it. I *wouldn't* feel it. I had a 'hands-off!' attitude and nobody got close. That, I guess, is the major change in me today. I'm giving off different signals. I'm letting people in. And let's face it, I'm letting Lena out—the Lena previously reserved for maybe two or three people in the entire world." And she is learning people like her, that they have always liked her. "I see it at the NAACP, Baptist Church, and Hadassah luncheons at which I speak. The women there accept me as a woman. And many not only accept but like me."

Her anger, however, is far from gone. It is not even dormant and barely controlled. "This country is in the midst of a revolution and anyone hiding from that fact had better find a new country to hide in. Oh, the mood has calmed considerably from a few years ago, but when that wind stirs up and gathers force again, it is going to result in an awesome storm. It is either that or a repressive state. I am not for bloodshed but I am against talk at this stage. I've heard *all* the talk, enough talk, in my lifetime to know it makes for very little change. So, if it takes blood . . ." Her sentence goes unfinished but not misunderstood.

As she tours, she meets many of the young people—black singers and dancers—and finds they still believe that communication can effect change. "They seem so naive, so trusting. Yes, they are angry but they are not hopeless. Well, who knows? Maybe I'm just tired and cynical. I'm just so sick of words, of bigots and well-meaning white liberals who will never understand how a black person feels. Never! And no white person wants to accept this. And until they do, until they accept we are different, that black and white are *not* the same, there can be no communication; no reaching across to one another in some realistic gesture of understanding."

She remembers when her Broadway musical, *Jamaica*, closed, and the depression into which she sank. "I just knew all the black gypsies [chorus kids] would have a terrible time getting jobs, whereas the white kids would find work in a matter of weeks. After the play closed, I sat in my kitchen day after day wanting to do nothing but scream. The years of frustration had caught up with me. It seemed like nothing had changed, not one damn thing, and that we were still coming through the back door; that we hadn't advanced one lousy friggin' step. I was so angry I cried. All my damn 'representativeness.' And for what? I had denied openness for usefulness, and it had all proven to be a crock."

That day, she says, "I entered a new age. I saw I had my own living to do and to hell with what anybody thought was or *would* be useful."

And then Medgar Evers was murdered. She had been working at NBC when word came of his death. She reacted as though she had been physically assaulted. Only weeks ago she had been with the black leader. This time she couldn't conceal her rage. It was seen and felt by televiewers and radio listeners for weeks to come. It spilled from her and onto printed pages all over the world. For the first time in her career Lena Horne was telling it like it is, or as it *was*, to her.

But it was the racial strife in Birmingham which she says brought her fully out of the closet and among the living blacks who protested. She was at home with Lennie Heyton, watching the horror on television, and as she watched "the children, *my* children, fighting what I so deeply felt was also my fight, I suddenly felt a hatred for the man sitting next to me—a white man. It was no longer the man who was to be my husband for twenty-two years but 'whitey.' I just couldn't help it, couldn't see Lennie clearly. And I'll always feel guilty about that," she says sadly. "He was compassionate about my anger. If I had said that day that I hate all white people, he would have understood. He would also have known it was not true."

Birmingham produced a storm that had her raging

and not hiding that rage for months. And as the anger flowed, "I became different, felt different, younger . . . freer, more me. It was then I became approachable. It was then my work changed. I began giving something, sharing that part of me that had previously been either nonexistent or closed off. Who knows which? It was also then that I began to receive as I gave."

In June of 1972 Lena Horne experienced mass love for the first time in her life. It occurred at a benefit performed for Phoenix House. The audience, composed of all ages and colors, sat on the vast dance floor of Roseland—many were in formal attire—just to be near the "fabulous Lena Horne" as she was introduced.

"That night was a coming together. I felt them—*really* felt them—their respect and their love. And I gave them mine. Finally Miss Calhoun and Lena had gotten it together—had *come* together."

No one ever called her Miss Calhoun except Lennie or Gail or someone truly close to her. "Miss Calhoun was for us; Lena was for those others. I don't know when that began—I guess when I started to protect the inner me, the real me, from the world. Professionally I learned early this is a lousy business filled with spoilers and takers. Show business is a rotten profession for a woman. You have to hold on to your softness by your fingernails. And it is twice as hard for a black woman. Someone really has to be in your corner to survive; someone who is there solely for you. I was lucky. I had that in Lennie. And I'm also coming to realize I had it in myself."

She doesn't quite yet understand her need for self-protection on a personal level. "There is the obvious—not having a home of my own, moving about, never feeling I belonged, but then, there was my daddy. My gorgeous daddy whom I wanted to marry. I loved him so and I always felt he loved me. He just seemed to know about things. He was there for me all my life. When I first went to Hollywood, Daddy left Pittsburgh, where he was doing his number, and demanded to meet Louis B. Mayer. And he did. He told Mr. Mayer exactly what his little girl *would* and *would not* do. 'No maid. Do you hear?' And Mr. Mayer heard. My daddy was very special." Her mother brings up more painful memories and feelings. "I always wanted my mama to love me . . . still do. Can you imagine? Fifty-five years old and still wanting to know that feeling before I die." She remembers her grandmother differently today than she did five and ten years ago. "She taught me wrong. People *can* be strong *and* loving . . . can be strong *and* affectionate. I never knew that till Lennie."

Of her late husband Lena says: "He created the middle part of my life. I was nothing until his influence. He taught me to sing . . . taught me music, actually. The truth is Lennie taught me, period. Sometimes I think I married Lennie under false pretenses. I was cold-blooded about it. I liked his talent and the doors it and he could open for me. But I also liked his strength. I felt he could take the crap I often pretended to handle. And he could. Lord knows he took mine. I was such a bitch at times. When the white world bruised me, made me bleed, I took it home and did to Lennie what my black husband had done to me. It was so undeserved.

"You know, my respect for that man grew with every year we were married and it has continued to grow despite his death. I owe Lennie a great deal. Wishes are only that . . . wishes, but I wish I had been less cruel to him—more able to separate the man from his color. He had such warmth, and when I allowed myself, I felt it. And it was then that we were wonderful together. Lennie cared for me. Lennie loved me."

His feeling for her was reciprocated but "I had difficulty showing it. Oh not just with Lennie but with anyone who mattered to me. The worst hurt I've ever known was when Gail told me that although she felt I had always been her best friend, she nonetheless felt I hadn't loved her—*didn't* love her. I just didn't know what to say. How do you tell your daughter that you didn't just love her but you adored her? How do you explain? How do you say to someone you love, 'I don't show it because so little was shown to me.' Love was wiped out of most black people and this black person is through blaming herself for seeming to be or having been unloving. I try today to be different and Gail is very sympathetic toward me and my fumbling attempts at affection. And it really isn't so difficult, not now that I feel I have something to give. Never mind labeling it, it's enough that it is there and that I am not afraid of it."

Despite the tragedy that has filled her life (she lost her father, husband, and son all within recent months of one another), Lena Horne looks ahead, not backward. "I am determined to make a life for myself—one other than just being another lonely woman singing her life away to strangers . . . and friends. I find I've been thinking a lot about a second career. My thoughts keep coming back to school. My mama and I were the only family members not to be educators. Wouldn't it be funny if that proved to be my real vocation in life? I mean that has to be laughs for someone who has been so anti-intellectual all her life; who can barely spell and who isn't too together with higher mathematics. And . . . I'd love to be a college graduate. The thought scares me. It makes me say: 'Oh, c'mon girl,' but the thought persists. I know I'm going to do something in addition to performing. I have to. I can't sit back anymore and sit out my life. I feel too much a part of it. But I don't feel I have to prove Lena to anyone. Lena just *is*, baby. She just *is*."

ANN-MARGRET

Ann-Margret is reflecting. "Sometimes I feel like I've made three comebacks. Sometimes I want to stand up and shout . . . I'm still here!"

Did she ever doubt she would be?

"Yes," she says softly. "It was only a few years ago that I thought I was going down the tubes; that I was coming apart."

She is not referring to "the accident"—the one that saw her topple from a twenty-two-foot platform during her Las Vegas act, fracturing her face and jaw and arm. That was six years ago. Ann-Margret, as she reflects, is thinking of much more recent events in her life. "But it's okay," she muses. "I'm feeling so much better about myself."

She both looks and acts it. I have known Ann-Margret eleven years. I still remember the afternoon when an elegant clientele in an elegant Manhattan restaurant stopped their elegant lunches to stare at an incredibly beautiful young girl who was trying to be unobtrusive as she made her way to her husband, Roger Smith's table. When he introduced us, I was struck by her sweetness and discomfort. Over the next decade I would always be struck by her sweetness and her discomfort. I would also be struck by the way she would paste herself to Roger and the very caring way he would shield her from a world she so obviously found terrifying.

She is alone this day and immediately that denotes change in Ann-Margret. In the past Roger has hovered about in the background, protective and supportive. But this afternoon Ann-Margret is braving it solo. She is long and lean. Boots, into which well-fitted pants lose themselves, add several inches to her 5 foot 5 inch frame. A loose-fitting sweater cannot hide her ampleness. Her famous mane is hidden by a bandanna. She is quite simply gorgeous and I tell her so.

"Oh, no, not me," she says, embarrassed. "I'm not beautiful. I never was and I never will be. Oh, I can be striking if I have my hair done up and if I'm wearing the right clothes, but beautiful? No. Not me." Suddenly she becomes aware of what she has just done. She shrugs her shoulders and sighs. "I've always been lousy at accepting compliments. But then, I've never really thought I was very good at anything."

And so the book reveals its cover has been false. Ann-Margret is not as motorized or as revved up as the motorcycles she rides in her nightclub act. The garish glitter so often associated with the lady is pure veneer. Underneath is an Ann-Margret who still finds it difficult to enter a room filled with strangers, who still avoids parties unless the guests are known friends, who admits "confidence remains a big, big thing with me. I still lack it—am still fighting for it."

We don't think of the Ann-Margrets of this world needing to battle for their lives. Ann-Margret is battling. She began seeing a psychologist two years ago when she felt "like a pressure cooker about to explode. I realized I was filled with pain . . . with rage. Far too often I have pretended—have acted 'nice' when I didn't feel it and have done things I didn't want to do. No more. I'm finding out about me and frankly it's about time."

She chose a psychologist, a woman, whose clients were very much like herself—entertainers and actresses. She found instant relief "in being able to talk with someone who understood conflicts I felt as a woman. Just having someone who not only under-

stands what you are saying but who often understands even more about what you're saying than you do is incredible. With each session I learn more and more about myself. I'm learning how to be kind to me. I no longer feel the Ann-Margret Case is hopeless, never to be solved. I now know I no longer have to be anyone's vision of Ann-Margret but my own. I am learning how to be!"

As she freely talks, it results Ann-Margret has been . . . "a nervous wreck." Her billing could have been Anxiety-Margret. There were bouts of depression and fear. Always fear. Before going on stage, her insides would convulse. She would freeze. Only when in character, being someone other than Ann-Margret, was she comfortable. Even today, she reveals, when she has to address her audiences as herself, her voice fades. The insecurity rises and she must force herself to speak out.

Ann-Margret chastises herself for "not being more verbal. It is still difficult for me to put into words all I feel but at least I'm feeling." This is said when she cannot yet explain or trace her negative feelings. She is still finding her answers. Many are at rest in her childhood, which was difficult in some ways.

"I came to this country from Sweden when I was six. I dressed and spoke different than other children my age. That made me self-conscious. My parents, who I loved and who loved me, were very Old World. Very Swedish. Which means very stoic. I was taught to be a good little girl . . . to always be obliging and to *never* express anger. I learned never to speak unless spoken to. I was very passive and very polite. I learned early to keep everything to myself. I had but one goal: to be pleasing. I would do *anything* to please even if I hated what I was doing."

Which explains why Ann-Margret went along with the early years of her career. Back in 1961, 20th Century-Fox signed her to a contract. Their initial plans were to star her in the ingenue role in a remake of

State Fair. That plan remained intact until the studio brass saw Ann-Margret in action as a singer-dancer. They instantly switched her role to that of the "other woman" in the film. They dyed her hair blond and with that. . . the dye was cast. From then on, in almost every film Ann-Margret played, she was, as she puts it, "the bitch." She accepted her lot in life because she never thought to protest—"that I had the right to."

Perhaps no star since 1961 has hit Hollywood with the ado caused by Ann-Margret. Overnight she was the new kid in town that everyone wanted. Then, "once I made it, the knife went out and I was cut deep. And I bled." Because she usually played some sort of sexy swinger on film, she was portrayed as being the same off the set. Magazines and newspapers had a field day with their Ann-Margret sexcapades. She was openly ridiculed, both personally and professionally. She went into hiding. She avoided all interviews for five years and thus won Hollywood's Sour Apple award three years running as the nation's least cooperative actress. "They were killing me with that horrible picture they painted of me," she explains. "I was never trashy and that's what they made me out to be."

She did date many men but not because she was "frivolous or flighty. When I was growing up, my parents wouldn't let me go steady in high school. They wanted me to know many boys so I would have some basis of comparison before I chose one to marry. In Hollywood I dated to find myself. I didn't want to be married eighteen times. I wanted one marriage and one marriage is what I've got. I've been with Roger fourteen years now—eleven of which have been legal."

These many years later she still shudders when she recalls her humiliation at her public ridicule. "I always, *always* cared about my work. I have never walked through a role. I'm too insecure to do that. I was always serious as an actress but no one ever believed me. Not for years anyway. I was just a joke. And I hated it! And," she adds softly, "I was always a 'nice' girl . . . a 'good' girl."

Stanley Kramer was the first to take a chance on something other than Ann-Margret's considerable physical attributes. In an unsuccessful film, *R.P.M.*, in which she starred opposite Anthony Quinn, she was required to act. And she did quite well. Next, Mike Nichols gambled on her in his *Carnal Knowledge*. The "gamble" resulted in her earning her first of two Oscar nominations—the other for *Tommy*. Ann-Margret's image and career turned around with those films. Today, of course, she is considered one of our leading entertainers and actresses.

"The nominations, and whatever awards I've won, have helped me a lot," she says. "I know they shouldn't have—that esteem and confidence should come from within but . . . having praise come from others has bolstered me. It still does . . . even if I *am* lousy at accepting compliments. I've always wanted people to accept me . . . to like me. And there has always been this paralyzing fear that they wouldn't. Even today. Which probably explains why I'm afraid of meeting strangers."

The irony to all this is that Ann-Margret is one of the best liked, even loved, performers in the world. A talk with members of the Rockettes, with whom she danced on her recent TV special, or with any of the performers with whom she has worked in Vegas or elsewhere yields nothing but warm feelings. Even the once hostile press, now that they know Ann-Margret, more than just like her. It is impossible not to like her. She is that most overused cliché . . . a *real* person. But she is first discovering this for herself.

"Therapy is making me see me. I'm even learning to express how I feel. Which shocks people. It used to be that once a year, I'd explode. Now," she says proudly, "the bomb bursts much more frequently. I'm not so afraid of anger anymore. I no longer have to be that 'good little girl.' I'm a woman now. I like this change. Roger likes it too, although the first time I disagreed with him, he was shocked. But he encouraged me just as he encouraged me to continue with my therapy. It's funny. The more I emerge as me, the better I feel and yet the more frightened I am. It's very scary to take long, hard looks at yourself—to finally meet and *accept* the person you are. Like I'm accepting my shortcomings. I've a confession. I'm messy. Actually, I'm a slob, but for print, let's say messy. And here I am, the daughter of a woman off whose floors you could eat. She is *that* clean and tidy. For years I would put myself down 'cause I wasn't. But now, I accept it. And besides, I have tables you can eat off so who cares? And so what if I'm a lousy cook. There are worse things in life." And she is laughing. "I have other strengths. Like I've been in this business seventeen years. Not bad for someone thought to be a flash-in-the-pan. I guess I do something right."

The proof of how "right" was in the thousands of letters that came to her from strangers everywhere after her freak accident of years ago. "People told me they cared," she says softly, "and they told me at a time when I really needed that kind of support." It results the injuries of the accident were not as painful as the emotional turmoil she experienced as she recuperated. "People would only have to look at me and I'd cry. All the joy had dried up—gone out of me. Then the letters would arrive—extravagant outpourings of affection. They helped me through. They made me feel . . . maybe I've been good in my work. I've never known. I can't be objective about what I do and since I lack confidence, I always feel someone else could have done it better. It's a tough way to live when you keep beating on yourself. I don't do bad things like that to myself anymore. I had reached a point once where I was so fearful of everything, so insecure about me, that I had made my circle so small I could hardly move. Now, as I've relaxed, come to terms with me, it's widened. And my life no longer feels frenetic because it isn't. I'm actually taking five months off come January!

"I can do that now," she says, her face glowing. "I now can believe that . . . I am here . . . and that I hold some kind of place with the public. I don't have to work twelve months a year to maintain that place. I won't be forgotten . . . won't lose that place. Ann-Margret will not go down the tubes if she stays home for a while doing simple things as Ann-Margret Olsson Smith."

Home for Ann-Margret is in Beverly Hills, where she lives with Roger Smith and his three children from a former marriage. Roger is the focal point of Ann-Margret's life. "When I met Roger, I was living in a cocoon, afraid to go out, afraid to live. He understood me instantly—understood how ravaged I had felt by my 'image.' He was kind. He *is* kind. He knows what I like and what I need. He is very much a father figure to me. He makes my life safe . . . comfortable. We have a good marriage because we want to have a good marriage. It is that simple. We are nice to each other every day. We talk. We communicate. We care."

The one element missing from the Smith marriage is a baby of their own. It is a painful subject for Ann-Margret. Nearing forty, her chances are diminishing rather than expanding. "We have been trying to have a child for four years now and I *think* we've been trying correctly," she adds, trying to make a heavy moment lighter. "But we haven't been successful. Frankly, one of the things I'm going to take a long, hard look at during my five months off is why I haven't conceived. Is it perhaps psychological? Or is it just possible that it is not intended for me to have my own child. But," she says, her voice fading, "not having a baby has been a source of pain for me

. . . and failure. That, too. But, I haven't given up hope."

As one observes Ann-Margret as she momentarily draws into her own thoughts, one sees she has not given up anything—*least of all* hope. There is a strength to match her vulnerability. This is no longer a frightened child afraid to face grown-up tasks but a *woman* searching to find her own maturity. Partly she is the result of her therapy. And partly she is the product of a brush with death. She shakes her head in agreement. "When you come that close to dying, you begin to live. So much of what once bothered you, no longer does. You recognize it for what it is . . . basically unimportant. Life is the most precious gift. Next is love. Both happen now! Perhaps they also occur in the future but no one owns the future. There is no 'for sure'! I live for today, for the 'now.' My life is about my husband and family."

She listens to her words and goes behind a cloud that covers her eyes. When she emerges she adds: "I'm first learning to live for me. I have this need—this very great need to feel cared for . . . loved. I find people do care for me, which is wonderful because I care for them. You know, ever since I was a little girl all I ever wanted to do was go out on a stage and touch people. That is *still* all I want to do as an entertainer. People tell me I do it: that me, Ann-Margret, contributes to their happiness. Well, that makes life good. Since there is Roger, my marriage, and my work, there is only one thing more I want from life—me! And I'm going to get her."

CHAPTER SIX

SARAH VAUGHAN

Shortly after noon on a rainy Saturday in California, Sarah Vaughan, wearing a big after-a-nap and my-didn't-it-feel-good smile, shuffles slowly from her off-the-kitchen bedroom into her living room. She carefully plops onto an overstuffed couch, then looks about contentedly at the family activity.

Her husband, Marshal Fisher, is pouring coffee. Her mother is doing busywork in the kitchen. Daugher Debbie is unhappily but necessarily removing the "souvenir" left in the hallway by one of their four dogs.

The "Divine One," as she is frequently referred to professionally, is dressed in an electric blue pants suit and is wearing a wig that *had* to be borrowed from Flip Wilson. She is feeling good. Suddenly she becomes aware that the open fly on her pants is permitting Sarah Vaughan to let it all hang out.

"Well, that takes care of any attempt at class," she says. "Never was one for that star shit," she continues, as she zips up in one quick motion. "Actually, I hate the word. Star. Ugh! What broad in her right mind would rather be that than a woman? This crazy business often forces a gal to make that choice. But not me. Status never did do for me. It's not what you have materially or what titles are attached to your name that matters, but who you are as a person."

Her home bears witness to her words. It is a "home gorgeous" rather than a candidate for a "house beautiful," and the good vibes that permeate it are obviously more important to its occupants than good taste. She is totally comfortable in her surroundings, that rarity, the celebrity without pretense, the woman who is.

The Vaughan/Fisher home is somewhere over the rainbow and its remoteness makes the way to San Jose seem simple. It is as high as one can get legally, resting on a series of mountains that make up the community of Hidden Hills. Appropriately named. It is also apropos that Sarah Vaughan should live there, as, despite thirty-two years of nightclub, concert, and TV appearances, she has remained hidden from public view. She may be show business's most successful shut-in.

Because of the distance between Vaughan and the public over the years, there has been much speculation (a euphemism for gossip) about her. Some think her to be standoffish and rude; others maintain she is none too bright; while most whisper she is an alcoholic.

The truth is Sarah Vaughan was shy and . . . she *did* drink. Until recently her communication was strictly nonverbal. Today she talks. "And if that comes as a shock to some folks, it damn near scared me to death!" says Sarah. "One day I quit drinking and the next, these strange sounds started coming out of my mouth. I thought maybe I needed an exorcist until a friend said, 'Hey Sarah, them is words!' "

She is aware that many believe her to have been an alcoholic "and only the good Lord knows why I wasn't. I loved my booze; needed it to make me feel *real* good. But when I quit, I quit. No pink elephants. No shakes. I used booze to hide my shyness, and I was bombed half the time I was working. That's why I sang with my hands anchored to my sides. I was afraid if I moved a muscle, I'd upset my balance and fall on my ass."

Today Sarah Vaughan is upsetting everyone's balance by coming back from near obscurity to where she is now one of *the* most in-demand performers in America. "Actually I was never away or in retirement. I just stopped recording."

When she returned to making albums, she was instantly rediscovered. Now she has climbed to legendary status in the music industry. "Yeah," she comments. "People keep rapping about me and an institution. I don't know if they mean I am one or that I belong in one."

If course they mean she is one. With Ella, there is Sarah and after Ella and Sarah, it's all second best. At fifty her voice is as rich, pure, and perfectly pitched as it was when she began her career at eighteen singing with the Earl "Fatha" Hines Orchestra. She finds the renaissance of Sarah Vaughan, the singer, unbelievable. "I can understand the oldies-but-goodies digging my work, but my new audiences are their children." She enjoys her new acceptance to the point of "having worked thirteen months in the last twelve. I'm not getting older, just better and . . . a little rounder 'round the edges."

The actual comeback took place in Los Angeles at a club that caters to the youth-rock crowd. She was second-billed to a big rock act and to her amazement, she "turned the place out. I didn't understand it. Those kids weren't even born when I was first doing my thing." She also didn't understand "but wasn't about to question it, honey," her rousing reception at New York's Continental Baths, whose clientele launched Bette Midler to stardom. "All those boys running around in nothing but towels! And everyone in the swimming pool naked! You just *know* I was dying to take a peek. A peek? Sheeit. I wanted to stare. Yes, to stare! But I didn't. They paid twelve fifty to get in and I'd like to think I gave them their money's worth." Within that last statement is the new Sarah Vaughan. Today her performances lack her onetime narcissism. She is energetic and "out there," giving to her paying patrons. She is no longer afraid to touch or be touched; her shyness is buried with her past.

"I never knew you to be shy," says Marshal Fisher quizzically.

"You never knew me to be drunk either," Mrs. Fisher responds. "Honey, I was so scared of the folks that I used to do my interviews in sign language. I'd shake my head once for yes and tap my foot twice for no."

Fisher shakes his head in disbelief. The couple has been married for four years and the Sarah Vaughan his wife describes is not the woman he has known. "I gave up drinking 'cause it trapped me," says Sarah. "But it is more than just giving up booze that changed me. For the first time in my life, I feel free, and I owe it to Marshal. He is the kind of man any woman would want. He's honest, stubborn, and typical Aries."

The Fishers met in Las Vegas. Sarah was performing while Marshal was employed as the kitchen manager for the Starboard Tack. At his urging a mutual friend introduced them. "I had been Sarah's fan for years. I figured I'd just say hello to an idol and here I am still saying hello and planning on doing so for a long time to come."

The "idol" beams. "Imagine getting a peach after two rotten apples," she says, alluding to two previous marriages, the very memories of which make her shudder.

Although both recall an instant attraction to one another, both deny there were any bells ringing around Las Vegas. "We dug each other," says Fisher. "We felt similarly about lots of things. But we were both cautious and had reason to be. I was wary of Sarah because I had met many entertainers in Vegas and found them shallow, wrapped up in themselves. Sarah was real. She didn't have that need, that sickness so many have, to run others down. She's been through a lot but she really isn't bitter. Actually you really can't say what Sarah is. You can't dissect her. It's the toal woman who is extraordinary."

The "extraordinary" one is beaming again, radiating a home-and-hearth-and-husband happiness. With a man she hopes will be husband number last—a man who is white—Sarah Vaughan goes deaf at the noise her intermarriage has caused.

"That rolls off my back like so much water," says Fisher, who previous marriage was also to a black woman.

"It doesn't come close to touching me," adds Sarah. "I don't see color when I meet someone. That Marshal is white and I'm black, well, my head just doesn't turn in that direction."

Fisher nods his head in agreement. "A friend recently said to me that it must take great strength to be married to a black woman. I couldn't explain to him that if you're into that kind of thinking, you're just not ready for it. Special strength? What does that have to do with loving someone?"

Sarah deals with racism by ignoring it. But when it gets heavy, so does she. "I'm not known for my mouth but in that kind of situation, I can be very loud. My life is nobody's business but mine and my Maker's. And Marshal, he is a good man, a nice person. He respects and cares for me. I have learned through him that not every man rips off his woman . . . steals from her blind. Marshal makes me feel just plain good. I'm supposed to walk away from him just because he's white? No way. Absolutely no way!"

She is not and never has been actively involved in black causes, movements, or organizations. "A lot of them ain't too together," she says, "but if they need me, I'm available just as I have been in the past."

The "past" found her responsible for the integration of a formerly segregated movie theater in her hometown of Newark. With her other preteen friends, she was relegated to sitting in the balcony, as the orchestra was "For Whites Only." To show how they felt about this second-class treatment, Sarah and friends would throw "stuff" into the seating section below. At first ole "Divine One" is reluctant to define "stuff"; but when pressed tells of doses of night-before Ex-Lax and day-of paper bags, filled "when the spirit moved us," and then tossed with youthful abandon down on the orchestra below. And thus almost immediately and without violence, integration came to that particular theater.

She has no bitter memories about Newark, and certainly none about her childhood. Her father, a carpenter, "picked guitar a little" and loved his daughter "a lot." His recent death is something she still cannot discuss unemotionally. Her mother was and is her friend. "Not too many girls can say that about their mamas. I sure hope Debbie can some day. We never went hungry. Mama knew how to make one good meal last a week. We had our struggles but we were happy."

At an early age she was skillful at both the piano and organ. She was also a soloist with the church choir. Her shyness, she says, was always with her and she knows of no explanation for it. "Just seems I was born that way. It didn't matter much, as I was never unpopular. Not that I was the queen of beautiful downtown Newark either." Dating was done in groups and there was never a steady boyfriend. "A steady? You must be kidding. Not even the married folks had that."

She was not keen on school but as a matter of pride wants it known she did not play hooky until her senior year in high school. "Then I'd show up for my music class and split." She never thought of being a professional singer. "I wanted to be a hairdresser. Still do. I offered to do Carmen's [McRae] hair for nothing and that's what Carmen said; 'Not for nothin'!' That girl is evil."

At eighteen Sarah entered amateur night at the Apollo Theatre in Harlem, not in hopes of launching a career but "to win the ten bucks they offered as first prize. In those days you could throw one helluva party with that kind of money." She wore a skirt and blouse, a little lipstick, and with teeth chattering, went on to "wreck the place" and took first prize, which included a week's singing engagement at the theater. Headlining was Ella Fitzgerald, and Sarah remembers her as being "very nice and very encouraging. Ella is one terrific lady and a great singer but she sure is hard to get close to. I think Ella and I are a lot alike: shy. Only I used booze and she didn't"

Sarah was accidentally discovered by Billy Eckstine. He had come to the Apollo to cash a check and heard "a girl who sang on key! Not too many could do that. She was incredible then; she's incredible now." His enthusiasm landed her the Earl "Fatha" Hines job. Ten days after the conclusion of her Apollo run, Sarah Vaughan was in show business, "scared to my socks and mad as hell as I never got to throw my party with my ten bucks."

Her family was also "scared to their socks. Ma kept wishing I was two instead of eighteen. She was moaning all over Newark about her baby being on the road with all those men in the band. She should've saved her breath. Being on the road first with Hines and then with [Billy] Eckstine's band was the most fun I have ever had in my life. In fact, it's probably the only thing in my life, up until my marriage to Marshal, I would do over again. It just had to be good, right? Being the only broad with all those guys, how could it be bad? They taught me everything I knew about music and life. It was more like having fifteen fathers, all demanding to know where you were, with whom, and why. But it was a ball, all tens of thousands of miles of it."

Yet she must be prodded to speak about "the road" in detail, and when she does, the memories, despite her admission that "there was an awful lot of shit going on down South" are bland. "It never got to me," she offers as explanation. "We just laughed at that crap. Billy and I would go around putting everyone on, saying 'yassuh' and 'nossuh,' and then running like hell. Like in Wilmington. While at the train station, Billy tried to get a shine but this punk said he don't wipe no nigger's shoes. So five minutes later the entire band hits this creep for a shine. To this day I don't know if that dude's ass is alive or dead but we sure left Wilmington in a hurry.

"Actually," she continues, "we left a lot of towns in a hurry. Most of them had only one general store and they wouldn't serve colored. We would damn near starve to death until Willie [Smith] would do his thing. Willie looked white so he'd go into the store and rap with the owner. After a while he'd ask if he couldn't bring his darkies in for a treat, and usually the guy would agree. Then while Willie gassed with the cat, we robbed him blind. Sometimes we took so much stuff we wouldn't need to get off the bus to buy food for a week. One thing about the South though, they may be a bunch of bigot-bastards, but at least they be honest about it. Up North it's another trip."

She is referring to her first engagement at New York's Copacabana. It is the late forties and she has attained national prominence. A big deal is made about a breakthrough—Sarah, a black woman, performing at the Copa. Yet she is not allowed to use the club's dressing room. She is also informed that she is not welcome in the cocktail lounge. No mingling and use the back door, please, are the house rules. She speaks of it all dispassionately. "There was no sense in being uptight about it," she says. "Sure I didn't like it, but I got 'round it. My musicians and I would hang out at a corner bar and come back loaded and feeling good. That's what it's all about, isn't it, feeling good?"

She didn't "feel good" a decade later, when at the height of her popularity she played the Empire Room at the Waldorf Astoria Hotel. "Those dudes didn't really dig my thing. They paid big bucks to see Sarah Vaughan because they thought it was wonderful that a black 'lady' was playing the room. It's that liberal shit—and it's horseshit. I wasn't comfortable there. My thing was smack crosstown at Birdland where folks didn't have a lot of money and knew where I was coming from. Together, we sure had a lot of fun."

Her memories as a black woman in the business are seemingly without bitterness or rage, as Marshal Fisher has stated. She accepts the past and lives in the present. "There are white people I hate but certainly not because they are white. I hate only those people who do me bad. Put me down and you're on my shit list no matter what your color. I also believe in retribution. If you treat me bad, I'm no good at turning the other cheek."

She does not feel that she has been particularly abused by whites, and she doesn't see the white man as the cause of her youthful despair and near disintegration. "It wasn't that tough for me," she maintains, "but I can see where it was tough as hell for someone like Lena [Horne]. Now she is one gorgeous woman, a real beauty, and I've never been known for my natural beauty—which is one of the world's great oversights, but maybe I was lucky. Lena had to deal with that black sexuality thing. White men went after her, and white women found her a threat. That gal took a lot of crap. I sometimes wonder how she survived but she sure as shit did. And with her beauty and femininity intact. A lot of ladies—and quite a few of the 'boys'—have tried to be like her, but there is only one Lena. Just as there is only one Ella, one Carmen, one Aretha. What I'm saying is, sure, things were tough, but we made it, didn't we? We're still here, aren't we?"

But at what price is a question she neither asks nor answers. She sometimes seems oblivious to her own self, to her own sufferings. "With my first real earnings, I bought my folks a home. It was also for me too, I guess. I wanted to make sure that if I ended up broke and alone, I'd at least have some place to go." And in another breath she adds, "Funny, no matter how miserable I would get, I refused to go home and cry. And I used to be miserable a lot. But there was no way I would let anyone in on that. Not me. Instead I'd go out and swing, and I do mean swing. I had me good times, no matter how I felt. I'd get drunk two and three times a night. Never falling down drunk, just high as hell and feeling good. I hung out with the guys—musicians mainly—because I learned early that a lot of females tell your story on the street the next day. Yep, men were my friends. Too bad my husbands weren't."

After a very long pause she continues. "Things are very different for me today. What I did then I wouldn't dream of doing now. I mean I used to hang out. Just hang out. Anything to avoid going home. One bar after another. One drink more. I just kept moving, searching for laughs, having a bunch but never quite having enough. And when I think of some of the joints I hung out in, if I did that today, they'd haul my ass into jail by morning."

She is back *there*, confronting what was her life. "I had my bad times," she says in a near whisper. "Night would come and I'd be wondering who I could hang out with that might buy me a meal. Truth is, I played a lot of bum clubs in my day that gave me a lot of bum checks. I've been hungry a lot in my life. And lonely. Lonely as hell. Why else does a gal hang out? But no one ever guessed I was lonely," she says as though her deception was something to be proud of. "No, never did anyone ever guess that. There were always the drinks and the laughs. I just wasn't the kind who could say to someone, 'Hey, man, I'm broke and hungry,' or . . . 'I'm lonely.'

"There were months on end when nothing was going on. And my love life stank too. But through it all, I don't have one single regret about anything that happened. It made me what I am today." And she laughs. "How's that for a line. Actually I do have a regret or two. I'm sorry I didn't kick a few guys in the teeth." She is referring again to the former husbands.

She does not choose to divulge further details about her marriages, but she does see parallels in hers, Dinah Washington's, and Billie Holiday's.

"We chose lousy men," she says. "My first two marriages were like a matching set to Billie's. I don't know what it is with us broads. Maybe we're dumb or too nice or too trusting. Each time I married, I really thought I had a winner, but in each case, as soon as I said, 'I do,' he didn't *do*. So I worked—had to because there were bills to pay. Both of them, with their expensive tastes, lived in the till. For every dime I earned, they'd spend a quarter."

She believes Dinah's case was different. "She was 'Big Mama' to her men. They sat back and let her work because she enjoyed doling out the dough. She was a helluva woman, Dinah was. A nice lady. Not too many people knew that because you had to know her to love her, as the expression goes; and Dinah wasn't about letting too many people come too close. She was a strong woman, and when she got shit from an audience, she gave it back. She was never a sad woman. Never Billie-like sad."

She dismisses the swipe Billie took at her in *Lady Sings the Blues*. "I *knew* Billie. I was her friend just as she was mine. We worked together. And at no time did I ever avoid her because she had been in jail."

Sarah is thoughtful and her face is as momentarily clouded as the sky surrounding Hidden Hills. A horse whinnies and she smiles. "That's ours, part of the household," she says. She has closed the door on the past—her own and that of others who shared it. "I always wanted a horse and a garden and trees and here they all are," she continues. "Today is an all-new life, filled with a magic I used to think only came in bottles. I have nothing to feel bad about.

"I'll be going out on the road soon," she says, "and as much as I love my work, I cry every time I leave my home. This is the time of my life. Everything I have ever wanted I have now. I'm fifty years old, a beautiful woman living with her beautiful husband and beautiful family in her beautiful home. That's what most of us women want."

And on a rainy afternoon in Hidden Hills, California, Sarah Vaughan, from the far reaches of an over-stuffed sofa, hair somewhat askew, looks across the room at her husband, sees his appreciative smile, and beams. And as she does, she is a beautiful woman indeed.

CHAPTER SEVEN

KATHARINE HEPBURN

I don't like my phone to ring at 9:00 A.M. By that time I am already two hours into my writing and I do not enjoy being disturbed. That morning, however, my phone rang at precisely 9:00 A.M.

"Yes!" I growled.

"Mr. Ebert, this is Katharine Hepburn," said the voice briskly.

"Now look!" I thundered just as briskly. "I have no time for jokes. Who is this?"

"Mr. Ebert, this *is* Katharine Hepburn," replied the unruffled voice that I suddenly realized was unmistakably hers. "I understand we have an interview to do. Can you come to my house at two this afternoon?"

Impossible, I said to myself. Unrealistic. Not with my deadline on still another magazine feature.

"But of course," I heard myself cooing. "No problem. Looking forward to it. Wonderful!" I crooned, big phony that I can be.

You have to "be there," as they say, to fully understand what happens when one unexpectedly receives a call from Katharine Hepburn. *The* Katharine Hepburn, who just set National Secretary Week back a decade by dialing her own phone and making her own appointment for an interview. That just isn't done when you're a legendary movie star.

So what did I do? I panicked. I couldn't collect a single thought or question in my head. What do you ask Katharine Hepburn? You've read that she refuses to talk about the late Spencer Tracy and Howard Hughes, with whom she had "involvements." Somehow you just don't ask Katharine Hepburn, "Do you sleep in the nude?" And oh-my-gawd, what do you wear to a Katharine Hepburn interview? White tie and tails? A three-piece suit? Do you kneel, bow from the waist, and kiss her hand (or ring) upon meeting her? Do you pretend cool sophistication with a "Hiya, Kate," or do you murmur something more reserved and elegant like "Charmed, I'm sure."

I settled on jeans and a turtleneck, a simple handshake, and all-encompassing, you-can-never-go-wrong-with (according to Elizabeth Post) "Hello."

Katharine Hepburn's New York City residence is a typical Manhattan brownstone surrounded by iron gates, which supposedly protect Ms. H. from the outside world. But a quick check of her neighbors proves that Ms. H. doesn't need or want protection. After a snow *she* shovels her own walk! And, the local supermarket manager reveals, *she* does her own grocery-grabbing and *shleps* her own grocery bags.

Katharine Hepburn *shleps*????

When ushered through the front door, the first thing that strikes you about Katharine Hepburn's home is that it smells like a baker's kitchen. Ms. Hepburn has been baking brownies, you are told.

Katharine Hepburn bakes brownies????

But didn't you know, she is famous for them, is the reply. Almost as famous as she is for her chocolate-chip cookies—but not quite, continues your informant.

Her second-floor living room overlooking the garden is filled with early American—good stock—furniture. The wood-burning fireplace makes a warm and cozy room even more homelike. Not one of her three Oscars is displayed. In fact, the room does not contain one memento of a career that began fifty years ago when Hepburn first stepped upon a stage in

The Czarina. The room is a blend of aromas:—fresh flowers and fresh brownies—the brownes win. You grab a handful. After all, one does want to tell one's grand-children—and anyone else who will listen—that one ate a Katharine Hepburn brownie.

Suddenly there is a stampede on the stairway. A stallion is thundering down. No, it's Hepburn in her trademarks—a turtleneck and slacks. Her hair is swept up and piled atop her head. That famous ruddy face, cheekbones rising sharply above a jutting chin, is with-out makeup, alive, vital, and pretty. I say so.

"Oh, I was never pretty," she says, "never con-sidered a beauty. In fact, at one time I was considered quite sexless. Not by me. Actually I always thought I was quite passable. I always tried to make up for my lack of looks with a stunning personality."

She whoops with laughter. When it subsides, so does she. Sort of. It becomes apparent that she is ner-vous, as nervous as I am. Whereas I'm catatonic in her presence, she is jumping about, fluffing up pil-lows, rearranging flowers, and pushing brownies.

She has granted the interview, she explains, be-cause she loves *The Corn Is Green* and hopes people will watch it—more for the play, she quickly adds, than for her. That she speaks to the press at all is still somewhat of a modern-day miracle. What has hap-pened, she says, somewhat embarrassed, is that she re-alizes that she does indeed "matter" to many people, and that a "certain amount" of her, but not much, should be available to the public. Yet she feels the fuss made about Katharine Hepburn is much ado about far less than people think.

"I don't think Katharine Hepburn is that special," she says. "I don't even believe in *that* Katharine Hepburn. She doesn't exist. I'm me and very few people know me. But the actress—although she did accomplish a lot—could have done forty times more than she did. But I will not lacerate myself with that. Let's just say I could've done better. Which, perhaps, is why I'm always amazed when people treat me with reverence. Who are they referring to? It is all very lovely, but it often seems to me to be about someone other than me. Yet," she adds, "I am touched by it."

Hepburn still has "hopes of improving," she says. Without a sense of age (seventy this year) or of time running out, she intends to work for many more years. She also intends, "with the good Lord's help," to "improve my tennis game." She does not plan to have another "relationship," she says, aghast at the mere mention of such an idea. But "I need people. I need my family—Oh, I have such a large and lively family—And I need my friends and the people who assist me in my homes. They all care for me. And at any age you need to be cared for physically and emotionally. One must allow that or one cuts off from life."

Katharine Hepburn believes she was given a "gift" in life. "Being able to make people laugh and cry—and I can do both—*is* a gift. Not a terribly important one, mind you, but a gift nonetheless. I enjoy my work. My career has been fun. It still is. I have great enthusiasm. That's me, Kate Hepburn—great enthusiasm and a great appetite for life. And for sweets too," she adds, laughing as crumbs from the brownies she has been munching fall into her lap.

"What you see before you today—me—is the result of chocolate," she laughs on. "What a pound of it per day—often at one sitting—can do for you! I eat whatever I want because I don't have to watch my figure. Never did, as I never had one to watch. So I am a heavy eater, but I also do love my exercise. I play hard, meaning I enjoy myself at what I do or I don't do it. I like to pick up and go . . . in my work or in my play.

"I'm a very active person physically," she continues. "Actually I'm so darn active that I ache in every joint from all my constant moving about. But I refuse to change. I treasure each and every ache because I love my tennis and my swimming. And I even enjoy getting down and scrubbing my own floors."

If you believe that, I think, you might just as well believe in Santa Claus.

"I don't believe in retirement, you know," Hepburn continues. "People of all ages must belong to society—must feel they are contributing so as not to feel alienated. Retirement can do that. One can continue to contribute in so many different ways at so many different ages."

Her phone rings and she excuses herself. When a housekeeper enters to clear away the coffee cups, I say inquisitively: "My, but this place is spotless! It must take a lot of help."

"Oh, no!" she replies. "Miss Hepburn does it herself. Every Wednesday when she's in town, she scrubs and polishes all the floors."

> *Dear Santa: I have been good. Very good. Would you therefore please arrange for me to have, at your convenience of course, the latest-model Jaguar. Blue would be fine. Thank you. Alan.*

CHAPTER EIGHT

KATHARINE HEPBURN

Youth and youthfulness are treasured in this society, as well they should be. But why is the opposite end of the spectrum not treasured? Perhaps it is because some call it the *declining* years. To many, growing older means growing less useful, less needed, less productive, less involved, but . . . more dependent. Aging is often viewed as a time of regression when one despairs, is ill and lonely. Thus when a someone dares to prove this view is indeed one-dimensional, we take pride in this person. We rejoice in her. Certainly we rejoice in Katharine Hepburn as we *think* she is and . . . as we want her to be—a crusty ole gal of a fierce, independent nature. For it is reassuring to know that at seventy, one can be "crusty" and "fiercely independent." Kate, as intimates call her, proves the so-called declining years can be active and not passive—as much on the *in*cline as one is inclined to make them.

Katharine Hepburn, the legend, is as in demand by the public and her industry today as she ever was. Why? Because Katharine Hepburn is as demanding of herself as she was when she first stepped upon a stage *fifty years ago* in *The Czarina*.

Often she reads like a great fictional heroine from a romantic novel. To many she is still Jo of *Little Women*, but one of her screen triumphs. To others, she remains Spencer Tracy's romantic lead through nine films and through many, many years of *real* life. Her studio biography so aptly describes her as "tem-

pestuous, unpredictable, free-spirited and vibrant."
She is timeless, ageless. But how? And Why?

Katharine Hepburn's town house on Manhattan's
East Side smells like the kitchens of Sara Lee. The
aroma of freshly baked Hepburn brownies competes
with the aroma of the fresh flowers that adorn her
second-floor living room. An old-fashioned fireplace
and furniture that is more Americana in style than
English or French give the Hepburn home all the
remembered warmth and comfort one associates with
childhood visits to a favorite aunt. Even the winter
frost that collects on the windows overlooking the
ample backyard garden cannot detract from the
room's warmth. Interestingly, whereas she proudly
displays her brownies on end tables and the mantel-
piece, she does not her awards. No shrine or museum
here. No evidence of the three Academy Awards she
has won for her starring roles in *Morning Glory,
Guess Who's Coming to Dinner?* and *Lion in Winter*.

She thunders down from her upstairs suite of rooms
and barrels into the living room, her blue eyes
brighter than the afternoon sun. From her almost
bawdy entrance and then from her firm handshake it
is evident this is no "sweet little ole lady." But from
her shy, hesitant smile, her very obvious nervousness
as she flits about the room, propping up pillows and
pulling up ottomans, it is evident this is no "crusty
ole broad" either. Hardly. In fact, one of the first
qualities one feels from Katharine Hepburn is
softness. Next . . . vulnerability.

Wearing beige slacks—a Hepburn trademark—a
black turtleneck sweater—another Hepburn trademark—and a bright red sweater draped casually chic
about her shoulders, Katharine Hepburn looks terrific. She has added some weight, which has
youthened the look of her body. That famous face
of rising-cheekbones above-a-jutting-chin is without
makeup, and . . . still beautiful in its very unique

way. She attempts to sit but bounds up immediately upon doing so to serve coffee. Seated again, she unseats herself to lead us now into temptation by bringing a plate of brownies directly into our line of vision. She insists we eat, which proves, even in the Hartford, Connecticut, born-of-Irish-parentage-Katharine Hepburn, there is a little bit of the Jewish mother.

She laughs when she is told this—a big gut roar rather than a polite chuckle. It results that Katharine Hepburn laughs and roars frequently. And nothing strikes her funnier than the Katharine Hepburn image itself. Except perhaps life. The joke is often on Katharine Hepburn as told by Katharine Hepburn and the laughs are more of wit than wisdom. This is unexpected. Much has been written of Hepburn but almost never has her humor—her ability to laugh at herself—been mentioned.

She dislikes this, dislikes that she has been lionized by the press and nearly canonized by her fans. She is not comfortable with her image because it is not her, she maintains. Which is why in recent years she has become somewhat (but not much) more available to interviewers. More confident of herself today, she would like to be known for *who* she is rather than for *what* she is in the minds of many.

When Katharine Hepburn finally throws herself down into a chair, successfully, but with great difficulty, temporarily harnessing her great energy, she turns to the questions and the question*er* face-on. Her expression is one of curiosity; her posture, as she sits, is proud. This is Katharine Hepburn who is not, at seventy, less useful, less needed, less productive, but more dependent. And with the disappearance of "but one more" brownie, she is prepared to tell *how* she is, *as* she is, ageless.

Do you think of yourself as "ageless"?
I never think of age at all. Age has absolutely no sig-

nificance in my life. In fact, two of the world's dullest subjects are one's age and one's health.

But they are realities.
So is death but one shouldn't waste time thinking about things one cannot change. I certainly don't fear death. Why should I fear something inevitable and unchangeable. Besides, perhaps death is great—a lovely, long sleep.

What do you see when you look in the mirror?
Me. As I am. I hope I'm not interested in fooling anyone—least of all myself, by having my face done. As you see, I wear no makeup. But I do try to look clean. I think that's the best that can be said of me: that Kate Hepburn looked clean [laughter]. Frankly, at this stage, I don't think people pay any more attention to my looks than I do.

Shouldn't one be concerned with physical appearance at any age?
Yes. But not excessively or obsessively. One should take pains to look best for oneself. What I am saying is . . . those people who concentrate *only* on how they look and how they feel are barking up the wrong tree. If they're my age, they are simply not going to look all that gorgeous. So what? Who needs to? Sad are those who want to look at sixty as they looked at twenty. Common sense should dictate what you were then is what you were *then*. I say one should just be the best person one is whatever one's age. Be a great sixty . . . a sensational seventy! But get on with it. Never look back.

Is that what you do?
Well, I certainly don't look back on my once great beauty because it was never there [laughter]. I was never considered to be beautiful. Actually, for a time, I was considered quite sexless. Not by me, heavens knows, but by motion picture makers. Actually I always thought I was quite passable. I also hoped to

make up for my lack of looks with my thrilling personality [laughter]. I also hoped the freckles on my **face would make me appear friendly. Sort of like** . . . Huck Finn.

Friendly is hardly a word or a quality that one has associated with the legend of Katharine Hepburn.
[Laughter]. Yes, I can understand that. I wasn't exactly available to the press or to the public, for that matter, for many years.

Why now?
I guess I've become sweeter [laughter]. But in truth, I discovered "me" is not just my business but theirs [the press's and the people's] too. Also, I have far more confidence in writers today. Now that they've stopped concocting stories about my supposed mad love affairs I'm not so skittish about interviews. Writers now concern themselves with real issues when talking to me. I guess they think I've reached an age when a mad affair is no longer probable. Now that I think about that, I'm not so certain I like it [laughter]. But seriously, the press has become far more sensible.

And "sensible" is important to you?
"Sensible" sounds somewhat righteous. The ability to *think*, that's what's important. It should be important to people at all ages. I believe most people want to use their minds, want to improve their knowledge. I think media, and in particular television, does an injustice to people by not providing programs of a more informative nature. Programmers seem to be unaware that people want to learn . . . want to grow. At all ages people need to feel they are improving and that this improvement helps them to live a fuller and more productive life.

You are speaking here of the more mature.
Of *anyone*. The mind, like the body, must remain active or it will wither. Even if you're six, the mind

must be exercised. More so perhaps if you are sixty. I think the lack of mental stimulation—boredom—is the greatest "destroyer" in life.

You have definite ideas on aging, then.
Oh, dear. What is "aging" or "youthening"? I simply don't think in those terms, which probably is a statement in itself. But I don't think of myself as "ageless," "aging," "old," or "elderly," or any of those labels. I put my efforts into living . . . into learning and concentrating . . . into work and what fun work is. Fun and stimulating. I never lose sight of the fact that just *being* is fun. I'm not as much for thinking sometimes as I am for doing.

You enjoy being Katharine Hepburn.
Who else should I enjoy being?

I mean being that Katharine Hepburn, public personality.
Whoever, or *what*ever, she might be. I am constantly astounded by the impression of me created by others, or perhaps which I unwittingly have created of myself. Such rubbish has been written! The Katharine Hepburn I know simply isn't all that special. And *that* Hepburn you ask about doesn't exist. I'm me and very few people know me. Now the actress—not the legend—accomplished a lot but she could've done a helluva lot more. Forty times more. But I will not lacerate myself for that. I could've and should've done better. Enough said. Besides, it isn't over yet. Perhaps I'll still redeem myself [laughter]. But that other Katharine Hepburn, all that fuss always struck me as much ado about very little indeed.

Do you resent being that Katharine Hepburn?
Not anymore. I used to think people, like critics, were my natural enemies. But now, oh my, but I'm so often touched by people—touched that they want to know about me and touched that they are so gen-

erous in their outpouring of affection toward me. That is [pause] . . . lovely [pause] . . . you know . . . very moving. I've come to realize and to trust that I matter to people. But I do wish some would stop treating me with such reverential awe.

As though you were not quite real or of this life?
That and more. People mean to be very sweet to me. They offer me their parking places, which is unheard of in New York. When they see me carrying bundles home from the market, they rush to relieve me of the burden. When I'm shoveling snow from my walk— something I love to do—they wrestle the shovel out of my hands. This is lovely of them but . . . I don't need the help. I happen to like to shovel snow. I like the exercise and I like the variety it gives to living. We take so much for granted. In life there are many roadblocks. It is so much more rewarding to unblock the road ourselves. When we do, it gives us a sense of independence . . . a sort of do-it-yourself lesson in solving your own problems. I say, whatever the "road-block," don't wait for Uncle Sam or anyone else. Do it. And do it now. Seize it for the opportunity it is and *not* the chore.

Which is the oft-written-about "independent" streak of yours. Are you "fiercely" independent?
I am not "fiercely" anything. That's part of the myth. But I am independent and have been for a very long time. I was taught from childhood by very independent parents to be a very independent person. My parents were highly intelligent and accomplished people. My father was a surgeon—a urologist—and my mother was college educated, very liberal, particularly for conservative New England. Why, my parents were hurrahing for women's rights, social hygiene, and birth control way back then! They were free thinkers, which was quite alarming to a large body of the Hartford, Connecticut, citizenry. But their sense of independence—given to me—fixed in the minds of folks

forever that I, as their daughter, was one of the Fighting Hepburns. And I was . . . am, I suppose.

So your independence is a "gift" from your parents?
A great gift. One of the greatest. That and freedom from fear . . . freedom to state what I think and be fully aware of the price affixed to being honest. But that's also about being independent, isn't it?

Do you pride yourself on your independence?
Good Lord, I don't think about it! I can't take credit for it. I simply inherited my parents' backbones. I've always said God gave me remarkably good health and good genes. I had a privileged childhood. I was a girl and yet I was extremely well educated—which in those years was not always afforded a female.

Which also added to your sense of independence?
Exactly. Education always does. As the mind is freed, so is the person. I *am* a very independent person but . . . and this is very important because it belies the myth about me . . . I am not totally independent, and more important, I would not want to be. I need the people in my life—the people who care for and about me. My family, my friends, my staff in my home who are family-and-friends in their own right. I *need* these people. We *all* need people. At all ages we need to be cared for physically and emotionally. We must feel that we are attached to significant others. It would be unbearable to feel cut off from such a necessary part of life. Although I belong firstly to myself, it is also true I feel a sense of belonging to family—to my sisters and brothers—and to friends, to those people who make me *me!*

This sense of belonging is important, then.
Definitely. People of all ages must belong, particularly to society. It is very important that people do not feel alienated. And our society can be very alienating for people past a certain age. Everything is geared toward kids in this country. People *must* feel

involved, a part of life. That is why retirement can be such a negative turnabout.

Retirement can lead to alienation?
Exactly. People, to feel important, vital, must feel they are part of a working society. People need to feel useful and that they make a contribution. And at any age, in so many different ways, one can contribute.

You are maintaining that to feel part of life, of the mainstream, one must feel useful?
Yes. People who have retired—women whose children have gone off in search of lives of their own, leaving their mothers, in a sense, in retirement—must be occupied productively in some way to be happy. One *must* feel necessary. I cannot imagine life without feeling important or feeling that one *matters* in some way—that one's presence and abilities contribute. How does one live without that sense?

Retirement therefore should not be about building a better bridge game or improving one's golf swing?
At least in the specifics you mention there is a goal, a purpose that might sustain one. But frankly I do not see how one can just play a better game of bridge in life. I believe one needs an activity that contributes— that makes one feel useful.

It sounds as if the "Christian work ethic" is integrally woven within Katharine Hepburn.
I believe work is man's salvation. I also believe concentrating on something other than one's own self is salvation. I find it sad that to many people work is a burden when it should be a joy . . . fulfilling. For far too many retirement brings a living death. Particularly enforced by age retirement. People are made to feel old. Worse, they are therefore made to feel they are useless, as if they've come to the end of the road. How humiliating to be thrown on the junk pile! And

to be thrown there, arbitrarily, because of a number known as age! Ridiculous! It can kill a person.

Do you find nothing positive about retirement?
For those unfortunate people who have hated their jobs, it is perhaps a good thing. For those who fall into that category and who now look forward to doing other things—things they really want to do—retirement can be wonderful. For these people retirement actually means a reentering of the mainstream with new interests. These people will become involved in living. But sadly, I believe, for most retirement means just that . . . a retirement from life, a withdrawal from being alive.

Obviously retirement is not a word in your dictionary.
I never think of retiring. I love to work. I'm an active person, as you've undoubtedly noticed by now. I do move around a lot, don't I [laughter]? I happen to thrive on mental and physical activity. Actually I'm so damn physical that every joint in my body aches from overuse [laughter]. But I refuse to change. I love tennis, swimming, walking. I also enjoy scrubbing my own floors.

You don't!
I do! And I launder my own pants and shirts several nights a week. Why not? As I said: I am able to do for myself and I enjoy the doing of it. Besides, I'm a compulsive worker and I love being a compulsive worker. And I'm handy. I can fix things around the house. I do very nicely, thank you. One usually can, *at any age.* To believe otherwise is to fall victim to the propaganda.

Do you watch your diet carefully to maintain both your health and your good physical condition?
What you see before you, my friend, is the result of a lifetime of chocolate. Viennese chocolate. A pound a day often. And cookies. I do so love cookies. Obviously, I don't have to watch my figure as I never had

much of one to watch [laughter]. Exercise, which I love, keeps me in shape. And I do get sufficient rest. As heavy as I eat, that's how heavy I sleep. I guess whether I am eating, sleeping, or working, I enjoy myself fully [laughter].

Is your work still challenging?
If it wasn't, I wouldn't do it. Not only is it challenging but it's fun. I bring enormous enthusiasm to it but then I'm very enthusiastic by nature. And happy. I am one of those who greet the dawn, and all that, which can be perfectly nauseating to those who can't stand cheer or noise early in the morning. But I am of boundless cheer and I do enjoy my enthusiasm. Without it, there would be no colors to life.

You are talking about an attitude as well as basic "born-with" traits.
Yes. My attitude keeps work fun. I have learned that one can always bring something fresh, something new, to one's work. I have also learned one has never discovered all there is to learn about one's work. I learn something each time I do a play or a film. I could never let my work go stale. It matters too much to me. *I* matter too much to me. *Mattering*, again, is a key word here. As I said: young or older, how does one live without a sense of *matter?* . .

So . . . my work matters to me and so do the people who now must pay outrageous prices to see my work. They are entitled to the best. Nothing stale for them! Not ever. They are entitled to a fresh and vital performance every time. I want that for them. And my wanting that keeps my work fresh.

So there is no resting on one's laurels.
I never saw a laurel one could rest on comfortably or for long. A laurel can be a dangerous thing. Some people take liberties with them. And they suffer for it. There are no laurels in my life, just new challenges. Nor do I believe that age entitles one to any

extra benefits. Saying something like . . . "Oh, isn't she marvelous for her age" is about as condescending a remark as I can think of. There should not be a separate set of rules based on age. Nor should there be separate considerations. I don't wish *ever* to be patronized.

You are asking for no special considerations because of age.
I didn't at twenty so why now? I'll get by on my abilities, my efforts and . . . my canniness. I'm very canny, you know. I really have but modest talent but lots of canniness [laughter]. And health. Really. Early on I decided to keep all my doors open—to be able to flit back and forth from screen to stage and now to television. That was canny of me. And I've always been curious—always wanted to explore all avenues of my work. Canny and curious. That's me. And I love being curious. It often takes me places that others dare not go. I love to take chances.

You enjoy the dare?
Yes. And why shouldn't I? I'm not brittle. I won't break easily. And if I am, or if I will, don't tell me [laughter]. I refuse to "act my age." What a dreadful expression! I suppose that's why some think of me as a "free spirit." The truth is I can't imagine life without challenge . . . without a little danger. How else is one to grow if one doesn't try new things . . . dangerous things. Like when I appeared on Broadway in *Coco*. Now that took some nerve! Audacity, really. I dared to sing—although I'm still not sure what I did could be called singing by any stretch of the imagination. Oh, but that was scary. But I do love to scare myself. I do love the scare in a challenge of one's abilities. For me the fun in work, in my life, is in the trying rather than in the arrival itself.

Do you ever just relax?
But of course. I never allow my passion for work to

weaken or drain me. I allow me time to refill my reservoir. I must do that. No matter what one's work, one needs to replenish oneself by doing something totally different, something that freshens and revitalizes you. For me, it's many things. Painting, writing, driving around town in my car, swimming, tennis—all refill my cup. But nothing refills it quite so satisfyingly as doing something or learning something new. Nothing opens the doors to life . . . to *living*, more than learning. And no one is too old to learn. Lord, how I hate the rubbish about how the mind supposedly deteriorates as one grows older! This propaganda foisted upon us is so deadening. One can learn at any age. And learning unlocks so many doorways in one's mind—opens such new passageways. When one's mind is open, life is open. It's a crime that people stop using their minds past a certain age. A crime! And they are their own victims.

Does it take more work to enjoy life past a certain age?
Life, whatever your age, is a gift, the most precious one we will ever receive. And, to coin a phrase, life is what you make it. I am never bored and find it difficult to understand boredom in others when there is so much to do and see around us. Boredom probably kills more people than all other diseases combined. And it can so easily be cured if one just opens oneself to new interests, to life. I don't care if you're one hundred twenty-seven. There must be something you haven't experienced that you would like to.

Are there "somethings" that you look forward to accomplishing?
Good Lord! I never think of "futures" Only *now!* There are no particular parts I covet, if that's what you mean. I just want to work in good productions. I strive always to be better. I still strive for that devastating serve in my tennis game. I truly hope when I get to heaven the good Lord will bless me by making

me a tennis champion. Not that I've given up all hope of attaining such a goal while here on earth [laughter]. **I still hope. Oh, yes. I have always great** hope for myself. I always feel that whatever it is I want to be or do is within my grasp. Which either proves how hopeful or how foolish I am [laughter].

If you don't think of "futures," do you then also not think of the past?
Hardly at all. To what purpose, except to learn from one's mistakes. People who live in the past have given up on their lives in the present. Who cares about "the good ole days" when it is now, the present, that is here. The present is all any of us has. It is certainly all I have. The past is gone, so it doesn't belong to me or to anyone else. And since none of us is assured a future, I say . . . let's get on with today. One can sit in one's chair and think about how pretty or how active one was twenty or thirty years ago but to what purpose? How active you are today, *that's* what matters!

Do you analyze the past?
I analyze practically nothing. The problem with all that dwelling on one's past is that it makes you tend to take yourself far too seriously. And if you do that, misery will be your constant companion.

Have you no regrets or second thoughts then, particularly about not having married?
None.

About growing older alone . . . without a mate?
I never think in those terms. And frankly I often look at some of the mates that are available and I think: "You are lucky, Katharine" [laughter].

Would you entertain the idea of a relationship with a man today?
Good heavens, no!

Why?
That's far too personal a question. I may have grown
"sweeter" but not that much sweeter.

Are you ever lonely?
Never! I am always so busy and I have so many interests and such a large family that just the opposite
is true. I find time I can be alone is a blessing. I seem
to be involved in a great many people's lives. Which
is good . . . lovely, actually. To be involved with
others is to be alive. But I never seem to have enough
time to do all I would like. But my family is part of
my joy. Although I make my own security, safety, and
comfort—I think everyone should strive to do that—
my family and friends do indeed contribute to my
sense of well-being. But I don't feel they are responsible for my welfare in any way, because they are not. I
feel we must be responsible for ourselves, whether we
like it or not. Family is the background and friends
the decor in one's portrait. But at any age, the foreground is *oneself*. And the picture is what you make
it.

CHAPTER NINE

DIAHANN CARROLL

Diahann Carroll's house is known as "the vault." It is *that* protected. More than just another beautiful home in Benedict Canyon, where it is camouflaged on the side of a hill and invisible from the roadway, her home is an inner sanctum. Much of her time in recent years has been spent here alone, at the side of the pool, thinking. She has had much to think about. A romance, a marriage, and a career have come and gone, and only the last is now being resurrected.

Until the recent release of *Claudine*, Diahann Carroll was a Hollywood has-been casualty—another used and discarded symbol. Long before black became beautiful, her basic beige was permissible, acceptable to a white America who sniffed and then decided she would neither contaminate nor offend. Beautiful, sophisticated, and chic, she was as relevant to blackness as the pages of *Vogue* from which she frequently smiled. The crucial issues of her life seemed to be: the Dior or the de la Renta? The Mercedes or the Rolls?

Of course, in her show-business infancy she was compared to Lena. Anyone black and beautiful and talented was. She became Broadway's brown darling with *House of Flowers*. Truman Capote adored her, and Marlene Dietrich, so stricken by her beauty and talent, gave her the black pearl ring from her finger. Richard Rodgers put his adoration to pen and created *No Strings* solely for her and the Broadway audience.

And Hollywood allowed her to be her image in a series of forgettable films when she was not being used in such picturesque "colored folk" epics as *Porgy and Bess* and *Carmen Jones.*

That was in the fifties, and if a black entertainer sought success then, it was done *their* way. Soul was not sold at the Plaza or Waldorf hotel supper clubs. Soul was not for sale anywhere but in black clubs. Lena pioneered the Waldorf and Eartha the Plaza, but soul differs from sex—the latter used by both women, while the other had to remain hidden. Diahann Carroll was only the second "one" to play the elegant Plaza's Persian Room, then the epitome of downtown chic. She sang Harold Arlen and Cole Porter—*that* people remember. But she also sang Oscar Brown, Jr.'s "Brown Baby," and that most people—particularly blacks—forget. What was not known is that hotel management, ever so nicely, requested Miss Carroll remove that song from her repertoire, and Miss Carroll, ever so nicely, refused.

Although not an overnight success, Diahann Carroll never struggled. Stardom was attained through a series of efforts beginning with *Chance of a Lifetime,* a one-time TV show that launched her as a singer and led to supper club appearances in Palm Springs where the neighborhood folks (Judy Garland and Dorothy Lamour) would drop in to hear her sing. "But my dear, you *must* come to Hollywood!" was the usual fuss, and at eighteen she did just that, to audition, at friends' urgings, for the title role in *Carmen Jones.*

Diahann recalls that Otto Preminger, the producer, "took one look at my eighteen-inch bust, which matched my eighteen-inch waist, and screamed: 'Whoeffah told you you vuh sexy?'" In hysterical fright of the Teutonic Mr. P., Diahann blurted out: "No one. I swear. Absolutely no one." Her answer satisfied Preminger, as he hired her for a lesser and definitely nonsexy role.

Many years later, when "times were right," she was the logical, survey-evaluated, time-tested, safe choice to play television's *Julia*. She was noncontroversial and nonthreatening, and to many, nonblack. She was tepid tokenism, network-style. And if she was irrelevant and not useful to a black America who in the sixties suddenly found its blackness beautiful, did white America care? No. As a must-be-nameless network spokesman says, "Our concern was not the black community but Main Street in Mobile, Shreveport, Memphis, and similar towns in the U.S. What they thought mattered because it would influence Madison Avenue. And that's where the money is."

The Main Streets made *Julia* a national success and an American paradox. *Julia* was a starring role without star billing, because America was not ready for that. "Starring Diahann Carroll" had to be sneaked into the credits.

Almost immediately, Julia and Diahann were attacked for being "whitey's cop-out." Both were judged and found guilty of being white middle class. The jury rendered its verdict on circumstantial evidence. Few came to their defense. And even now, no one wants to acknowledge that without her "basic beige" the bigots who rule prime time would never have permitted a black woman on the air.

It is slow in coming but she finally admits "the criticism got to me for a very long time. It made me unhappy and uncertain." Today, she feels "immensely proud of both my own and the show's contribution. I know that a program with more of a ghetto attitude would never have gone on the air at that point in TV and American history."

She knew *Julia* had built-in pitfalls—the stereotypical black woman without a man in the house— knew the show was more white middle class than black, but, "I believed if a black could enter people's homes week after week and be watched and accepted, that was reason enough for *Julia*'s existence. I still believe that. Yes, *Julia* assuaged guilts of the white hierarchy but on a larger and more important scale, I knew if *Julia* was accepted, successful, it would open the doors for blacks in television that were previously closed."

Which is exactly what happened. Shortly after *Julia* the networks scheduled *Sanford and Son, Good Times* and others. *Julia* and Diahann were canceled simultaneously. White America grew tired of the former while the latter was nailed by black America to a very popular cross and crucified with David Frost and Frederick Glusman, her most recent ex-husband, who, like Frost, is white. The crucifixion had as many reruns as *Julia*. It went on and on and thus, until *Claudine*, Diahann sat in "the vault" thinking. Down the hill, others were "thinking" too, but their thoughts were verbalized as "thoughts" about symbols usually are. Drugs, liquor, and sex-to-ease-the-loneliness was what they were saying about Diahann.

The public doesn't know what to think now that *Claudine* has reestablished Diahann both professionally and personally. Compounding their confusion is Diahann herself. She has begun to fight back, to strip away the Saran Wrap in which she has protected herself. Her hostile press relations, caused both by her own insecurities and by the past maiming of her feelings after the Frost-freeze, are easing. She is still overly mistrustful and her fear results in broken appointments and demands (made upon the interviewer) that no self-respecting journalist would honor.

She is still not without her barriers. She will not discuss freely Frost or the marriage (to Glusman) she wishes everyone, including herself, would forget. She has not yet removed all obstacles protecting the *real* Diahann Carroll mainly because she has learned from her experience why she should not. But to the disappointment of those who would wish otherwise, she is not going the route of Billie or Dinah. Despite an admitted self-destruct button, she has far more ego strength and intelligence than neurosis.

More importantly, she doesn't hide from herself. Long ago, she says, she learned that "a black woman's fight is both racial and sexual." Long ago she learned "both are painful and enraging." And long ago she learned that she is "not a lady to lose her pain in drugs." The woman has gladly and willingly earned the reputation in Hollywood of being a pain in the ass by doing what no other black woman has—speaking her mind, making waves, and questioning decisions of people who happen to be white. Professionally, and even personally, she no longer knows how to be subservient, but she does not deny she is still a person with problems.

In speaking of the last few years of her life, she sheds the layers of "beautiful" and "chic" and "Ten Best Dressed" when she says, "Thank God I was in analysis. I'd never have made it otherwise." She knows she is less than loved by "her own," but she can handle it. However, that her blackness is questioned disturbs her. It brings her back to the day in New York when they were filming *Claudine* in Harlem. The studio provided a limousine for its star, and one day at noon she sat in its backseat, snug and secure, directing the driver to a restaurant suitable for uptown, midday dining. But then, she was not doing that at all but directing the car to a house on 148th Street and Amsterdam Avenue where she had been raised by her parents. As she sat there recalling her childhood, she waited to feel joy but it never came. Only disturbance, a gnawing annoyance that she could not immediately identify. And then she knew she was a stranger in her own hometown.

In actuality, that should not have been surprising. She has always been a stranger in her own hometown. As a child she felt she was being groomed to do something with her life and that being raised in the middle of a ghetto was part of the training. Middle-class values, which she says her parents imposed on her, contributed to a feeling of separateness. "We were the 'haves' of Harlem. No bill collectors camped on our doorstep." And she had parents—two of them—and this, too, she says, was unusual for the ghetto. All combined, they made her feel "like an outsider, not comfortable with my given circumstances."

She was born at New York's Fordham Hospital, July 16, 1935, to Mabel and John Carroll. Her father, employed by the Transit Authority, was "a proud man who insisted on paying his own way in life but who found it necessary to maintan a shell of non-feeling.

"My father would have been destroyed if he allowed every incident that hindered him from being the provider to get to him." Specifically, she speaks of job opportunities and promotions, bank loans and buying property—"those things whites take for granted but which no black man can.

"But he kept us at an upper-middle-class living standard." The cost to him: "He closed off to shut out many of the hurts in his life." Yet, she insists, she felt his love for her, and for her younger sister, Lydia.

Although not stated, it becomes apparent that Mabel Carroll was a more shaping influence in her daughter's life. She was one of those you-can-be-president-if-you-wish-to-be mothers. She was also overly protective. She did not trust her daughter to "the elements." She took Diahann to and from school and demanded that each second of the child's time be accounted for. "I couldn't have a friend in the house without my mother wanting to know: who are they? where are they from? who are their parents?"

It was Mrs. Carroll who encouraged Diahann's attendance at the High School of Music and Art, a middle-class proving ground for talented youngsters.

Although never a "street nigger," Diahann recalls that she was "one of the kids" until she made the move to downtown education. There, at Music and Art, where nearly all the students were white, her values and interests were to change. Her alienation from ghetto life became complete. Where previously education was an enforced institution to be swallowed like castor oil or cod liver oil, in her new environment Diahann found her peers enjoyed school and used it as a tool of further socialization. At first she found it difficult, as she had never learned to study, but "rather than risk the embarrassment of deportation back to the old neighborhood," she applied her energies and learned quickly.

Upon graduation she enrolled at New York University, where her parents hoped she would enter the field of medicine. But Diahann, not quite so ambitious, chose psychiatric social work because "the job sounded important and I knew it would please my folks." However, she never earned her degree, as part-time modeling soon led to full-time employment in show business.

In looking back, her tendency is to dismiss the past as just that—past. Her childhood emerges as problemless when she first speaks. Only later does she admit that there is as much pain as there is joy in her remembrances but that "analysis has taught me to let go." It is no longer necessary for her to place blame where it may belong. She now assumes the responsibility for her own life. "Whatever mistakes my parents made were the result of ignorance, not malice. I have long since forgiven them."

The problems she experienced with her parents she defines as generational. "I liked to talk things out but I was constantly being told I was fresh and too outspoken." Eventually all communication between the generations broke down. The family became aware of Diahann's frustration when they came home one evening to find she had torn apart all of the furniture. "The total frustration of not being heard or listened to got to me. The *you-wills* and *you-will-nots* were punishing . . . killing."

By her early twenties, when the world was defining her as "the beautiful" and "the talented," she was defining herself in analysis because "I was operating totally without self-esteem, unconsciously seeking and finding business and social relationships in which I would be put down. I discovered I inwardly felt I deserved no better. I lacked a real belief in my intrinsic worth." She holds the environment responsible, believing its whiteness breeds feelings of inferiority in blacks.

But a family friend believes "the problem began at home. That child was pushed by her parents, who were determined that her life, whether she wanted it or not, would be different from theirs. I don't believe they allowed their girl to be what she was, only what they wished her to be. If she received an A in school, they wanted an A+. Diahann was under that kind of pressure from the day she was born."

Diahann insists she is free today from feelings of worthlessness and that "no one—not even me—is allowed to put Diahann Carroll down." She refuses to play the submissive role, "which is truly not my personality," but which she once felt was her duty as a woman. Today Diahann Carroll is, she says, first with Diahann Carroll. "Even sexually. I have learned if you don't know what you want emotionally from sex, you deprive yourself of the ultimate—orgasm. Once you find *your* needs and fulfill them, then you can open up and help to gratify your partner's."

The condition of being "the beautiful Diahann Carroll" is also a solved problem. Years ago, when she felt there was nothing underneath the exterior, it took her several hours "to pull myself together" before she could even make an appearance at her local supermarket. People would frequently stop and stare at "the beautiful D.C."; and she remembers one woman in particular who was insensitive but honest in her admittance of: "I just wanted to see how beautiful you *really* are."

"I couldn't handle that then," she says. "You can't imagine how it feels and what it does to the you inside, to the human being you are. It's like you aren't a person but just some beautiful object without feelings."

Strangely, despite no longer feeling that way, today's Diahann Carroll often appears to be an object without feelings. When she speaks of hurt, it is as though she is speaking of someone else's. She is seldom present in the emotion of her own life. She accepts this criticism, knows its truth, and after considerable deliberation, hesitantly explains what she believes is its cause.

"When I was a year old, my mom, dad, and I lived in one room. I guess times must have gotten bad because a day came when both had to work. They took me to my mother's sister in North Carolina. My mom put me to sleep and when I awoke, they were gone ... gone for an entire year in which I didn't get to speak with or see them.

"I know my mom did what she thought was best, but then that wasn't clear to me. There was just this feeling of not understanding why I was separated from them; this feeling of not having been told. I've lived with this all my life."

Her parents say she didn't cry at all during the year they were gone. "I don't know what I did to get through," she says, but later adds: "I shut off." When the Carrolls did bring their daughter home, she reverted to animal behavior, was afraid of the bathroom, and in subtle ways punished them.

She says the behavior of that one-year-old, "that inability to cry and say, 'You hurt me!' " is still with her. "I shut down that feeling. I still protect myself from feeling hurt, from feeling devastated to the point of I don't know what. I allow myself to feel so much and no more." She is difficult to get close to and knows it. "Trust has been the hardest thing for me to deal with in my life." The expectation is that those she loves will leave—without word or warning.

As she speaks, the hurt she says she shuts out makes a surprise appearance. She *looks* devastated even though she does not act it. Tears cling to the corners of her eyes. But she does not allow the emotion to rule. Instead, she suddenly speaks of her daughter, Suzanne, and of their relationship. "She'll be forty this September," she says of her thirteen-year-old. "She lives on the phone and is my other self."

Diahann is glowing, and the spark is Suzanne. Suddenly she giggles. "Just the other day my dear daughter was laying it on rather thick—a real heavy rap—when I spontaneously said, 'You know, that's bullshit!' It knocked her out, partly because I don't normally use language like that with her—I'm old fashioned that way—and partly because of her own response, which was, 'You're right. That *is* bullshit!' "

The moment is precious to her and she savors it, saying nothing for a while. It is proof of the communication that *can* exist, of the furniture that need not be turned over or broken in fits of frustration, when parent and child communicate honestly. She thinks of another moment, now past, when Suzanne was communicating dishonestly, using the divorce of her parents as a wedge to get what she wanted. "But Daddy said," went her divide-and-conquer whine until Diahann one day suggested, "We both get on the phone with Daddy and hear, first hand, what he and I and you have to say." And that ended that game. She speaks lovingly of former husband Monte Kay, Suzanne's father. "He is one of my best friends— always was. If our parents had left us alone, not objected as strongly as they did to our relationship, we probably never would have married."

She knows of the difficulty in being a parent and she does not deny that, as a child, Suzanne went through a difficult period. "It frightened me, but it changed as soon as I realized it was me she wanted, and that I had been selfishly doling me out to her on my terms and not hers. Well, I've frequently been selfish as a mother. I know it, and Suzanne knows it. But she also knows I've been there for her just as she knows much of what she now enjoys is because I, as Diahann Carroll, entertainer, have been selfish in my need to work." It is with considerable pride that she adds, "I have never lied to Suzanne, and there is no pretense between us."

Much of what she must give to Suzanne is evident in *Claudine*. There is something beyond acting in what Diahann, in the title role, gives to her six children; something deep from within that explodes in frustration, anger, and hurt when she learns one of her daughters is pregnant; something equally deep, which she conveys, that *knows* of the difficulties when a black man and a black woman try to make a relationship work beyond the bedroom.

"Claudine is very special," says Diahann. "She is part child, and has made every mistake a woman can make. But she has a sense of humor about it all." She stops, hears her own words, and laughs loudly. "Well, I guess we can see why I love her so."

In speaking of Claudine, she could have been speaking of herself, and when she is asked about her former love affair with Sidney Poitier and whether its demise was a down period in her life, she echoes, "A down period? I thought the whole world was falling down . . . around and on me. But you know, it had a lot more to do with Diahann than with Sidney. I mean it had to do with *all* of me and not just the end of a relationship."

Relationships do have a way of ending for her ("Basically I'm a marrying woman, but I've never seen anyone fight it as hard as I do"), and when she is asked if she really expected to marry David Frost, she flippantly replies, "Honey, I've learned not to expect one single thing."

Initially she speaks of Frost and their relationship honestly and with warmth. Only later does she ask that she not be quoted, which is surprising, for at no time—not even at her most relaxed and unguarded—does any bitterness or negative feeling emerge. "I cannot and will not discuss what it was *exactly* that came between David and me. In fact I've promised myself I wouldn't discuss David and Diahann *at all*. It's just *too* personal and belongs solely to us. What was, was."

And what was, was a "lovely communication" that lasted two years, and a concern for each other's well-being that was based on mutual respect. There was also that seemingly rare ability to laugh together. Yes, she admits, she would have liked a fairy tale ending, but long ago she learned that reality differs as often as not from fantasy. There were hurts she had to live with, but regrets? "Not a one."

She is still stunned by the "exceptional amount of attention" given to their relationship. "Was it due to our respective statures in show business, or because we were an interracial couple?" Far less attention was given to her ensuing marriage and divorce to what's-his-name. She will not discuss it *at all* except to angrily deny that she married on the rebound, and that she most definitely did misjudge his character, "which was unfortunate."

She is beyond feeling any kind of embarrassment over her more recently publicly displayed "love life."

"Why should I be? Every time I make a mistake or misjudge someone, it's just another lesson in living. I'm not much for the 'If-I-had-onlys.' I allow me my mistakes. My greatest and only concern was for Suzanne, but I found she understood a great deal about what was happening long before I did. She was able to analyze personalities and to recognize that my needs were operating."

What others thought, she writes off as meaningless, just as they "wrote off" meaningless but hurtful copy about her. Only once was she "practically moved to violence" and that was when Hollywood columnist Rona Barrett quoted Suzanne without ever having spoken to her. "If I'd have come face-to-face with Barrett, I'd have killed her. *I* chose to be in the public eye and I accept that, as such, I am fair game. But there are limits, and to use a child is way past those limits."

She is aware of what is written, not written, said, and left unsaid about her as a black woman. The criticism leveled at her by the black community—the "white Diahann Carroll"—both haunts and angers her.

"There is no confusion in my mind that I am black. And if confuson exists—and it obviously does—in the minds of some blacks, then I ask them: What makes one black more black than the next? Even if I were the kind of black who turned her back on present-day pressures, that still wouldn't make me any less black, just uninvolved. And that is one's choice. Whether I am or am not involved is no one's business. I refuse to discuss what I do or do not do for blacks. I will not appease *anyone* to prove that I am black."

From their respective beginnings, she has been involved with SCLC and the Black Economic Union. Both, along with her meetings with Shirley Chisholm, are a matter of public record. But she is not a soapboxer and she does not permit her public relations firm to publicize that aspect of her life. She suffers the consequences, and remains outside the black community. "But I have always been that," she says and then adds, "but that doesn't mean I am or have been

unconcerned." She wonders why blacks judge, rather
than allow her her life-style. "Why this need for con-
formity? Is it that blacks have not yet reached the
point where they can allow for individual differences?" she asks, answering her own questions. "Blacks
are still demanding: 'We as blacks should do it *this*
way and this way only.' Well, other than doing things
collectively—like not buying products from known
racists and boycotting those firms where blacks are
not given equal opportunities—I don't believe there
is only one way. I'm with Sly Stone: 'Different strokes
for different folks.' "

The accusation that as Diahann Carroll she has
never had to enter and live in the black world draws
her humorless and derisive laughter.

"You never, but *never,* walk away from being black.
It stays with you all the way to Beverly Hills." In her
mind she is back in Miami Beach fulfilling a supper
club date at the plush Americana Hotel. The year is
1958 and although she is the headliner, the hotel requests that she live elsewhere. She refuses. When she
demands accommodations, they attempt to discourage
her by quoting a daily rate that is so exorbitant that
only a very determined woman would agree to it. She
was *that* woman. Her engagement in the main room
is successful, but the hotel lounge is dying from starva-
tion. No people. Would Miss Carroll visit it after her
performance and perhaps sing a song or two? Miss
Carroll would, as would her friend, Johnny Mathis,
who is appearing elsewhere on the beach. Later, they
are enjoying a pre-dawn breakfast at the coffee shop
when a redneck policeman barges in and says, "You
and you," meaning Diahann and Mathis, "you're
going to jail!" She seeks help from the hotel management, but only an "aide" can be sent. Out of nowhere
she is charged with leading an "interracial orgy" and
ordered to "come along, miss." She refuses. "You'll
have to shoot me first," and the cop pulls a gun. She

and Mathis flee to her room and they wait as the squad cars wait in the street during the long night.

She thinks of that moment now and says: "He would have shot me. I just know that. If people—tourists—had not been around. But I had to face him. *Had to.* And I went right on facing all the *hims* until each damn one understood."

Then her eyes widen and she remembers when she finally *understood* why she could not appear on the then highly popular *Dinah Shore Show.* The sponsor, Chevrolet, she was told, feared the repercussions from dealers if they used a black woman married to a white man. And she *understood* all too soon and too clearly the meaning of the "we-will-let-you-knows" she, a black woman, received when she apartment hunted in neighborhoods where blacks worked as domestics but didn't live as people. And she *understood* why a private school she found acceptable for Suzanne did not accept her daughter.

"How dare anyone think I'm not black!" she challenges with rage not identified with "the beautiful Diahann Carroll." "There is no such thing as not living as a black when your skin is black! When will we stop? When will we blacks stop taking every opportunity to put one another down? 'Cause till we do, we will remain separate, and that means without. We must learn to defend rather than destroy one another."

But she should be used to being put down. It started as far back as *No Strings,* when she was the first black woman to star in the first interracial love story. The pot-shotters said she should have insisted that her co-star be black. Only the ignorant could think she was in a positon then to demand anything. It is highly questionable whether even today, where Broadway is concerned, any black can demand anything other than decent treatment.

"Let's get to where it's really at," she says abruptly.

"No matter what I do, in some sectors, enough will never be enough, my 'blackness' always questioned. It's about my dating white men," she says. "The black community resents it. There is a feeling blacks share that says anything we have that is worthwhile, the white man will take away. Blacks want to keep the goodies in the family. I understand that, but it is not always possible."

She works in an industry that is overwhelmingly as white-populated as the country in which she lives. And it was even more so back in the fifties when successful black entertainers could be counted on fingers and toes. Because of circumstances, or necessity, a black worked and played with whites on Park Avenue or in Beverly Hills. It was either that or loneliness.

"Early on in this business, you learn that success means isolation from your own. You also learn that if you don't want to be alone—lonely—you better judge people for themselves, rather than on a black or white basis."

She found that as a celebrated, high-income-earning black woman, her male/female possibilities were narrowed considerably. In the case of herself, a successful black woman who begins a relationship with a black man, "It becomes a loud reiteration of the 'deballing' process that the white society puts him through daily. The black woman becomes the enemy, the scapegoat for her black man. He goes after her out of frustration and anger at the whole environment. It's so damn difficult. If you, as a black woman, bring home the bacon better than he, then he has to deal not only with your capabilities, which may be overpowering and frightening, but also with his own, which, more often than not, are stifled. Thus, doubt creeps up on his masculinity. It's a lot easier for a white man to deal with this, as his balls and ego are more intact."

Which is how she explains her coupling in recent years with white men. "Sure there are successful black women who have taken on and conquered this enormous problem. But I find with black men who are successful that they, too, most often feel that it is easier *not* to deal with the insecurities of the black female. Instead he chooses a white woman. And so what? If that works for someone, so be it! Damn! *Any* two people in a relationship have troubles enough . . . any relationship is so damn difficult, that if you find someone, *anyone* who makes you happy, why let color matter?"

But she knows why it matters to many blacks, and she even thinks the anger is righteous. "Whitey has denied so much to so many blacks—has mistreated and abused us so—that any black woman who becomes partner to a white man is seen as having joined the enemy."

She regrets that some see her as having gone behind the enemy's lines. "I'm sorry they feel that way," she says, "but I ain't-a-changin'. There is no such thing as one way. I refuse to prove to them, or to anyone else, how black I am. To some, I am a cop-out; always have been and always will be. Again, I'm sorry they feel that way but I have to live my life. My personal style is *my* personal style. When they put you in that box and lower you six feet down, you go in alone. Nobody goes with you. If you don't recognize this while you're alive—recognize that it is your responsibility, *yours* and not others', to make you happy—you'll never make it. I've learned that if I try to please others and not me, I'll never find my own happiness."

And she believes in happiness just as she has come to believe in herself. "The miracle of miracles: liking yourself—believing in you. To be black in this society and to be able to do that . . ." She trails off. Her eyes fade as if going backward over the years. The people and the pain. The hurt . . . humiliation . . . and still, the happiness. Her face tells more than her words. "It can be done. You can learn to like yourself," she says. "Look at me. In the past fifteen years I've lived a b-i-g life . . . nothing small about it at all. If Diahann here had to 'go' tomorrow, no one could says, 'Poor thing. She hardly lived at all.' Hell no, they couldn't." And she is laughing, slapping at her thigh in delight, hooting even. And then, abruptly, there are tears hiding in the corners of her eyes. "Hell no, they couldn't," she says again. But it sounds different. Very different.

CHAPTER TEN

FAYE DUNAWAY

It is often stated, as fact and without feeling: Faye Dunaway is crazy. In Hollywood her spoken-of demise into sex and drugs is an old story, one in which many a film goddess has starred. At first when her *Chinatown* director, Roman Polanski, declared Dunaway "demonstrated certifiable proof of insanity," Hollywood was titillated and her "irrational outbursts" and subsequent marriage to that *young* man were nibbled at like so many peanuts at a cocktail party. Then Hollywood shrugged, "So what? Of course. Next!"

Faye Dunaway lends credence to the rebounding rumors of her instability by both calculated inaccessibility and behavior. Months of "Is it yes or no?" pass before she agrees to interviews in May. Come spring '67 phone calls are left unreturned. Finally word is sent through representatives that "Miss Dunaway regrets but she is out of town." Thinking the issue closed, the out-of-town Miss Dunaway answers her telephone and is trapped by this irate and near obscene phone caller into a meeting—now reaching summit proportions—to take place in July.

On the appointed day Faye Dunaway attempts to cancel. "I am afraid," she says bluntly. Asked of what, she responds, "Of your hurting me. I have given you cause," she adds simply. Assured that is *not* the writer's purpose, she just as simply enters her living room later that afternoon in what is definitely an unstarlike entrance. Baggy black slacks and a sleeveless beige sweater fall haphazardly on her 5 feet 7 inches.

Her long, naturally brown hair is as casually worn as the friendly, but not very, smile on her totally make-upless face. There are no needlemarks on her arms and no glaze to her eyes.

To say Faye Dunaway is beautiful says nothing. Facing you, framed by the New York skyline, she is seemingly as "cool" as the steel-and-glass decor of her overlooking-the-park apartment. But she is frightened, unable to explain to you or to herself why she has finally consented to the meeting. The fear, tinging her green-gray eyes, explains her behavior of recent months better than words. Despite her uncertainty she asks for no special considerations, which is surprising considering how she has refused to discuss Polanski and their *Chinatown* contretemps, her past love affairs, and her marriage August 7, 1974, to Peter Wolf, the lead singer with the J. Geils Band.

She has been on the run, she explains, setting up a Boston residence for her and Peter, as that is where the Geils Band is based. Yes, he is younger—twenty-nine to her thirty-four—but "he has a maturity some men reach at forty while others never do." No, it most certainly was not love at first sight. "Hardly," she says with an almost bitter laugh. They had met through friends in San Francisco but it was only later, after she had seen him work, that she felt "this might be a man worth knowing." But she was wary of relationships. "I had just spent my first eighteen months living alone and had made the most remarkable discovery—that I wouldn't fall apart without a man to take care of me."

Her words are spoken so unselfconsciously that they nearly pass unquestioned. Were her other relationships then "crutches"? She is uncomfortable. She does not wish to discuss her past affairs. Must she? She makes her own decision. With an almost weary sigh, she debunks the legend that maintains she was Lenny Bruce's last great love. "Untrue. We dated maybe ten times before he died. He was brilliant, soft yet strong. And boyish. He was very endearing." Jerry Shatzberg, then a photographer and now a producer, was indeed, however, "a great love. I still love Jerry but differently, of course." And Marcello Mastroianni? She stiffens. Their affair made international news. "Does anyone still care?" she asks impatiently. "Well if anyone does . . . Marcello was enormously kind. Such a bright man, witty, and he enjoyed women, particularly a woman with a mind. And a gentle man," she adds almost to herself. What happened? She shrugs. "He was caught in his Catholic-Italian heritage which was burdensome to him and then to me as it spilt onto our relationship. But it was quite lovely for a while and then . . . quite painful. There is always that in the end. He has a nice wife, you know."

Then with actor Harris Yulin, she withdrew into a self-imposed retirement, thinking that necessary for the relationship to breathe. After eighteen inactive months she learned otherwise. "To give up my work was to give up a chunk of me and thus bring less, not more, to a relationship." But her actual reasons for leaving Yulin and setting off on her own remain secreted, as she suddenly balks at any further intrusion into her past. "What's important is that I went out on my own and survived. I learned to live alone. What's better, I learned to like it."

But still the question remains unanswered. Were her relationships crutches to prop up an insecure Faye Dunaway? "Yes," she says abruptly. "In many ways, yes, I was a dependent child-woman in need of protection and nurturance. And I stayed in relationships long after they were over because I was afraid to be alone. But I regret none of the past, although sometimes a woman does give too much of herself in a relationship to discover who she really is. When all that success after *Bonnie and Clyde* didn't make me feel happy or fulfilled, I turned too quickly to relationships to fill the void."

She discovered the void was within her and spent three years in analysis to discover "what was image and what was me. I didn't know what I really wanted. I was obliterated by the 'shoulds' of my southern background and the film industry. One insisted I *should* be married, a mother, and settled within the bosom of the family. The other demanded I be blond and beautiful. Eventually the only *should* I accepted was . . . I *should* be whatever *I* wish to be. To do that, I had to leave the lonely, frightened child I was and become a woman. That feeling of being alone, helpless, and adrift in a hostile world is one I have had to continuously fight."

She cannot trace its derivation. "Maybe I was frightened in the womb." She explains that her parents, Grace and John Dunaway—he a military man—raised her "in an atmosphere of enormous love. Maybe I was overly protected." But when she speaks of her childhood, first spent in Bascom, Florida, where she was born, January 14, 1941, it is with both fond and painful recollections. Her father could not express the love she insists he felt for her. He was remote although her mother maintains, she adds, herself confused, that she was Daddy's little girl. Her mother gave her "the gift of aspiration," defying her own southern background to suggest to her only daughter that life was perhaps more than being a cheerleader and beauty-contest winner—both of which Faye was—and even more than a wife to the local football hero. "Yet," she says, "I think my mother would have been much happier had I stayed close to home."

As an army brat her life was in constant transit, leaving her somewhat "anxious, unsettled, and as though I were not centered in the world." She had very few friends. "You learned early in that life not to get too close to people, as they or you were always leaving."

One who left was her father, and the scars of her

parents' subsequent divorce remain even today. She hated his leaving but could not tell him so. She felt irrationally responsible for the dissolution of her parents' marriage and she "cut off" from them and herself. Years later she had to relearn how to cry. She could not admit to pain, to having been hurt. She grew up "thinking divorce was inevitable and that everything in life is but temporary."

Scholarships and summer jobs saw her through the University of Florida and the Boston University of Fine and Applied Arts, where an instructor arranged for her to audition with the newly formed Lincoln Repertory Company in New York. Accepted, she studied for three years before starring in an off-Broadway production of *Hogan's Goat,* which brought her to the attention of those who manufacture stars. She admits she was a product, produced and packaged by expert agency men who whisked her through the forgettable *Hurry Sundown* and *The Happening* to *Bonnie and Clyde.* She never struggled, and despite her beauty, the casting couch was never a prop in the production of Faye Dunaway, Movie Star, because "I was protected by agents. I never needed a job. One was always waiting. Thus, I wasn't vulnerable."

But she was vulnerable in other ways. She knew nothing about her business and unwisely was managed at first by a man expert in the construction business but not in the construct of a film star. It cost her $500,000 to sever the relationship. On her own she discovered painfully that hers is a business and not an extended family; that her worth was as a product and not as a person. Love was how much of you did ten percent buy. It was a shock realizing "that few agents cared about me personally. Just as few cared professionally. Oh, they cared that I received top dollar because they fed off that, but they didn't care about my work as an actress."

She made some bombs, before her eighteen months of retirement and afterward. Eventually she learned to choose her own scripts. Today she even sets her own price although others do the actual negotiating. When she came to *Chinatown,* she needed a good film.

Two years after the making of *Chinatown,* Roman Polanski still maintains Faye Dunaway displayed "psychotic and ritualistic behavior. Before the scene, after the scene, she'd smear Blistex on her lips. Then she'd gulp Coca-Cola when she wasn't chewing gum, which was always. One after another. Over and over. Crazy. Totally crazy. Also, without provocation, she would rant, scream at me, and then rush off in tears. A totally irrational woman."

Was her behavior possibly drug induced? he is asked.

"Drugs? What drugs? There were no drugs. Blistex and Coca-Cola, yes. Drugs, no! She's a crazy lady but she is not *that* crazy."

Jack Nicholson, Dunaway's costar in *Chinatown,* insists, "Roman and Faye . . . two swell kids. And they're really in love. Crazy about each other. All great lovers fight. Faye is a throwback to the great actresses of the past. She's *heavy* man, *real* heavy. She's also a little nuts, but find me an actor who isn't. She's a good broad. I love her . . . I honestly do and I'd make another film with her tomorrow, tonight even, if you could get her away from her ole man."

She relaxes when read Nicholson's words. The subject of her craziness and Polanski has returned the veiled look to her eyes. Her arms are protectively folded across her chest and the debate taking place within her is obvious.

"Roman and I had a terrible time," she begins softly, breaking her long-held vow of silence on the issue. "He works within a rigid framework, maintaining a dictatorial atmosphere on his set. His need is to control every aspect of his film. I resist being controlled. I hate it, actually. I found Roman strange. I didn't know how to react to him. If a man jerked a hair out of your head—which Roman did—wouldn't you assume he didn't like you? But it turns out Roman didn't dislike me, not personally [he agrees]. We just had no communication professionally. I didn't know what he wanted. He would scream and I would scream back. The fights were awful. And yes, I cried. Why not? I was hurt. But I never slapped Roman, as one columnist wrote," she adds, although it is obvious from her expression that the thought is not repellent to her.

Paradoxically, *Chinatown* resurrected the Dunaway career—earning her an Oscar nomination—as it nearly destroyed it. Her rumored instability and addiction scared off many producers and directors. Gil Cates was nearly one. "We had but twelve days in which to shoot *After the Fall*," says Cates, who directed Dunaway in his two-hour TV version of the play. "If she was absent but once, we were in trouble. But she was never absent, never late, and never less than professional. Drugs? Forget it? Yes, she was difficult but only as befitting an actress who is determined to achieve her best performance." Sidney Pollack, who also hesitated before directing Faye in his *Three Days of the Condor,* found "the stories are totally untrue. Yes, she will fight for what she believes to be right professionally, as she is no mass-produced windup doll. She is an actress. One of the best. I would hardly call her difficult and the only thing she is addicted to that I could see was perfection and not just her own but the entire production's."

Roy Scheider proves Dunaway did not do an abrupt about-face after *Chinatown* to shape up or be shipped out of her industry. He met her when both were struggling, aspiring, and understudying at the Lincoln Repertory Company. Four years later he was featured in her film, *Puzzle of a Downfall Child.* When asked if Dunaway was ever unprofessional, Scheider explodes, "Never! She was always prepared

and always respectful of her fellow actors. She was
dedicated to the point of ridiculousness. Nothing in-
terfered with her work. The only times I ever saw
Faye stoned was on pot and that was at a private
gathering years later in Hollywood. Faye is being tar-
geted," insists Scheider. "In no way is she a trouble-
maker. There are actresses who don't like men, who
feel threatened by them professionally, but not Faye.
If she reacted badly during *Chinatown*, I'll bet she
was treated badly."

Both Pollack and Cates, separately, stated that the
best way to reach Faye Dunaway is through kindness.
Both hinted that kindness was not one of Polanski's
professional strengths. "Faye responds to consider-
ation. Kindness of any kind gets to her," says Pollack.
"Without kindness, or within an insensitive setting,"
says Cates, "Faye is going to be in a lot of trouble."

Apprised of what both Cates and Pollack have said,
Dunaway is for the first time *visibly* moved. She has
difficulty speaking. "Kindness touches the major
problem for me," she finally says softly. "I want people to be kind and I want to be kind to people. I
cannot understand why we all aren't nice to one
another. I find life so often assaultive and it is so
much safer to react to the assault with rage than hurt.
Who wants to be *that* vulnerable? I don't." She stops
and struggles for a composure that is almost escaping
her. Once again in control, she adds, "I'm afraid my
view of how the world should be is very childlike. We
should all be nice and play. Why can't we?" she asks
as though there is some answer that has escaped her.
"I had such enormous love as a child. Such kindness. I
think what has shocked me so all my life is not finding
that in the world."

Since *Chinatown* her world has been hostile to her.
She has reacted with an equal hostility. "I really
should have returned your phone calls," she blurts
out. "I meant to but I didn't. I just didn't want to be
picked apart any longer. Yes, I had heard all the sto-

ries about that crazy Faye Dunaway and how she
smacks, snorts, and shoots up. I smoked pot five years
ago and quit when I read it could possibly cause
chromosome changes. I wasn't about to risk that, as
having a baby has always been in my mind. Yes, I've
heard all the stories," she says again but this time in a
much too quiet voice. "And they hurt. They all hurt.
Nothing rolls off my back. Rumors like that kill and
they are circulated by those who feel they made you
and thus have a right to break you. It's awful and
that is why I stay mainly to myself. I don't want to be
maligned. No more."

Why didn't she speak up and out against the stories? "Because it is *still* so damn hard to admit 'You
hurt me. I hurt.' There is nothing more terrifying
than opening yourself up like that to others who may
not care even if they do hear you."

But she says it now, clearly and loudly, and I am
moved in spite of my previous prejudices against her.
"If you are conning me," I begin defensively. "I don't
know how to con," she says angrily, hurt again, and
closes off as she closes the interview for the day.

At our next meeting Faye Dunaway reacts to a
"kindness." I bring her flowers as an expression of admiration, affection even, for what had been her unexpected openness. She responds much as a child might
to an unasked-for ice cream cone. Delighted. She links
her arm through mine and very personally escorts me
to her kitchen where great pains are taken at a floral
arrangement. She is chattering about Peter's return in
a few days from a week-long tour and how separations are always difficult. "You would like one another," she says suddenly. That is her reciprocity, her
gift, in return to me.

We settle in her living room; she fighting her
needlepoint, which is her new adventure, while I
again notice she has made no effort to look beautiful.
She just is, the little lines about her eyes and slight

sag under her chin making her more the beautiful woman than the pretty girl. Several scripts lie about and she explains that she is in the selection process. Now a factor in her choosing is how long she will be required to be separated from Peter.

"Long periods of time in which we would be apart might be harmful," she explains. "I will not risk that." There is no conflict, however, between her work and her marriage. Peter does not suggest she stop and she does not feel divided between the two. "One complements the other. I could not be happy, not ultimately, without my work. But Peter does come first," she says with finality.

It is an often-stated-but-seldom-meant statement by star actresses. In Dunaway's case it is possibly true. Says Gil Cates: "Faye is determined to make this marriage work. She has picked her husband with great care. He is a nice man, devoted to her, as she is to him. The affection between them is quite touching. If a choice between work and marriage ever become necessary, I believe Faye would choose Peter every time." Sidney Pollack adds: "When we filmed *Condor*, Faye would rush from the set each Friday to fly to Boston. Where Peter is, is where Faye wants to be. She is happy in her marriage and will fight like hell for its survival."

It is with difficulty that Faye Dunaway speaks of Peter and their marriage. She is not a dimestore novel, *True Romances* heroine. She guards this part of her life as she feels it is hers and not, as is her work, in the public domain. As she speaks, the feeling is they "fit" together. They do not live on the "grand" scale but enjoy "doing the museums, walking through the park, concerts—mainly rock, and . . . just being together." Repeatedly she uses the words *nice* and *kind* to describe Peter. Without actually stating it, she implies that Peter may be the first man who truly listens to her and the first to whom she has truly talked.

"If I had married ten years ago, it would never have lasted. I needed adventure before settling down," she laughs, an almost self-deprecating chuckle. "Well, I sure got that. Which was good," she adds thoughtfully. "I waited a long time to find the right person. A long time. Luckily, and happily, I found a man who is concerned not only with his wants and needs but with what *I* want to do and what *I* want from life. We have a very give-and-take relationship. In the past it seemed one person always needed and took the upper hand and that person was never me. I blame no one, as it was then my need to be a dependent child. I used my men as buffers against the world. Keeping Faye Safe, it is called. And I kept Faye safe at all costs. I never walked away bleeding from a relationship because I allowed them to continue long after they were over so I could prepare myself for the moving on. My bleeding took place while they were ending. I have always, in retrospect, been able to pinpoint that exact moment when a love affair was essentially over for me. But I couldn't let go. I was so afraid of being alone."

But that is not what motivates her today. "I am married because I need to share me, my life, my accomplishments. I need to give and be given to. Yes, marriage is scary; frightening as hell to let in another person as you let yourself out. And you must do that in marriage. I married Peter, rather than lived with him, because marriage means commitment. It is another door closed, one that *can* be opened but not quite so easily. You must work harder in a marriage. Obviously I believe it is worth the extra effort but not because *being married* allays my fears. Marriage does not make me feel safer, just happier. That part of my life now has a shape and a focus. I do not expect Peter to protect me from the world. But he is a friend who can help me face it. He is *not* my protector and not placing him in that role makes the relationship that much more stable. I now know that loving someone who loves you back doesn't entitle you to dump the responsibility for your life on their shoulders. In some way I always resented the men I leaned on. I think dependency leads to resentment on both persons' parts. I have my own sense of safety today. Even when I feel adrift in the world, which is no longer often, I know I will swim and not sink. I do not need a man to be my daddy."

But "Daddy," in the form of old bugaboos, continues to plague her. When she married, many of her old fears returned. "We won't last," she thought. "Peter will up and leave without a word. I will be hurt." She was paralyzing herself and the marriage until she returned to therapy "to separate the reality of today—my life with Peter—from what happened yesterday with my father. Yes, Peter will hurt me because in the process of living, people hurt people. But today, if he does, I can tell him. I can shout. I can cry. I have words and emotions. I also have a man who will listen." She is hopeful that Peter will soon consent to joint consultations with a therapist. "Not because he is neurotic but just as another measure to keep the communication between us alive and growing."

Her needlepoint rests in her lap. She rests with it, her mind elsewhere. "I was thinking how I would like to have a baby," she says upon her return to the now. "I know there are no guarantees but I hope this marriage will be my first and last. I am happy. My life today is better than it has ever been and it is going to be even better," she says in a tone that defies doubt or contradiction. "Everything I have ever gone through in my life—*all* of it—was necessary to bring me to where I am today, which is only the best place I have ever been." She again puts down her needlepoint. Between tears and laughter, she hides neither. Instead, "crazy" Faye Dunaway just smiles, one that widens as though to meet the solitary tear that gently drifts down her cheek.

CHAPTER ELEVEN

GOLDIE HAWN

"I was anxious . . . depressed. I went from my home to the studio and back again. That was the extent of my functioning. I was terrified."

Of what, Goldie Hawn?

"Of just *that*. Of being Goldie Hawn. I was twenty-two when *Laugh-In* exploded onto the American scene. I was a very young twenty-two. Success . . . Hollywood . . . they were very frightening to me."

But of what were you frightened?

"Of drugs, of sex, of falling apart as so many women in Hollywood had. I was afraid the *me*, the little Goldie, would get lost; that I would change or worse . . . be consumed by the business. I felt split as a personality. On *Laugh-In*, I was carefree, a bubble . . . zany. Off camera I was a wreck. I was so nervous, I had trouble coping with day-to-day living. I lost my smile, something I had always had."

Goldie Hawn is talking quite unlike the girl we think of as Goldie Hawn. There is no golden giggle punctuating her words now. She is thoughtful . . . serious. Was she ever her image? "No, not really," she responds evenly. "Although there is a tickle inside that bubbles up and out of me, I am basically a serious person. However it is my sense of humor about life that keeps me bright and balanced." And seemingly the darling of many. Seldom is heard a discouraging word about Goldie in an industry that delights in rumor and innuendo. Instead one is bombarded with a stream of clichés ranging from "she's wonder-ful" and "she's wonderful" to "she's so honest" and "she's so honest," when gathering research about the lady. If one listened only to others and not to Goldie, she would emerge as less than real.

But on the eve of the release of *Foul Play*, an old-fashioned thriller/diller in which she costars with Chevy Chase, and a transatlantic flight that will deposit her in Rome and into the arms of Giancarlo Giannini, with whom she will costar in *A Trip with Anita*, Goldie Hawn is very real. She explains it took seven years of analysis to become so—seven years to discover "I could be famous and still be me."

It was her *Laugh-In* success and the insecurities it dredged from within her that made Goldie seek out the couch. Yet she feared analysis, thinking "It might make me lose what I liked best about myself—the fact that I am a little person who delights in little things; a woman who doesn't need diamonds and furs to be happy." She discovered "analysis made the little me bigger . . . stronger. After seven years I came away with more awareness and confidence."

And with one divorce, one baby, and a marriage to the baby's father, Bill Hudson of the Hudson Brothers, "I was a child when I made it as Goldie Hawn. I was a child when I married. Today, at thirty-two, I'm a woman who is no longer afraid of her success. The 'little me' has her priorities screwed on straight. Many say it but I mean it. Much as I now enjoy my work, my marriage and family come first. If Bill asked me not to work, I wouldn't. From the moment I met Bill [she was a captive audience to his amorous advances on a cross-country flight], I felt this was a man I could be with. Within weeks to months, I felt being with him was more important than working. So I stopped working. [*Foul Play* is her first film in two-plus years.] Bill is a very solid man. He is super bright and secure within himself. We are not in com-petition with one another. What Bill and I have together is an awful lot of love and friendship. And oh, God, how important it is to be friends with the man you love! Frankly there isn't anyone I would rather be with than Bill. And it pains me that our work will keep us separated Mondays through Fridays while he films in London and me in Rome. Bill makes me laugh. I make him smile. Whatever success I might achieve as the public Goldie Hawn cannot affect this marriage."

As it did her first. In 1969 Goldie married Gus Trikonis, a Greek-American choreographer/director. They separated in 1973. Goldie, at one time, blamed her success for killing her marriage. "Gus couldn't cope with it," she stated, "and my money . . . the house . . . and all the pretty things that he couldn't afford and which I bought." Today Goldie believes it was not her success alone that precipitated the breakup. "There were too many other big differences between us. I had married an older man who I proceeded to fashion into a father figure. I was his little girl. I didn't know then about real love. But then one day the little girl grew up and that's when the fireworks began."

Although Goldie admits she was once quite bitter about the marriage's demise and the divorce, today she insists the bitterness is gone. She rationalizes the $75,000 price tag Trikonis put on her freedom by saying, "All of us have our own way of reacting to anger and hurt. Perhaps that was Gus's way. I really don't know, as we never spoke. But I do know I could not have been the only one who walked away feeling hurt. Sure I hardly enjoyed giving up seventy-five thousand tax-free dollars. But you know, if that's the price of freedom, it's cheap at the cost."

Although she says she is free of bitterness and anger, when Goldie Hawn is asked what she learned from her first marriage, she snaps: "Nothing! Nothing other than it is all right to make a mistake." One of those mistakes was her publicly endorsing open marriage. She cringes at the remembrance and explains: "I would have said anything then that would have rationalized my staying in the marriage and that might have helped make the marriage work. But, in truth, I don't believe in open marriage or in the No Fault/No Guilt . . . Do-Your-Own-Thing type of relationship. I *do* believe in fidelity . . . commitment, in giving yourself fully to a relationship and using all your energies—particularly sexual energies—to make the relationship work."

And how important is sex to a relationship?

"Sex is only an extension of a relationship," says Goldie. "If the couple feels good together, if there is warmth, comfort, excitement, in their relating, then the sex will reflect this. What happens during the day between two people is what tends to happen later between the sheets. A lousy marriage usually produces lousy sex. But I do not believe sex makes or breaks a relationship, important though it is to it. There are other things that are equally important, like friendship, trust, respect, and caring. All take work. All take knowing yourself. I think if you're mistrustful of your own integrity, it's easier to put accusations on another rather than to deal with yourself. I had to learn that *me*, the little person who is Goldie Hawn, is most comfortable in a traditional marriage to a man who shares my traditional, conventional values—even if we haven't exactly done things in a traditional, conventional way."

She is referring to the fact that the Hudsons planned their baby before their marriage. When the couple did walk down the aisle in the backyard of Goldie's childhood home in Takoma Park, Maryland, she was "very pregnant and very glowing with eight months of baby. My daddy gave me away. Like my mother, he was beaming. Both knew how much I had wanted a child—had *always* wanted a child. I see now that I always knew—although I wouldn't admit it—that my first marriage was bad because I never felt the time was right to have a baby. With Bill, almost immediately, we began talking children. Within a very short time I felt this man would be a wonderful father. And that he has been!"

Goldie is still somewhat surprised at the flakless public reaction to her visible pregnancy-without-marriage. "Not one irate letter," she says. "Even in Hollywood no one chastised me, or suggested that I was wrecking my career." And had they? "I would have laughed and said: 'Okay, so I'm wrecking it.' I never thought in terms of what repercussions my pregnancy might have on my career. It just didn't matter in comparison to the feeling I had as the baby began to grow within me. Also what others thought meant little to me. They could not have known that Bill and I had exchanged our vows long before we were legally sanctioned as husband and wife. All I wanted was our baby. That meant happiness and fulfillment to me."

Happiness and fulfillment in the name of Oliver Rutlege Hudson was born September 7, 1976. "With Bill and Oliver, I feel insulated by love," says Goldie. "And safe. And complete. Being a mother has made me feel as if I've lived out, completed, a female function . . . as if I found a missing part of me. I am totally committed to this little person's well-being. When he calls me Mama, I feel utter joy."

The Hudsons plan to have another child of their own—"It will again have to be by cesarean section"—and then hope to adopt still more. "And it will not necessarily be an infant who we take in. Our family is blessed in that we have both love and financial security in our lives," explains Goldie. "It would be nice to share that with some little boy or girl who has known neither."

Currently, the Hawn/Hudson residence is somewhere in transit between Malibu and the Pacific Palisades. Goldie believes the Hudsons have purchased a new home in the Palisades area but its current occupant believes otherwise. He refuses to get out, which prevents the Hudsons from getting in. Meantime, as they make their respective films in Europe, the Hudson home is in brown boxes waiting to be established somewhere. But not anywhere within the typical Hollywood/Beverly Hills environment, insists Goldie. She does not explain her personal antipathy toward the film colony but instead speaks of "lousy values." One gets the impression that at one time Goldie may have been wracked up against hot Hollywood coals but today she simply says: "Bill and I want our kids to grow up in a regular neighborhood with regular kids. We don't want their heads filled with box office figures or with the whispers of who-is-doing-what-to-whom-and-how-and-how-often.

"We want our children to grow into caring human beings," continues Goldie. "We want them to accept the little persons that live within them. I have such a pleasant feeling about life. I always have and I believe it comes from having had a warm and loving family. I want to give that to my kids. I want them to be able to say, as I am saying now, 'I am sooo happy. My life is sooo good!' Did I say good? The word is Great!"

CHAPTER TWELVE

EARTHA KITT

"I am here!" says Eartha Kitt passionately in the privacy of her backstage-at-*Timbuktu* dressing room. "I survived while the people who contrived against me are either dead or gone. The truth won out, as I knew it would. I survived as I always have . . . as I always will."

She sits facing herself in her dressing-room mirror. With her lashes applied for her upcoming performance, she looks *fiercely* beautiful, her manner that of a cat about to pounce on its prey. At approximately fifty her face is like a great piece of sculpture or architecture. It can be admired from most any angle, and at most any angle it changes. The face is not unlike the person.

"Survival is what life is about. I prove that," she says with intense pride. "In 1968 I was an international star, a legendary great. Then it fell apart as I was pulled apart by forces greater than I. Eartha Kitt was banished from her own country and all because she dared to speak out against her country's political policies. They put me down but I was never out. My public kept me alive. They never forgot me. Now, LBJ is dead and Nixon is gone. But . . . *I am here!*"

Which are the words Eartha Kitt announces to a gut-roar audience reaction when she makes her entrance in *Timbuktu*. The people are responding to "the dream"—the one amongst us who has met and beaten "the man" and his system. Arms and smiles open wide to welcome Eartha back home. Which is strange. Till *Timbuktu,* Eartha had no home—not among blacks, nor amongst whites. What a difference a decade and a little banishment-and-exile make! The onetime "black sheep" is now the prodigal "son." More, she is the conquering hero, and the public, instead of the scorn many once heaped upon her, bestows flowers and accolades.

Eartha Kitt has come full cycle. No one is enjoying it more than Eartha herself. She is once again The Star—although in her own mind she always was. She has returned to former glory—although she will insist it had never faded, which it had. Through it all she has remained as controversial as ever. Long before Eartha and *Timbuktu* came to Broadway, rumors arrived that spoke of Eartha's "temperament." But then no one has ever accused Eartha of being Mary Tyler Moore.

And Eartha has been accused of many things . . . many times. She has always been one of our most "rumored" performers. She emerged in the fifties, predating Ann-Margret as the original sex-kitten. She slinked and slithered out of *New Faces of '52* purring promises of promiscuity. She was a major recording artist and the first to put sex between the grooves of an LP. Her songs were about sex and the pleasures—like diamonds, yachts, furs, and cars—that sex could bring. She was temptress and adventuress, the embodiment of black exotica.

She dated white men and accepted their presents of . . . diamonds, yachts, furs, and cars. Often Eartha was photographed with these gifts, her white teeth flashing and her eyes always with that curious blaze. She looked successful but she never looked happy. People, and in particular black people, resented the white men and the gifts they brought but they resented even more the smiles Eartha wore as she accepted both. Whites thought Eartha was her image and dismissed her as some-kind-of-trash. Not her Oscar nomination for *Anna Lucasta,* her Emmy nomination for *I Spy,* or her Tony nomination for *Mrs. Patterson* could turn around an image Eartha had so artfully created. The sex kitten was trapped in her do-it-yourself cage. But for a period from 1952 till the early sixties, Eartha Kitt was a star. But as the country and the times went through changes, Eartha, artistically, did not. Her style belonged to another era. In the fifties people "played" at sex as Eartha did, but in the sixties, when the hard-rockers took over, they were doing *it* and taking it seriously. As Eartha failed to grow, her recording contract with RCA was dropped, her nightclub appearances diminished. Her work was sporadic. There was a season on the trendy *Batman* series and semiregular appearances on *Hollywood Squares.* But not much else.

By 1968 Eartha Kitt was, as she has stated, "an international star," as she had always maintained a huge European following. But a "legendary great"? Hardly! Americans had simply grown bored with Eartha's "thing." Aretha's was more honest; Diana's more beautiful; and who and what was an Eartha Kitt in 1968 anyway! That is what the late President Johnson decided to find out after the now "legendary" Lady Bird luncheon at which Eartha made a scene. And what a scene! Lady Bird had invited a group of "distinguished ladies" to discuss what was then a burning social issue—juvenile crime. Eartha was one of those distinguished ladies. She had earned her right to be there. Not known to many has been Eartha's participation in many socio/political projects. One of her pets, Rebels with a Cause, was a Washington group, mainly of black youths, devoted to getting ghetto areas better street lighting, among other crime-prevention and neighborhood-improvement techniques. Eartha came to Lady Bird's luncheon ready for battle—not with Lady Bird, as it later resulted, but with the problem at hand . . . juvenile crime. Eartha, who has never been thought to be naive, waited, she claims, throughout the luncheon for the ladies to *get down*. When they did nothing more than sigh tremulously, scratch the surface with polite observations, she became enraged. When she obtained the floor, she spoke with the typical Eartha Kitt passion, which borders on ferocity, about American involvement in Vietnam and "the toll it is taking on the best of American black youth."

You would have thought Eartha had unleashed a volley of four- and five- and eight-letter "dirty" words, the way the press carried on after they received the *official White House story*. Lady Bird had been insulted in her own home, reduced to tears, they said. Lies, retorts Eartha. Lady Bird did not cry, she insists, and her intent was not to insult Lady Bird or anyone else. But LBJ didn't agree. Before Eartha could burp, the luncheon broke up into horrified gasps and whispers that caused LBJ to phone the FBI and the CIA. Our late president actually ordered a dossier be prepared on Eartha that would prove she was not of this democratic process but some kind of degenerate dissenter. The dossier, which Eartha obtained and which she carries with her today with disconcerting pride, is terrifying proof of the lengths to which this country went to discredit those who disagreed with its policies. The dossier, brandished by Eartha, reads like a very bad, five-and-dime pulp novel. But it served its purposes. According to Eartha, along with other LBJ machinations she was forced off television and out of nightclubs and into work in foreign countries. She was systematically eliminated from the American scene, she says. Interestingly, no one of note came to her assistance.

With the end of the Vietnam war and LBJ's death Eartha tested the tide of public opinion in 1974 by concertizing at New York's Carnegie Hall. She was well received. Merv Griffin and Mike Douglas began showcasing Eartha once again. By 1975 *Timbuktu* was in the talking stages. Three years later it is here!

Here with it . . . Eartha. The once banished queen has regained her throne. She issues statements from it which curiously the press does not challenge. Her career, she would have you believe, was at its zenith when it was torpedoed by LBJ. She was a star, a legend, a legend, a star, she repeats. And the press concurs. Perhaps like so many others, they too are acting out of guilt for not having defended not just Eartha but the supposed American way of *free speech* when they should have. Perhaps they reason that Eartha has suffered enough and is thus entitled to her minor trespasses on truth.

And indeed, Eartha Kitt has suffered greatly in her lifetime. One must understand Eartha's roots to comprehend the many angles of her personality. She was but a child when she watched *and felt* her mother give her away because her lover-to-be-husband did not want another man's offspring, and in particular a white man's offspring, in his home. And her mother's family would not accept her. They literally, physically, threw her out because she was "yellah"—also known as not black enough. Then there was the family who so "kindly" took her in. The older children, twelve and thirteenish, would tie her to a tree, wrap a bag around her head, and then beat her. And if she told—not that anyone would listen—they would beat her even more severely the next time. The child Eartha learned to spend many hours hiding under the house. Because a child, to survive, must have something that dimly resembles love, she would court the woman-of-the-house's approval. She would do anything for those rare pats on the head. Any gesture that could be interpreted as positive, Eartha decided, was love. "When you have nothing, you take bones, any kind of bones," she explains.

As she reached puberty, she was sent to live in Harlem with an aunt, a woman Eartha depicts in her autobiography, *Thursday's Child*, as a psychotic. The woman starved, beat, and abandoned her ward, and to lord only knows what purpose, as she was, above all else, a churchgoer . . . a God-fearing woman.

Thus Eartha's childhood is filled with rejection: pain, unexpressed rage, and resentment. It is absent of any kind of kindness, acceptance, and love. One can only imagine the wounds that don't heal from this kind of childhood experience. And thus one can only marvel and yell a cliché-ridden, "Right on!" when Eartha Kitt takes center stage—at the theater and away from it—and proclaims "I am here!" Damn right she is and more power to her!

Facing that mirror in her dressing room, in her throaty growl, she insists her experiences have not made her bitter, resentful, or mistrusting. Her words say one thing while her actions say another. She has barely said a hello when she entered the room. Air conditioning certainly isn't needed, as her chill could freeze over hell. Hostile, Eartha Kitt seems to dare you to like her. Yet she says she is easy to be close to, that she likes to be touched. Then suddenly she changes. Kitt McDonald, her seventeen-year-old daughter, walks into the room and melts her mother's icy exterior. The "legend" becomes human. Looking at Kitt, one can see why. This is a beautiful child-woman. Very tall, slender, and *naturally* blond, she is another "gift" from a white man, or as Eartha puts it: "The dividend from an otherwise bankrupt marriage." Kitt does the seemingly impossible. She brings softness to her mother's face . . . a sense of vulnerability, a trait Eartha admits to hiding. "I will not allow myself to fall into that trap," she explains. And yet just by the way she changes in the presence of Kitt, she has "fallen," if indeed it is a fall to be vulnerable to another. A week later on a rainy afternoon that finds Kitt marching off "to do Bloomingdale's," Eartha is still looking vulnerable as she curls up on her living-room sofa. She seems so much smaller amidst the steel and glass of a New York high rise than she did in her dressing room. And she *acts small-*

er. A complex creature, this Eartha Kitt, who in her biography admits she is two people. Eartha Mae, the unwanted "urchin who fears she will one day return to eating bread, sopping molasses, and being hated," and Eartha Kitt, The Star. Eartha Mae will still accept bones; Eartha Kitt demands the entire carcass. Eartha Mae's ghost is her past and she is haunted by a fear that she is nothing and nobody and will thus ultimately be abandoned and rejected. This, Eartha Mae admits. But Eartha Kitt is fierce . . . defiant. She believes, because she *must*, that she is rare . . . special . . . legendary. Because Eartha Mae's ego is damaged, Eartha Kitt must act as though it were not. Sometimes during the course of an afternoon that talks its way into evening, it is difficult to tell with which Eartha one is speaking.

She is very at home in the palatial cooperative apartment she is subletting. But luxuries are not a new companion in Eartha's life. Early in her career she implored "Santa, baby, leave some presents under the tree." He, and many others, did. With a wry laugh Eartha says: "I never bought my own sables or diamonds, as admirers gave such things to me. Why, I even owned a Jaguar before I could drive." Obviously "bones" come in many sizes, shapes, and colors. Eartha Kitt sees her image as fun and insists "I never took it seriously and am amazed when others do. I laugh at that Eartha even when," she adds somberly, "she has made me cry."

And *that* Eartha has made her cry frequently. "I was a sex symbol and proud that I was," she begins with her usual defiance. "And I was the first black woman identified with the word *sexy*. Till me, black women were allowed to be beautiful, like Lena, or talented, like Ella, but never sexy. But I was never *just* sexy. Never. I was also known as one of the great actresses of our time."

By whom? one is tempted to ask until one realizes that it is Eartha Mae's insecurities that drive an

Eartha Kitt to make such an outrageous statement. She continues: "And I was never my image. I never dated white men exclusively. The press made it seem such because that sells newspapers, but so what if I did? It's nobody's business. Besides, I don't see people as black or white. I see them as human beings, male or female, hostile or friendly. And I belong to no one race but to all!"

Again the defiance, but soon another feeling follows. Matter-of-factly Eartha states sullenly, "Black people always denied me love. Always. First as a child because I wasn't black enough and then as an adult for the same reason. I was always too 'yellah.' Well, I can't cry over that anymore. I won't cry over any of the rejection I have suffered at the hands of black people. Today if someone sees me as not black enough, it is their problem and not mine. Isn't it funny that they used to think *I thought* I was white. Funny, too, how whites never thought I was."

And still, despite the tone in her voice, Eartha Kitt insists "there is no bitterness . . . no more anger. One forgives, if never forgets. One leaves the judgments to God. I am not a vengeful person. There is nothing to forgive of anyone. Not of Mrs. Johnson or of her husband. Fate takes care of all. You see, whatever has happened to me through the hands of others . . . well, I believe, what goes round . . . comes round. What that person has done, that person must one day deal with. Fate takes care of all."

She is a fatalist. "Fate tests you," she says. "The cards of life are dealt and one must simply learn to play them. I have learned to fight for my destiny—to be *that* Eartha Kitt. But then I have always fought for my life. I always will. I do not give up and that is why I have never been, nor will I ever be, defeated. Nothing defeats me. Nothing. I will not allow me to be unhappy for more than five minutes at any one time. Anything more is self-destructive. Yes, there is pain in my life, but why treasure it? Scream or cry it out, I say. I have; I do. But I never feel sorry for myself. That is a meaningless self-indulgence. Play the cards. Do the best with what is dealt. Go after what you want in life. Seize it! We all have the power to make our lives work . . . the power to survive.

"One must never cave in under pressure," she continues. "Give no one that satisfaction. When I was boycotted from working in my own country, I went where I was wanted—to Europe, Asia, Africa. I worked. What a mockery that boycott was, a mockery of everything this country pretends to offer its citizens: freedom from want, freedom of speech freedom of all kinds."

The laugh that follows her words is bitter, resentful. There is always a Vesuviuslike feeling about Eartha, a lid struggling to fly off the container. She says anger, like alcohol and drugs, is a weakness and thus she will not, she insists, be weak. She speaks of herself in the same breath with Judy Garland, Marilyn Monroe, and James Dean. She identifies with them—Piaf, too. They were, she says, "charismatic artistes but self-destroyed people." Where she differs from them, she says, is in her tenacious ability to "be in control of me . . . my life. From the time I was old enough to think I knew who I was and what was happening around me. I decided in spite of everything and everybody I would be happy. I am happy!" she says in a tone defying contradiction. "I am the last of the great international stars. There was Josephine [Baker], Marlene [Dietrich], and me. We belonged to the world. I still do. People beg me not to leave again—that the theater needs me. They say I am a great artist—that there is nobody quite like me—that I am a one-and-only. And yes, I do believe that!"

Do you, Eartha Mae? Do you really?

She answers the question obliquely, pushing aside feeling and vulnerability. "Eartha Kitt exists as a product of her childhood. She will always be afraid of rejection, of love that will be withheld or withdrawn.

That always hovers over me. But Eartha Kitt must be
great because if she is, she cannot be rejected. And
when great, she will be noticed. And when noticed
she will be loved."

But how permanent is such a love? she is asked.

"There is no permanence to love," she says evenly.
"Love is not something one can cling to. It is offered
by some and by some withdrawn. They come, they go,
bringing and taking their love with them. Love is not
a possession. It can be reclaimed by the holding company at any time."

And suddenly this proud, often vain, sometimes
pompous personage becomes painfully human. "I
would still accept a bone," she says quietly, revealing
her deepest need. "Yes, I would. A bone. *Anything*
that feels like love I would take. I am grateful for
whatever love there is in life." And almost as an afterthought she adds: "I need to be wanted."

Seemingly she is not aware of the barriers she
throws up against being wanted and receiving love.
Her attitude is a decided "Hands off!" She neither
acts nor appears as if she needs anyone, least of all a
man. Often it seems men who have glamourized and
even worshiped her have also been her destruction.
One of the dedications in her autobiography reads:
"To all my lovers who walked away when they
couldn't handle it."

Today Eartha says: "I will no longer deal with a
man who cannot see beyond my image to who I am. I
want a man who can handle his own weight. I would
like to be loved, but I do not look for marriage. I am
not afraid to be alone, as I am not lonely. In that respect I am free. I no longer have to be with a man
. . . any man. I know how to laugh and how to
cry. It would be nice to be with a man who can share
my tears and laughter and who would allow me to
share his. There are men in my life today. There is
always that." She laughs. "But I see now that I am
basically a loner and how being alone is very comfort-

able to me. I would like to be loved by a man but there is also that part of me that prefers hiding under the house in a place called Safe."

Throughout her life Eartha Kitt has not found safety with the men she has known and loved. She has suffered through numerous broken engagements. Before her men could say their "I dos," their families said, "You don't!" and they didn't. Today Eartha recognizes her image may be difficult for some men because "they expect me to be the sexiest thing in town. I can be but not at random. I must care for the man—must care deeply."

She seemingly did care deeply for Bill McDonald, whom she married in 1960. At the time of their meeting, McDonald, a Korean veteran, was intent on obtaining a college education. Eartha agreed to "see him through, as a man should have his degree." She did not mind being the breadwinner, as she believed that after McDonald's graduation "we would both put our shoulders to the wheel, combine efforts, to earn what we needed in life. I also believed a marriage is based on two people helping each other achieve individual as well as collective goals. That's what *I* believed. He, it resulted, did not share those beliefs. After he graduated, he chose not to work."

Initially she refused to talk about her marriage. "I have a child to consider," she explained, "a child who remains in touch with her father." But as time passes, Eartha remembers and allows certain memories of her marriage to trickle out. "Eventually he did work—did try, but the marriage failed."

And why did it fail? Again the wry laugh that says more than the tone of her words. "If a marriage is to work, both people must have a respect for and trust in one another. Perhaps it is foolish to think both should love in equal parts—maybe that's not even important—but there must be some reciprocity. I didn't feel that there was. I felt quite alone in my marriage. In fact, I felt I was married but he was not."

The couple divorced in 1965 when Kitt was four. "I didn't lose everything in the divorce. I kept my home in Beverly Hills, which is my refuge, my piece of this earth. And I had Kitt, who is the bottom line of everything in my life. She was the reason I married. She makes it all worthwhile."

She is also the reason why Eartha Kitt, beyond her own need to survive, weathered the holocaust created by her inflammatory remarks at the White House in 1968. "I was not a pauper when the word came down from LBJ to get-that-girl-off-the-networks," she says, "but I was not rich. I could not have afforded to wait out the boycott. I had made a promise when Kitt was born. She was never but ever to know hunger or poverty of any kind. She was never to know want. Kitt was seven when I had to work abroad to make a living. If I was frightened by what was happening in my life, she never knew it. Any anxiety I would have shown would have caused my child to be anxious. I was having none of that."

Kitt McDonald is Eartha's rock, her stabilizer. "She makes my life worthwhile," says Eartha. The women, when observed together, are as much like sisters as mother and daughter. They obviously like each other. "I've sown my seed well," says Eartha. "This is a good person, strong too. She will not abuse her beauty and she will not allow others to abuse it and thus her. Yes, there will always be those who will look at Kitt— her beauty, her color—and say ugly things. I hope I have given Kitt a foundation that will stand erect under the weight of rotten words and feelings. I think I have. But I would not want to spare her from that ugliness. No. Life should be experienced without protective shields. I don't believe in safety locks around children. Kitt will weather the storms. And there will be, just as there are, storms. I want Kitt to stand tall, so tall that nothing can blow her away."

Like her mother? "Yes!" says Eartha passionately. "My life is a lesson to Kitt in how to weather it out. I have six gray hairs on my head. I treasure them. I've earned them. I've earned my tomorrows. It will be wonderful. My life will be wonderful. I survived my childhood, my lovers, my banishment, LBJ and Nixon, and a war. Eartha Kitt will always survive. Always! Eartha Kitt is *here!* And *here!* is where Eartha Kitt intends to stay because *here* is where she belongs."

CHAPTER THIRTEEN

BEVERLY SILLS

"Mama, I think I've met a man I could marry," said
Beverly Sills, the morning after her first date with Peter Greenough. *"But there is a* small *problem,"* Beverly *continued just as "Mama" was about to do flips
and cartwheels as "Mamas" of twenty-six-year-old unmarried daughters were given to do in those days.
"He's married, has three children, is thirteen years
older than I am . . . and he isn't Jewish."*

It's typical of opera star Beverly Sills that she
would call such obstacles *"small problems,"* but then
Beverly Sills Greenough has a talent for making
mountains into molehills. What matter that she was
the daughter of Russian-Jewish immigrants, raised in
the middle-class mores of Brooklyn, a *"child laborer"*
on radio's *"Uncle Bob Emory's Rainbow House,"* and
Peter Greenough was a proper Bostonian, socialite,
and direct descendant of John Alden and heir to millions? Furthermore what did it matter that when they
met she was an aspiring soprano, singing for her
supper and reviews that would eventually catapult
Belle Silverman into international repute as Beverly
Sills, and he was associate editor and financial columnist for the family-owned Cleveland Plain Dealer?
None of these differences were really relevant—not if
you are like Beverly and Peter and possess their inner
strengths and capacity for growth.

The Sills-Greenough marriage is twenty-two years
"young" this November. The couple is growing old
together but not stale. Beverly's success, of course, is

virtually unduplicated in the operatic field. Yet where other marriages in which the woman has attained superstar status have crumbled under the weight of such pressures, theirs has not. Competition and jealousy, often unnamed "correspondents" in divorce hearings, are not evident here. Although Beverly walks in the spotlight, Peter refuses to follow in her shadow. The egos of both partners are intact. Thus the Greenough marriage has not only endured but flourished because "Beverly's priorities have always been, like her head, screwed on straight," says Peter. "On stage she belongs to the world. At home she belongs to her family."

The world's highest-paid opera star is looking for a handout. "I'm down to a dollar. Can you spare five?" asks Beverly Sills of her husband. Her entrance could not have been better timed if it were written by one of the composers whose dramatic works she sings. At that moment Peter Greenough was explaining the importance of his work as Beverly Sills's financial adviser—her money manager—a position he assumed eleven years ago.

As Peter fumbles through his wallet, his den-office comes into focus. On his antique rolltop desk are Lucite blocks spelling out the message "I love you" to his wife. The same feeling is demonstrated by scores of Sills's pictures and memorabilia adorning the den walls.

Clutching a ten to her ample bosom, "Bubbly," as Peter calls his wife, waves and departs. "Great singer but no business sense," growls Peter good-naturedly, which brings him back to his point. Eleven years ago Beverly Sills became "big business," with earnings beyond a quarter of a million yearly. At that point they decided that Peter would put his thirty years of expertise as financial editor of *The Cleveland Plain Dealer* and *The Boston Globe* to work for Beverly. "I decided to mind the store to protect Beverly's earnings. From the time we married, we've never used her money. I support this family. Beverly's earnings are in trust for her and Muffy. She'll never have to worry about money. Her energies are freed for her work," he said proudly.

Beverly herself corroborates this later on another day in their warm, comfortable living room overlooking Central Park. The apartment is one of three residences owned by the Greenoughs. The others are on Martha's Vineyard and in Miami Beach. All homes and furnishings have been purchased with Peter's money. Even Beverly's charge cards read "Mrs. Peter Greenough," with no mention of the more celebrated, credit-giving Beverly Sills.

While the outside world is far more aware of the tall, exuberant, outgoing, red-haired superstar, "No one in his right mind would ever think of Peter Greenough as 'Mr. Sills'!" says Beverly. "Not my Peter, I assure you." Beverly laughs. A big gutsy laugh as she sits nibbling away at a box of chocolates. Don't you watch your weight? she is asked. "Of course," she replies. "I watch it grow.

"Peter's the original take-charge kid," she continues. "In fact that's what attracted me to him. That and the fact that he was tall, blond, and handsome. Imagine how I felt when I discovered he was also rich!"

At that moment husband Peter—with arm-in-sling—enters the living room. He has just returned from the doctor's. "I'm told that I must learn to play tennis left-handed," he reports.

Beverly refuses to swallow this diagnosis. Aware of her distress, he expertly shifts the subject to her day, and in particular to her fund-raising activities for the New York City Opera, for whom she will soon serve as director.

"It looks good," she tells Peter. "My luncheon guests promised to look into their upstairs closets for a spare million." He congratulates her—and she congratulates herself by reaching for another chocolate.

As Peter leaves for his study, Beverly recalls their first meeting in Cleveland, where she was performing, and where he was living and working at the *Plain Dealer*. They met at a postperformance party—and there was an instant *click*—"just like in the movies," Beverly recalls. They were surrounded by other people, but Peter managed to slip a matchbook into Beverly's hands. On it he had written: "If you have any free time, I'd like to see you."

Beverly's reaction: "Corny but effective." Still, she decided not to respond. But the very next day, having taken pains to keep track of her whereabouts, Peter showed up at another social function Beverly was attending. He did not bring a date but decided instead to escort two of his three daughters, Lindley and Nancy. "It was as if he was trotting all of us out for mutual inspection" is the way Beverly describes it. "But he did it with such ease."

"Within minutes of our meeting, he told me that he was available—that he was in the process of a divorce. Soon afterwards arrangements were made for the two of us to have dinner the very next evening. There was nothing then—or now—indecisive about Peter. He's a very secure man. Even though we are both somewhat conventional in our outlooks, it never occurred to Peter—or to me—to forsake my career if I were to marry him. Quite the reverse. Peter encouraged my career, and together we have shared it and the world in which we traveled."

Peter also remembers their first meeting. "She was a very beautiful girl. When I saw her, I was in the process of a divorce, and not thinking of remarriage. Yet when we met, we hit it off instantly. I liked her mind, her sense of humor, and the fact that, unlike many people in opera, she has many interests . . . she even likes baseball! That clinched it. Imagine finding a beautiful, intelligent, accomplished woman who knew the difference between a fastball and a curve!"

He recalls the early years of their marriage and the ball games they attended. "We'd arrive at noon to watch the batting practice. Beverly invariably kept her eyes on Ted Williams, who tested every part of the field before the game started. Thanks to Williams, Bubbly developed her 'Ted Williams Drill.' Wherever she sings, Bev arrives early to test the field—to see exactly how her high notes are going to bounce off her 'ball park's' walls. My wife is a perfectionist," Peter proclaims proudly, "and an artist."

But even though their relationship was harmonious from the start, it doesn't mean that they haven't had their share of major problems.

Fortunately their wide cultural differences never posed conflicts. Only Beverly's aunt and uncles were heard from Brooklyn echoing a loud *"Oy Vay!"* when they learned that Peter wasn't Jewish. That the Greenoughs were based in Cleveland while their respective families lived elsewhere, Beverly terms "a blessing in that it gave us time to adjust to one another without the constant interference of family."

Still, there were difficulties. "The Silvermans [Beverly's maiden name] were never poor," she points out, but there *is* a difference between living in an apartment and a twenty-five-room château, particularly when the house originally belonged to another woman. "To tell the truth, I was never comfortable living in that house. I was jealous. I didn't like living in a home that had been entirely decorated by another woman—Peter's first wife. I sensed her presence everywhere." Apart from that, the bluebloods of Cleveland felt that Beverly-of-Brooklyn was not their type. "When Peter was transferred from Cleveland to *The Boston Globe,* I was relieved," Beverly admits. "I was glad that we could have our own home, could create our own atmosphere."

From the outset of their marriage, Peter's daughters from his first marriage lived with them. "I always thought of them as ours," says Beverly. A third daughter, Diana, was retarded and placed in a special school near Boston. Instant motherhood was not a problem, Beverly says, nor were there religious conflicts. Lindley and Nancy were raised as Presbyterians; Beverly is Jewish. They compromised by embracing the Unitarian Church. Peter and Beverly's daughter, Muffy, who is deaf, was educated in a Catholic school until she was nine. "It never mattered to me," Beverly remarks. "I was grateful to the nuns for all they gave my daughter, particularly her belief in God. Muffy, like her sisters, Lindley and Nancy, will make her own religious choice when she comes of age."

But while she prefers not to dwell on Muffy's disability (Muffy is now seventeen), Beverly admits that when she first learned that her twenty-three-month-old daughter was deaf, "those were difficult times." She not only had to adjust to this reality, but six weeks later she was staggered by another permanent fact—Their son, Peter "Bucky" Greenough, was hopelessly retarded. Beverly became severely depressed and ignored her career to work with Muffy on developing a sense of sound.

Initially she felt a self-pitying "Why me?" which later gave way to an angry and bitter "Why them?" But as time passed, she had to accept what could not be changed. "Peter and I drew closer together, closed ranks you might say, and vowed to make life as comfortable for our children as humanly possible. Throughout all of this, he was my rock. He still is," she adds softly.

Peter also talks with difficulty, but with candor, about his children. He admits that having a second retarded child troubled him. Today, with the knowledge he gained through his one-day-a-week involvement with the March of Dimes, he says: "Had we known then what we know today about birth de-

fects, we would have had arranged for genetic charts.
But," he continues, the words coming more slowly,
"if I knew in advance what was to be, I . . . we
. . . would still have had these children.

"Each has been tremendously rewarding in his or
her own way. Diana [his daughter by his first mar-
riage] has made a very happy life for herself. She
lives at the school and is unaware of her limitations.

"And Muffy, although she has only residual hearing, I don't feel sorry for her and she doesn't feel
sorry for herself. You see, in all other ways Muffy is
an extraordinary young woman. She's bright, creative,
nice . . . a joy. Oh, she could have been a terror.
If you let it happen, a handicapped child can become
very domineering. Many use their disability to manip-
ulate and control their parents. Neither Bev nor I
ever tolerated this. We raised Muffy as if she were a
regular kid—which to us she is. No special considerations were given and no tyranny allowed.

"Today Muffy is like most seventeen-year-old girls
who are beginning to date and want to do things on
their own. Beverly is such a Jewish mother. She gets
up each morning to make breakfast for Muffy. She
tells her not to talk to strangers. But then, she does
the same with me," Peter laughs.

When asked about Bucky, and his effect upon the
marriage, Peter's laughter becomes somber. He
remembers all too well the specialist who examined
Bucky when he was several months old, and abruptly
announced: "You have a severely retarded child." He
remembers all too well their shock and despair, particularly his wife's.

"Beverly was so distressed," he recalls. "Within a
six-week period she learned her daughter was deaf
and her son was retarded. What a terrible blow! So
difficult to absorb . . . to deal with. A man is lucky
because he has his daily work to go to. I was at *The
Boston Globe* at the time. I remember coworkers re-
marking, 'You look a little down.' I was down—not a

little but a *lot*. I'd already had four daughters and I wanted a son for selfish reasons. I wanted a son to take to ball games . . . on fishing trips. I wanted the same kind of close relationship with Bucky I'd had with my father. There was so much I wanted for the little fellow . . . so much I still want for him. Yes. I cried. Why not? I distrust men who never show their feelings.

"But I threw myself into my work. I also threw myself into helping Beverly out of her depression. She had stopped working to stay at home with Muffy. With Bucky they told us there was little to be done. But they were wrong. Thanks to some wonderful influences . . . particularly the special school we sent him to when he was six . . . he has learned simple things which seem like extraordinary accomplishments to Bev and me.

"Bev gave everything she had that year to her children," Peter continues. "Which is why I wanted her to resume singing. I felt that her going back to singing would be good therapy. Lord knows, she needed her career to take her mind off things."

Yet, as Peter admits, neither therapy nor work can ease or erase certain heartaches. They both often visit Bucky and take him to lunch and play in the park. Parting is always difficult. "I watch Bev as we drive away and there are usually tears rolling down her face. I feel so helpless at these times. I wish I could say or do something to make things easier for her. He's such a beautiful sixteen-year-old."

Peter does not believe that tragedy necessarily brings a couple closer together. "In my first marriage the birth of a retarded child never helped the relationship. When a couple is far apart, nothing short of a miracle can bring them together. Beverly and I were always close. We just moved closer . . . clung a little tighter and fought like hell. You see, we both believe that even when the going gets rough, life is too important to be ignored. We fight to enjoy life. We weather the storms."

Beverly agrees that a shared tragedy does not necessarily strengthen a marriage. "A marriage is either good or bad—with communication and caring—or without. Peter and I read each other—we are sensitive to each other's moods and care about each other's well-being. We are protective of one another.

"Those first awful months when we learned the truth about our child, we suffered. But then we decided not to give in or give up. We couldn't . . . if we were to make our lives and the lives of our children meaningful and happy."

Beverly has come to terms about what it takes to be a happy woman. "I once said that a happy woman is a cheerful woman, without cares. I guess I don't fully qualify, but I am cheerful. Peter and I love our children. We believe that God meant them to be ours, to be appreciated and loved by us. My children have been very rewarding. Anything Bucky does today— such as lifting a spoon to his mouth to feed himself (something doctors said he could never do) is a triumph, a miracle, to us."

There never was a question of blame or of "bad seed." "I believe that God intended for Peter and me to have these children. It was His will. That doesn't mean when I get to heaven—and I fully intend to get there!—that I haven't a few questions to ask Him. I guess you know," she adds softly, "I cannot bear to see children, any children, in pain." When pressed, she adds, "There's never a moment when I'm not aware that something is wrong. You can never brush off that kind of thing. It's a kind of hopelessness that you always carry around with you. I guess I'll spend the rest of my life shaking my fist at heaven and asking 'Why? Why the children?' "

Because he was so in touch with his wife's feelings, Peter pushed her out the door after her year of "coping" and back into the limelight. To allay her depression and get her going, he presented her with fifty-two round-trip Boston-to-New York tickets. He wanted her to resume her voice lessons, he explained. But neither anticipated that she would become the extraordinary operatic star that she is.

Still, as Beverly puts it, "Peter never competed with my career. Nor did he compete with the particular kind of love the public bestows on a popular artist. If he had ever said 'Quit!' I would have, but he never did. He was always aware that my marriage and family came first.

"In fact, I recall one particular Christmas Eve in London. It was very cold and dreary, and the two of us were spending Christmas all by ourselves, away from friends and family. As we huddled before a small fire, Peter turned to me and asked, 'Is this the way you want to spend Christmas Eve?' I said, 'No.' Then he replied, 'Okay then, no more Europe except for two weeks a year.' Since then that's the way it's been. Peter is head of the house. I'm still basically a conventional Jewish girl who sets the table for dinner each night and sets the place at the head for her husband."

While Peter enjoys the fact that Beverly is back in the swing of things, and that theirs is such a varied life, "even invitations to the White House, no less," he reports, he still manages to be "the rock." Six years ago another potential tragedy struck. While Beverly was performing in Texas, she discovered that she had uterine cancer. Within twelve hours, Peter had her on a plane and in New York Hospital for surgery.

"He was there for the run-of-the-play" says Beverly. Still, the doctors were optimistic from the start. "I would not accept the possibility that I might be in danger," Beverly relates. "*Cancer* is a dreaded word, but to me it was just an operation—and as it turned out, that's all it was. I refused to live in dread. Actually," she continues with that special Sills smile on her face, "there isn't any way that life will defeat me.

This . . . now . . . is the most special time of
my life. I live as I wish. There's nothing professionally left to prove.

"Personally . . . well, there's still so much romance in our marriage. We have a very old-fashioned
relationship . . . none of that open-marriage stuff
for us. I'm a one-man woman and Peter has never
given me cause to be jealous. We have had twenty-
two years together. Frankly I think it was God's in-
tention. Ours was a marriage made in heaven."

CHAPTER FOURTEEN

LEONTYNE PRICE

Leontyne Price walked through doors normally closed to blacks but held open for her by "guilty liberals who assuaged their guilt by allowing me, the token, to enter." She was further abetted by those who found her blackness an "exotica of sorts." Neither faction of the fifties had planned on "me surviving, not only intact, but with prominence."

She had been musically prepared to be "the token," and from the time she came to study at New York's Juilliard School of Music in 1952, her career had the Midas touch. Within the decade she made her debut in Paris, Berlin, Vienna, San Francisco, and New York; sang with La Scala and the San Francisco and NBC opera companies to arrive in 1961 as *the* prima donna of the opera world at its mecca, the New York Metropolitan Opera House.

Today Leontyne Price is one of the world's most famous women and the opera world's only recipient of the Presidential Medal of Honor and fourteen Grammy awards, a number unmatched by any artist—pop or classical. Legendary, she is both loved and loathed for what she is and for what it is assumed she is not. In actuality, with Leontyne you get two for the Price of one—the career woman, the superstar who "demands red carpet treatment" and the private Price, a woman emerging at forty-six to be "my own person" who "clings like glue" to her femininity and who sharply separates the love of the masses from the love of *her* man.

Both the *artiste* and the woman are evident in her Greenwich Village home, which is sumptuous and elegant and yet comfortable and vibrant. She has no house help, no servants. She cleans and cooks and "feels my own tomatoes" at the supermarket. She is the happy homemaker and the prima donna.

And why shouldn't she be the latter? No other profession in the performing arts demands the time, energy, and total all-consuming passion like the opera/concert world. It is not a charitable field. No one willingly gives an inch. Leontyne took inches, feet, and yards by force of talent—a voice that she describes as "unique. You have not heard it before in anyone else and when I'm gone, you won't hear it again." She is "nuts" about her voice, listens to it for hours, and even applauds it "like a fan" when she hears herself "doing something wonderful. My voice is gorgeous," she says with unflinching immodesty. Many an evening passes in which the famous diva sits with feet up on her elegant sofa, listening to her elegant voice or to "the one other woman who can upstage me anytime—Aretha [Franklin]. Rocking with that lady, you can let it all hang out."

She sees her own work as "soul in opera. There is an abandonment in my singing. I always spill over." Not so. Formerly self-contained, hidden as much from herself as from others, only within the last three years has she grown to be, as described by her friend, Pearl Bailey, ". . . more relaxed, looser." The change is credited to a growing understanding and acceptance of herself. "I have begun to discover who I am and who is image."

Until recently she felt herself to be only the singer, "only a voice and that if the voice was silenced, no one would so much as say hello. I doubted that I mattered to anyone as *me*. And that was a reflection of how I felt about myself. I didn't know who and what

Leontyne was apart from this publicly loved gargantuan image. I discovered I am a woman who needs to be loved apart from her work. The superficiality of being loved solely for my fame terrifies me. This lady doesn't want to hear the thud of herself crashing later."

From the beginning there was always fear, despite the fact that the last thing Leontyne Price looks is frightened. As she became increasingly famous, as she went from La Scala to open the new Metropolitan Opera House, the fear heightened. She was pulled at from all sides. Do this, do that. Be this, be that. She avoided everything by plunging further into her work and, by doing so, avoided the pain. But as she later learned, she also avoided herself.

"So much responsibility, so much," she says of those years when beauty—particularly black beauty—was in the eyes of the beholder. "Always the proof is needed, the credentials to show you belong. When you're black, yesterday's high C is just that—yesterday's. I was under constant observation and thus constant pressure. There was never any time left for me to be me. What I felt, *if* I felt, could be expressed only through my music."

She is minimizing what must have been a fishbowl existence at best. Although there had been Marian Anderson before her, there had never been the opportunities afforded to Miss Anderson that were dangled before "the girl with the golden voice," as Leontyne was labeled by *The New York Times*.

First at La Scala. *First* at the NBC Opera. *First* at the Metropolitan. *First, first, first* can create awesome recognition, responsibility, and burden. The voice received most of it; the person, only the leftovers.

Today, twenty-three years after it began, the shades have been lowered in the fishbowl, while the draperies have been opened to allow in the light for the woman herself. She is examining who she is and who she isn't and finding "being me is very challenging. I'm not many of the things I thought I was. Yes, by necessity I was self-involved, even selfish. As the one who came first, I had to be. But now I can be there for another person, for a friend; not just by phone or check, but in person. Where once, again by necessity, I wore blinders and barreled through to where I had to go, today I am a softer, kinder, more thoughtful and understanding person. Although I am still thin-skinned, what others think of me bothers me less than it used to." In the past many have thought she was petulant, arrogant, snobbish, and childlike in her constant need for handholding—the artistic temperament she admits to.

She has a tough manager, Hubert Dilworth, who for twenty-three years has fought for, babied, and nursed her career. The only black manager in the opera world today, Dilworth is known as Clyde to Leontyne's Bonnie within their industry. What she wants, he gets. Not because it is her whim, but because in that crazy world of "grand" opera, the "grander" one is, the "grander" the paycheck and the respect that goes with it.

Opera is no better, and no worse, than Las Vegas in that an act is merchandise, meat in the market. How it is displayed often affects its sale. And Leontyne Price, as her box-office receipts throughout the world reveal, is always well displayed.

It is more than possible that this elegant woman can be a number-one bitch when professionally pushed in directions she doesn't wish to go. Her strength hits you at the door. It's an immediate statement that can be confused with arrogance, which in a sense it is. Mainly, it is a healthy statement that says: "I like me and if you don't, screw it."

Her single-mindedness to "make it" cost her friends, but the pressures she felt as a black woman, and as the first black—and "petrified because of both conditions"—made that unavoidable. Hers was misconstrued as a "star trip." Many felt she made public entrances that rivaled Cleopatra barging down the Nile. Leontyne denies this, insisting she has always hated any entrances other than those on stage. "I am a terribly shy person. I dislike attention being focused on me other than in my work. I would prefer to enter a public place unnoticed. I literally have to pull myself together into this assured state of being in order to enter a restaurant. It may look like I'm barging down the Nile when in truth I feel as though I'm about to sink."

She is admittedly aloof. She takes no interest in the cocktail party syndrome. She finds the people who inhabit her professional world "not all that scintillating. You can suffocate on their talk, which is mainly of music. You can also get hurt. They play that terrible social-kill game where people verbally stick needles into one another. Why should I be torn apart or needled? Why should I have to wear a protective suit of armor?"

She shouldn't and she doesn't. She prefers her own company, or that of a few friends, to mingling with many. She is eminently self-sufficient and "all the talk about my needing to have my hand held and to have things done for me is irritating. People forget I helped put myself through college by working as a maid and by slinging hash in the school cafeteria. No one ever had to pry a silver spoon out of my mouth. Not ever!"

Suddenly she is enraged, her voice booming, breaking the "great lady" image and damn near the glassware, as it thunders throughout her home. "There is no privacy anymore," she rants. "None whatsoever. It's 'follow the yellow brick road.' Well I won't have it," she screams. "Not me. I'm an individual. I refuse to let *anyone* into my head unless I choose to. What I feel and what I do is nobody's business. *Do you hear?*"

Her rage is so sudden and so total and so unexpected that it is like a mad scene from one of her operas; only it's for real. "All that criticism," she begins again. "So awful. So untrue. How dare people think I could stop being black! Why should I have to prove to anyone where I'm at when I have been there all along."

She is reacting to that social-kill game, as she put it, that hinted Leontyne was black in skin tone only. It began as fame approached and with it the press, uncovering the fact that she had received financial assistance from a white family in her hometown of Laurel, Mississippi. A very big deal was made of this because any kind of black/white togetherness in the fifties was an oddity and thus suspect. The stories, unfortunately, placed her parents, James and Kate Price, in the background when in truth they were "center stage," doing what they had done since Leontyne's birth—"working their asses off" so their daughter could be well educated. That hurt her, as she remains, after their deaths, fiercely devoted to her parents.

That some people made it seem as though she were "tomming to reach the throne" also hurt. Still others made it appear as though she had turned her back on her roots. She never understood what was happening other than "something neighborly—one family helping another—turned into something ugly that made me seem ungrateful and incapable of making it on my own black feet. It also made me vulnerable to the vultures, those who measure a person's blackness. It makes me mad!" she yells again. And then suddenly she turns somber. "Funny, if I had lost my temper years ago, today no one would know my name. I wasn't allowed to express my anger then. No black person was. I had to keep cool because I was first and a lot of black folks were behind me waiting for their chance. Had I opened my mouth, we might all be still waiting. So I kept it shut and because I did, people assumed things about me. How *dare* they!

Don't assume anything about me. If you want to know, ask!"

She is raging again, fuming because "I have been unfairly criticized by my own people. I wasn't involved enough, they said, wasn't truly concerned with my fellow blacks.

"How can anyone say I could have taken a more active role?" she asked incredulously. "What right do I have as a famous singer to speak out politically. I have had to seek the advice of Whitney Young and Roy Wilkins to find my own truths. How could I have been politically involved when my own knowledge was fragmentary? *Didn't-get-involved; could've-been-more-active*—I tell you it makes me furious! What do they think I should have done—waved a flag? Never! I don't have to prove anything to anyone. I have my own way of expressing my involvement and if it doesn't fit an expected mold, that is not my problem."

Her involvement was quiet but meaningful. Initially it consisted of being professionally better than all others. As a black, center stage, she could never be less than great, and she never was. "Second chances are not extended to token blacks." She "snatched" every opportunity offered "not always because I wanted it but because it opened a formerly closed door. In proving to concert and opera goers that black is beautiful, I lost me in the process. All my energies went into being the best *artist*. Today my energies are into being the best *me*."

She thinks back to the early years, to the waiting in the wings, and the fear that held her hand. Together they would make their entrance before audiences of thousands where "I had not only to prove my worth but also the worth of black people. Being black, there were no laurels on which to rest. Each night was a new experience with new minds to conquer. Each night my talents and blackness—my right as a black

woman to be there—were challenged." She withstood
every test.

She made another kind of contribution to the
"cause." Wherever she performed, she insisted that
the chorus and orchestra be integrated. She would
not sign a performing contract unless guaranteed this.
Throughout the country she forced the issue and
won. Except at the Metropolitan Opera House.

When she opened the new Met at Lincoln Center,
there were numerous bomb threats. That kind of
open, racial hostility she could handle, but the more
insidious was the more subversive. It found a popular, esteemed, white female colleague insisting that
the reason Leontyne drew the honor of opening the
new opera house was because "she's a nigra, darling,
and *they* are in right now." The colleague was not
alone in her bigotry or jealousy. Many hinted that
the Met was indeed making a gesture to march to the
civil-rights rhythm.

She shut everyone's mouth by opening hers and de-
livering a virtuoso performance that made worldwide
headlines. The Met management took their deserved
bows and privately made it known to Leontyne that
they had given her the "plum of the century." She
saw it as the plum of responsibility and that the Met,
had they indeed done her a favor ("as they im-
plied"), had it repaid tenfold. After several successful
appearances there Leontyne took a leave from the establishment, tired, she said, "of being a symbol."

When the Met urged her to negotiate a new contract, she promised to open an ear if they would first
investigate why their orchestra has no blacks in it.
The answer was "the usual cop-out"—that there were
none qualified—and the relationship between artist
and Met management has never been the same since.
She doesn't know where the Met is at today. "I don't
appear there very much anymore and I doubt if that
is too upsetting to many of the board members who
weren't too thrilled with my black presence to begin

with. My name was only approved for the Met roster after checks of my box-office receipts made it obvious that I was big business. You know," she says as an afterthought, "I've told that story about the lack of blacks in the Met orchestra to several reporters and never once was it printed. Prejudice can be so insidious.

"And when it comes from your own, it kills. The biggest hurt I have known in my life was the unfounded and unjust criticism from my own people. I have never understood the nibbling we blacks do at one another. I cannot tell you how painful it is to think you are not accepted by your own."

Her "own" is what sustained her through those years. Her black roots grew deep from childhood. "In our home there was always the pride in being black and of being yourself. My parents loved one another—they made that obvious—and they made their love for us kids obvious too.

"I felt respected as a child and I have always believed that accounts for why I have always been a proud person. My daddy had great pride. He was king in our house, and his word was law. He would work sixty hours a week at the sawmill or as a roofer or carpenter, but he never complained. 'My life is my wife and my kids,' he used to say.

"My mama worked as the country midwife. She delivered more babies than the county doctor. She was everybody's mama and some mama to me. And some wife to her husband. My mother was a very strong woman, possibly the strongest I have ever known and yet totally feminine. She knew how to let her man run his home. My mama died over a year ago, but she has never died for me. Both she and my daddy were very special and they made my brother—one of this country's few black generals—and me feel special too. They never made us feel they were sacrificing anything for us, or that we should repay them for all they had given. And although I didn't know it then,

theirs was a sacrifice. I had to leave Laurel to discover we were poor—materialistically poor. Love-wise,
we were rich beyond belief!

"Laurel was a 'house divided'—*their* part of town
and ours—and never the twain did meet. It was always us and *them* and if *they* didn't want us, we
didn't want *them*. Instead we lived in a very close, ex-
tended-family environment. I never thought I was de-
prived as a child, and in some ways I wasn't; but in
others I was. I had none of the cultural advantages
that *they* had in *their* part of town. Only whites had
libraries, museums, playgrounds, and swimming
pools. I didn't understand until years later how that
kind of second-class treatment can result in a second-
class life for a black child because she is not given the
same equipment with which to deal with life. Like
when I came to New York, I realized how the division between black and white, like the one I experienced in Laurel, can bounce back at you. I discovered
I was uncomfortable when entering white establish-
ments, and in that respect it was still Laurel-time for
me. I have *yet* to enter *their* sector, the 'For Whites
Only,' comfortably."

Music, in the form of piano lessons, began at five,
and through her efforts in church she rapidly
emerged as the town's musician. She is today as
"deeply religious" as she was as a child with "the
same childlike belief in God. It is a very naive, simple
but precious belief to me. I know He is there and
ever present as He is in all people."

In an all-segregated, grade-one-through-twelve
schoolhouse, she was an honor student. College was
an assumed goal and her parents had been saving
toward that end since her infancy. Yes, she was
"pushed," she says, but "I was a very ambitious child,
quietly but deadly so. My mind was always smoldering, always working. I seldom felt the need for companionship. I was content playing with my dolls by
myself under the big fir tree in our yard. But if a

friend joined me, that was nice too. I am still very much that way. I was never, however, an all-work-and-no-play girl. I liked dating. When I was in high school, I had this mad palpitation for the school football hero. We would date in groups and I had a strict curfew. If when he and I sat outside past the appointed hour, Daddy would come around with his Big Ben watch and stand there as the minutes ticked loudly by. It didn't take too much sense to get his message."

Reliving her youth, she laughs and says: "I was so darn lucky. I had a complete childhood. My best girl friend then is my best girl friend today. I loved my life in Laurel. My roots are still there."

She does not feel particularly nostalgic about Wilberforce, where she attended Central State College and where her vocal abilities emerged. But she gratefully acknowledges that it was Clark Wesley, president of the college, who, upon hearing her sing for passing-through dignitaries, suggested she audition for the famous Juilliard School of Music, which she did. And it was upon her acceptance to the school that her previously mentioned Midas touch "midas-ed," and the rest is near fairy tale in history.

Professionally she has reached her fulfillment. Performing gives her a sense of completeness but "success by itself doesn't concern me anymore." She sings because she needs the artistic expression, certainly not the money. She is financially secure. "I am known as the laziest singer in town. I work when I choose to."

But she never rusts the talent. "I must always keep my voice in shape. It never stops needing care. Like its owner, it is temperamental and crazy. I wish I could, but I can't stick it in a case like a violin. I often test out the ole girl between the hours of three and five in the morning. Obviously I sleep late. It's the fulfillment of a promise I made to myself in college when my day began, rather than ended, at five. I said then, as I staggered through my work as a maid or in the cafeteria, that if I ever made it big, I'd sleep till noon whenever I felt like it. And this girl often feels like it."

Her challenge today is personal. "I have learned to wear my successes rather than let them wear me. I no longer need material things to make me feel good about Leontyne Price. I can now throw on a cloth coat and feel as good in it as I would in a mink. It's what you wear inside that matters.

"I—the *me*—the other half of Leontyne Price, the other self, work on being that constantly. I am a woman. The woman finds it impossible to function fully without *my* man. He makes me feel beautiful, alive. When you are a career woman, you learn that no man should ever have to face the 'image,' only the woman."

She does not believe that because she is a successful black woman, she is more difficult for a man to relate to. "That has nothing to do with color. Black or white, if the man is not together, if his ego is a sometime thing, he just isn't going to hack it. I am a tough symbol but I am not a tough woman unless the man himself is weak."

Although she has been involved with one man for many years, marriage is not contemplated. She tried that once, to actor William Warfield, and it ended in divorce "despite my adoring him. I married for love. We are still the best of friends, and exactly why our marriage failed is still somewhat of a mystery to me. It had nothing to do with a clash of egos. Frankly I think it had to do with the fact that I'm not the marrying kind. But marriage was expected of me—a pressure of sorts from certain family members I wanted then to please. Today I please me and I don't feel by being unmarried I am missing anything at all.

"My man is very important to me, but I cannot give up anything in the hope of having something more. And what I would have to give up in a marriage is my work, which is a part of me. So I am better off not married. I'm too independent. Most career women are. Happily, my man accepts me as I am. His ego is not on the line. Let me tell you, that is some kind of extraordinary man. We have a great physical and emotional relationship. He satisfies my needs, which are intellectual as well as physical. I enjoy a man, particularly a man who enjoys his woman. I suppose those people—and there are millions who think of opera singers as being sixteenth-century virgins—will be shocked by my talk, but I'm strictly a twentieth-century woman with needs and passions."

The relationship has lasted, she says, because "I never confuse it with my work. The love between me and five thousand others in an evening is hard to upstage, and I need that love, but you can't take it home to bed with you. I need love that is quite different from that which I experience as the public Leontyne Price. I need a nourishing love; one that is more real and a greater validation of myself. You see, despite that 'star trip' I am supposedly on, the truth is I'm really a homespun lady. My man is still *numero uno* with me."

She pauses, considers her words, and with a radiance no stage lighting could effect, concludes: "It may be late, but I am finally excited about me. I'm just so grateful to be alive, to be a black person today. We are positively unique people. Breathtaking people. Anything we do, we do big! Despite attempts to stereotype us, we are crazy, individual, and uncorral-able people. Yet," she says with a sadness creeping through her happy tone, "I still feel the need to prove on stage that black is good; black is capable. The need is more quiet now than before, but I wonder if it will ever disappear. Actually, I don't know that I could function on stage if it did."

CHAPTER FIFTEEN

JOANNE WOODWARD

The "public" Joanne Woodward, as defined by her press image, is "incredible" and "a miracle of miracles"—the "complete woman" who skillfully combines marriage and motherhood with woman and personhood.

To this, Joanne Woodward says: "There are days I wonder why Paul [Paul being Paul Newman, to whom she has been married sixteen years] doesn't take me out in the back and shoot me as you would an injured horse." Joanne insists most of what is thought to be true of Joanne Woodward is "rubbish." She insists she is not "incredible," "complete," or "cool" in any way and certainly no "miracle of miracles."

Joanne Woodward tends to see herself in a very dim light. The press, she claims, has been conned into thinking she is some superbeing. "Actors soon learn what is wanted of them and thus push a button during interviews which foster the fiction. I've done this."

Additionally she is, as her friend writer Gore Vidal says, "a remarkably private person." In recent years, other than to promote a film, she has dodged interviews. A top public-relations firm is employed to "keep the press away." A request for an audience with Joanne results in a mass and a maze of machinations that begin with "Impossible!" and conclude weeks to months later with "Okay but . . ." The "but" contains more stipulations, conditions, and clauses than an application for a bank loan. Examples: No interviews in the Newman home. No interviews with or pictures of the children. No joint interview with Paul Newman. No interview with Mr. Newman at all. And . . . no questions about Mr. Newman. However it is strongly intimated that Ms. Woodward *will* discuss the weather.

Due to the conditions and demands, a she-better-be-worth-it colors a first meeting with Joanne Woodward. She arrives promptly, looking gorgeous, which is unexpected. One thinks of Paul Newman as "gorgeous"—not Joanne. Wrong. Her eyes, a changing blue-green—which she says is consistent with her personality, "inconsistent"—are every bit as arresting as Newman's baby blues.

Instantly Woodward becomes the Queen of Chit-Chat. It's a trick, a device learned to keep the press at arm's length. When nailed to the wall, forced into revealing something, *anything* personal, she becomes a contributing factor to the energy crisis. Warmth does not flow from within to without. She becomes snappish, almost rude, but then explains: "It is not the interviewer I hate but the process. Why should I be picked and poked at? Why should I allow strangers to know the *real* me? And autographs? No! My signature, like my name, belongs to me. Besides, I don't give a damn what others think of me."

Doubtful. More likely Joanne fears the negative evaluations of others, which is an unrealistic fear, but as friend Stewart Stern says: "If Joanne owned a shooting gallery, she'd be all the ducks."

Reluctantly Joanne admits: "I do have this boring tendency to complain and whine about me and my shortcomings."

Woodward actually has difficulty accentuating her positives. She admits that a recently played parlor game, Torture, found her sentenced by Paul and her daughters to listening to an endless stream of compliments. Gore Vidal finds Joanne's tendency to downgrade herself "refreshing in a world where most people go the other way" but an anonymous female friend thinks otherwise. "Joanne is only gorgeous to look at, scintillating to talk to, and above all a genuinely nice, sensitive person. But to hear her tell it, she's impoverished. Frankly, her negativity is a bore!"

Joanne does come dangerously close to being any one of the dozen or so neurotic women she has portrayed on screen. Her performances as ladies with loaded libidos have won her numerous awards—including the Oscar—and a rather peculiar stature in Hollywood, where she is thought of as one of America's best actresses but decidedly not a star. Unlike her husband, no mystique surrounds Joanne Woodward. Interviewers do not ask of her: Do you sleep in the nude?

What they have asked and had answered is that Joanne Woodward was born February 27, 1930, to Mr. and Mrs. Wade Woodward, he a schoolteacher in Thomasville, Georgia. She came to New York via Louisiana University, from which she did not graduate but where she appeared in campus productions as she "majored in parties." Her formal acting training was at both the Neighborhood Playhouse and the Actors Studio. Her " big break" occurred when she understudied a lead in *Picnic,* a play notable for its artistic and financial success as well as for introducing Paul Newman both to the world and to Joanne. He discovered her almost instantly. Hollywood was somewhat slower. It took a hundred or more appearances on live TV shows before 20th Century-Fox signed her to a long-term contract.

Joanne Woodward insists she is reluctantly a working woman, an actress. "I act because I wouldn't know how *not* to act. It's like being born with a deformity: you learn not only how to live with it, but you wouldn't know how to live without it." She does not think she has accomplished or contributed anything notable as an actress. "I'm a good listener," she says, "and thus can be what the writer or director wish me to be. I don't seek perfection in my work. When the director calls, 'Cut! Print it!' I'm ecstatic. I never plead to do another take. Just the opposite. I just want to do it and go home."

The myth surrounding Joanne maintains she does a "miracle-of-miracles" juggling act. As the actress comes down, up goes the mother and homemaker. The "juggler" insists her acting career runs a constant collision course with her housewifely roles. She was raised "1940's style—to believe motherhood was a joy and its responsibilities sacred." She was also raised, she states, to believe "women should be both wife and mistress to their husbands and in that is their 'true' fulfillment." Today, she claims, media and changing mores have her confused. "Constantly I read how at forty-four or fifty-four I should be thin, desirable, vital, doing my own thing, and enjoying an absolutely terrific sex life. Without previous training that's rough as hell. I'm caught in the crossfire—somewhere struggling to bridge the generation gaps. And it *is* a struggle. My work has made me horribly guilty toward my daughters. I'm still seeking to balance actress and mother; still learning to leave the one on the set to be the other on the hearth."

She doubts her success as a mother. "I'd score myself a sixty-five percent but my kids would not be that charitable. There have been nights when I have returned from a day's filming and sneaked into my own home and hidden in my bedroom. The perfect mother, right? Not only not relating to her children but avoiding them." She still remembers when Nell or Mellisa or Clea, now fifteen, thirteen, and nine respectively, would inch up to her and say, "Mama, I'm lonely," and "Mama, why don't you talk to me."

"God, how that kills!" she says. "How do you tell

your child, 'Go away, dear. Mother's had a hard day at work and you're bothering her.' Children don't understand that and why should they? To them, you are mother and that's all that matters."

Only today is she coming to grips with conflicts as an actress/mother. "Whatever is good for me is good for my children" is something a friend once said to her. Then she thought the woman "awful," but today "I know she was right. Like it or not, I *must* act. If I don't, I'm going to be bitchy . . . displaced. My family will suffer for my not doing what I have to do." Then as though not quite convinced of her own logic, she adds, "Besides, it's highly probable kids get along just fine without the amounts of maternal devotion previously thought necessary in child rearing."

An objective party grades Joanne considerably higher as a mother than she does. Says Stewart Stern, "Joanne has a unique relationship with her kids. They dig her. Lots of kids *love* their mothers but how many *dig* them? Joanne is free with the girls and encourages *their* needs and *their* dreams rather than stamp hers onto them. She makes it possible to be her kids' friend. But, as she says, she could never be just a mother. That for her would be stultifying."

One would be hard pressed to find anyone less stultified than Joanne Woodward. In addition to presiding over a rambling Connecticut house that at last count included X amount of children—the exact number depending on whether Paul's girls from a previous marriage are living in or out—ten dogs, four cats, twenty-two pigeons, a skunk, a chicken, and a horse, she has studied or is studying French, piano, guitar, ballet, yoga, and needlepoint. Politically she is involved, although she claims that involvement is "an offshoot of Paul's. I'm too politically naive to take a firm position of my own." Since she is on one of his enemies lists, Richard Nixon would not agree. Additionally she is the current chairman of her local Planned Parenthood chapter but believes she is "lousy at it. I can never remember statistics or those marvelous pithy paragraphs from pamphlets that punch home their point."

Nevertheless her efforts resulted in a $50,000 take from a benefit she produced last fall and for which she secured such talents as Debbie Reynolds, John Gavin, Paula Prentiss, Richard Benjamin, and Hazel Scott. "I was scared to death appearing in my own skin. I got through the damn thing by pretending I was Betty [Lauren] Bacall—poised, chic, confident."

Indeed, as her anonymous lady friend stated, Joanne Woodward can become boring and irritating. Anyone who has so much, *is* so much, and makes so little of both soon becomes less than sympathetic. Challenged with a "doesn't anything make you feel good or fulfilled?" she spits back, "Yes, my hollandaise sauce." The suggestion that she is being facetious angers her. She is not, she maintains, and she cites how just-the-other-day, she was in one of her "why-do-I-bother-when-everything-is-hopeless-and-I'm-a-total-failure" moods when husband Paul suggested she "buck up."

"Why should I?" she whined. "I'm a failure, useless." To which Mr. Newman replied: "But you have a great figure and you make a helluva hollandaise."

"And he is right," she concludes. She thinks a minute and then softens. "I just thought of something else that makes me feel good: the term paper I wrote for History and Ideology and for which I received 'Good Thinking!' as a grade. No Oscar can compare with that!"

History and Ideology is but one course she is taking as a student at Sarah Lawrence College. Her return to school has been greeted by friends and press with an "Isn't-that-just-like-Joanne" kind of respectful and admiring awe. Those closest to her hope it will end yet another Woodward negative evaluation: that she is something less than bright. According to Stewart Stern, before Joanne married Paul, she took a battery of intelligence tests that, Stern maintains, "were as important to her and the marriage as the results of the Wasserman. They showed Joanne has a near genius IQ."

"I am *not* stupid," Joanne Woodward says firmly. "But I don't know anywhere near as much as I would like to know." She pauses, and for one brief moment looks about to cry. "Just once I would like to feel I can do something really well, something that is uniquely Joanne Woodward. I love my children but they are themselves . . . thank God. What I mean is, they are *not* me, not a product of my intelligence or creativity. As I said, they are themselves. My work as an actress is a product of the writer, director, and cameraman. Paul and I are a joint venture. So . . . where is the me?"

She believes she is far too dependent on Paul and the children for her happiness. "How I would survive if those I love suddenly disappeared from my life is a question that haunts me." She believes all her relationships would improve if "I needed me more and them less. The world's saddest people are those without inner resources. I always feel something lacking within me. I'm always stretching to be something more, stretching to find the limits of my being . . . to create . . . achieve . . . to be so many different things. I'm terrified of being *un*self-sufficient. I wish I had a sense of self rather than still searching for an identity."

Counters Gore Vidal: "Joanne may be unsure of her identity but no one else is. Despite *anything* she might say to the contrary, Joanne is a woman of great inner resources and of even greater strength. She isn't terrified of herself or of human relationships. Actually Joanne isn't terrified of anything."

Stewart Stern adds, "Joanne has an extraordinary value system based on her own inner decency, and people without identities don't have that."

She has been in and out of analysis over the years

and thinks about returning despite her admission "I'm not certain of what it has done." Stewart Stern doesn't believe "Joanne needs an analyst to help her make changes; she makes her own. Joanne today is a totally different woman from the one I met twenty years ago. Then she was extraordinarily mistrustful, hypercritical, and caustic. But marriage to Paul changed her. Each passing year with Paul, each new child, has made Joanne increasingly loving, open, and beautiful."

Inevitably, as any interview with Joanne Woodward must, the subject becomes Paul Newman and her life as one half of "the Newmans," legendary in their longevity as a married couple. "I cannot tell you how much I hate, loathe, and despise discussing my marriage. It's like opening our bedroom door for inspection," she bristles. She has stated she has long passed the identity crisis of being Mrs. Paul Newman, a title many would kill for, but she has not. Recently Barbara Walters on *Today* asked the "what's-it-like" hated question and "I wanted to knock her teeth out and told her I would if she ever asked me that again.

"What's it like, what's it like? It's damn hard. *That's* what it's like," she says in both exasperation and pain. "You can't imagine how difficult it is relating to Sam Superstar. Not because of Sam . . . Paul . . . but because of what the press and public make him. Sometimes it is horrendous living with this gargantuan and unreal image, this idol of millions of heaving-bosomed women. You forget who he *really* is."

Living with Paul Newman, "superstar," although difficult for her, is even more difficult for the children, she claims. Agitatedly she describes how the Newman girls have frequently been pushed aside by people hungry for a glimpse of their famous father. "It's like they don't count at all, as though they were nothing in themselves," Joanne says, speaking of "they"—the children, but also of herself, one suspects. "I can only hope that Paul and I have given something to our children that will help them withstand this stress. God what ego strength it takes to be the child of celebrities plus the daughter of a sex symbol! Has anyone ever thought how disturbing it is for a girl to hear how her friends have the hots for her father?" She does not comment on the effect it has on her—that *her* friends frequently "have the hots" for her husband.

Within the first minutes of meeting Joanne Woodward it becomes clear how she feels about Paul Newman. Despite all the stated conditions and warnings of how she will not discuss Paul or her life with him, *she* breaks all the rules, and not the interviewer. Paul floats in and out of her conversation without thought, unconsciously and naturally. "Paul is the most beautifully selfish person I know," she will say spontaneously. "He knows how to satisfy his own ego and thus doesn't need to have it massaged for him." And "Paul is a collection of habits, traditions even, that make him happy. Like his dunking his face in ice cubes first thing every morning or his one-hour shower." And "Paul gives to Paul and that makes him happy and because of that he is then able to give to me and his children."

Their marriage has been atypical in that there have been frequent separations caused by their respective work. This, she claims, has helped rather than hindered the success of the marriage. Togetherness, she believes, has been "blown out of all reasonable proportions. Why should husband and wife impinge their souls on one another day after day?" Both she and Paul have a need for aloneness, for a retreat into their own private worlds, and neither resents the other when this occurs. She is on a current campaign for separate beds but to date "Paul will have none of it. A double bed is fine for making love but not for sleeping. I like waking up alone, having time to fix my hair and my head before facing the man I love."

She is aware most women would think her bananas for wanting a bed separate from Paul Newman, but these are the same women, she maintains, who think of the Newmans as being what they are not: elite, a glamorous couple. According to Joanne the Newmans may be the world's most successful shut-ins. Despite the fact that columnists frequently have them seen at *that* ball or *this* gala, the truth remains that the Newmans are stay-at-homes. Paul prefers pretzels and beer to champagne and caviar and Joanne's idea of a big night is to stay up to midnight. This is totally counter to the underground but rampant rumors about the Newman's sexual appetites, activities, and proclivities.

"What are they?" she asks, fascinated, and when informed that gossip reputes them to be sensual sexualists, swingers, and swappers, she gasps: "Paul and I?" She claps her hands and screams: "How lovely. How absolutely lovely. And delicious. And elegant!" She is laughing, beaming, tickled by the salacious. "At last an image I can live with. Do me a favor. Tell everyone it's true. That's one myth I don't wish destroyed."

CHAPTER SIXTEEN

CINDY WILLIAMS

Although barely a hundred pounds, Cindy Williams is, in TV talk, "heavy." Which is strange, particularly to Cindy, as she thinks of herself as "movie-people." She has a long list of film credits including *Gas, Beware the Blob,* and *Drive He Said*—all of which barely missed being part of the cultural exchange to Russia—and of course the Oscar-nominated *American Graffiti* and *The Conversation.* So what's a nice "movie-people" like Cindy Williams doing in television and being "heavy" at that? She is, in spite of herself, portraying Shirley "Wait-for-the-Wedding-Night" Feeney, in *Laverne and Shirley,* which the rating services tell us is the "biggest smash" (TV talk) since *All in the Family,* its numbers far outdistancing *Rhoda* and *The Mary Tyler Moore Show.*

If you find that hard to believe, so does Cindy Williams. *L & S* was not a show Cindy wanted to do. In fact, she kept screaming "No!" to anyone who would listen until ABC-TV made her the offer she couldn't refuse. That, of course, means money—better than five but less than $10,000 per week. All that to play one of two "broads" in a beer brewery who struggle to keep bottle capped, chin up, and reputation intact! It may not sound like much but *L & S,* a spin-off (more TV talk) from *Happy Days,* another winning Nielsen number (which is actually a spin-off from *American Graffiti*), is a funny, funny show combining high camp and low comedy to glorify the "fabulous fifties." But the true "glory" is in its stars,

Cindy and Penny Marshall (Laverne). They are Lucy Ricardo and Ethel Mertz incarnate. To the question "Why would anyone watch a weekly show about two dizzy broads working in a Milwaukee brewery?" (the question, incidentally, was asked by Cindy as she fought *not* to do the show), *they* are the answer. Their collective "insanities" (much of what viewers see is improvised) is what has made—are you skeptics ready for this?—*Laverne and Shirley* the top-rated, or next-to-top-rated show since its debut.

What has all this meant to the twenty-eight-year-old Cindy Williams? Not much. She disbelieves it, as she sees no evidence to believe it. Actually Cindy sees very little except the freeway between her little nest in Beverly Hills and the studio where she puts in a five-day week, but one in which each working day lasts a minimum of thirteen hours. The only apparent change in her life is in the amount of telephone calls she now receives. The phone now rings off the hook with offer upon offer that she *can* refuse (and does) from men who wish to "date" (a euphemism) a celebrity. By the time this is read, she will have a new number. But other than for that newfound "fame," her life is hardly that of the celebrity. No diamonds, no yacht, and no runaway romance with Warren Beatty. She *shleps* to the studio and "crawls" home "too tired to do anything but fall into bed with a good fantasy." Saturdays are spent "sacking out" and "sorting out"—in that order—laundry and myriad other household chores which she, herself, continues to do as she finds it "embarrassing" to hire a secretary. Her one night to "make whoopee" (another euphemism) is Saturday. Then it is church-on-Sunday followed by dinner-at-Mama's. The Sunday-Night-Nauseas, suffered, she says by everyone who has ever made a TV series, closes out her *fabulous* weekend except for the prayer to her Maker that she get through the following week.

If all this sounds somewhat less than glamorous, it

is. She had a better time as "movie-people" because she was most often unemployed and therefore free to work as a waitress by day as she gloried in little theater productions at night. Just prior to *Laverne and Shirley,* she was living high on unemployment checks following her twenty weeks of work on *The First Nudie Musical,* a film that satirizes the porno people. It is just making the national rounds and as it does, it is "freaking" ABC executives and all those who hold Shirley Feeney close to their bosoms. *Their* Shirley would never be in such "bad" company.

"What a crock of shit!" says Cindy/Shirley, fanning the furor as she speaks such language. What has enraged the provincial press the most is Cindy's usage of the word *shit* in the nudie musical. *Their* Shirley, they insist, would never be so gross.

"That is *not* Shirley in the film but me," says Cindy through clenched teeth, "and how dare people confuse the two. But!"—and she rises indignantly to her full five feet three inches to cough up this one—"what makes me even angrier is the fact that if it were a man who had said 'Shit!' no one would say boo. But a woman using what some sickies think is a 'dirty' word, *that* becomes a cause. And," she continues now standing at about five feet seven inches, heat blazing from her dark eyes, "what makes these people think Shirley wouldn't use such a word? And just wait until they find out that Shirley may *not* have waited until the wedding night. It's going to blow them away. Good: A lot of nice girls in the fifties didn't wait, you know. It's time someone told *their* story." She stops, throws her hands up, and laughs. "What am I getting so heated about. Fuck 'em! How's that? That should send them running to the archaic typewriters. Fuck 'em! I guess that proves they didn't call me Ole Garbage Mouth in high school for nothing."

She is an absolute delight, this "surprise smash!" (more TV talk) of the television season. There is nothing fake about her, which accounts for the success of Shirley Feeney, who doesn't pretend to be anything other than what she is: an average girl wanting an average life—"but legal." Cindy describes herself as "not exactly a polished pearl. Actually I'm not a polished anything. I'm just me." Amen! She is without guilt, deceit, or conceit, and is therefore amazingly free of the annoying postures of the "actress." Perhaps as fame fondles her, she will change, but it is not likely. Her goals, like Shirley's, are admittedly and unashamedly middle class. She wants to marry and raise children. She also wants to be a working actress, which is not the same as saying she wishes to be a star. The fact that she is now well paid for her labors and is achieving great recognition is secondary to her employment in a job that allows her to use her talent. Shirley s-t-r-e-t-c-h-e-s Cindy's skills. "Initially I didn't know if I could make people laugh. Now I hear the reaction of the studio audience and know that I can and do. That's a wonderful gift."

Her previous comedic training began as a child in Irving, Texas, where the first ten years of her life were lived. Her father, a struggling electronics technician, would leave the poverty that "hung out" on the doorstep and the incompatibility of his marriage to play Sid Caesar to Cindy's Imogene Coca. The improvisations took place frequently. Even the household dogs were dressed up and pressed into service. "I often wonder why they didn't come with a big net for all of us," muses Cindy. Her mother was also humorous but "not with my father. They should have divorced but didn't. For our sakes—meaning me and my sister—they said, but that wasn't true. They were too frightened. My mother was a two-time loser and my father had one previous bummer. Yet in some strange way they were devoted to one another. But they never got along. Neither knew how to dream. Life somehow had robbed them of that gift. Early in my life I knew I wanted to act. They tried to stop me. They felt my

being an actress was like taking one's life savings to
the crap tables in Vegas. I fought them and I won. I
guess that marked the first time I ever said *yes* to
me."

She remembers her childhood as both a-yes-and-no
situation. Yes, she was frequently unhappy, particularly at her parent's bickering and their inability because of their respective jobs to spend any time with
her at the various parent/child school functions. But,
no, hers was not an unhappy childhood because "I
adored my daddy and loved my mother. I felt secure
in their love but I was always afraid one of them
would give up and not come home again. Sometimes
their fights were that bad. I still get very edgy at sunset. As a child that was the hour of day I was left
alone. My mother would have just left for her night
job and my father would still be at work for another
two hours. Funny, all these years later and I still have
a need for comforting when the sun goes down."

When she was ten, the family returned to California, where she had actually been born. In high school
she became active in school plays and pageants. Upon
graduation she "knew what I had to do" and broke
off an unofficial engagement to study dramatic arts at
Los Angeles City College. Her hard-earned degree
won her a job as a cocktail waitress. One of her many
jobs as she waited to be "discovered" was at the
Whiskey A-Go-Go, one of the Sunset Strip's more
colorful rock disco palaces, where she waited on the
late Jim Morrison and Jimi Hendrix as well as assorted other druggies, dropouts, glitter-freaks, and
groupies. It was an education Los Angeles City College had not provided. "There was an awful lot of
sex going on—*all kinds of sex*—behind closed doors, in
front of open doors, on the dance floor, at the table.
After my initial shock I found it rather beautiful. All
those people touching. The only thing that ever
freaked me was the knifing. Violence to me is obscene. Never sex. There was a time I thought bisex-

uality was bizarre. Actually I abhorred it. But in seeing a lot of it at the Whiskey, among other places, I stopped thinking negatively about it. Why shouldn't a person be attracted to both sexes? Besides, other people's scenes are just that—*their* scenes, and I say yes to anything as long as it is nonviolent and between two consenting adults. If all those people who wish to legally inhibit sex would just do it more and talk about it less, they'd be less threatened and more accepting."

She is not as liberated as she sounds and admits it. Almost sheepishly she reveals, "I still find it hard to call a man I'm attracted to and ask him out. I plead guilty but I prefer it when the man is the aggressor. That is not to say I haven't 'aggressed' in my time, because I think a woman today should feel free to initiate sex, but I prefer to be Scarlett to some man's Rhett Butler and be swept off my feet and into the bedroom. And you want to know something worse? There is no hope for me at all. I want to get married."

She certainly has made her stabs at it. Her first live-in arrangement was at nineteen. "That was the thing to do in the sixties." Did she love him? "I know now I didn't," she says. And what of her mother? How did she react to her daughter's "fall"?

"My Italian momma said but two things: 'If he don't treat you so good, remember, there's a lot of other fish in the sea' and . . . 'Make sure you are friends. No friendship; no marriage or else you be in big trouble.' She was right. I've had several lovers but few, if any, were friends."

The people who were her friends in the sixties were mainly "the poets and protesters—all very anti the war in Vietnam. I never marched in the demonstrations but I always wanted to. Rehearsals for one of the scores of little theater productions I was in always prevented me. I regret that. I wanted to raise my hand against war. I don't mean to be redundant but I cannot understand violence—cannot understand *anything* that maims or destroys children, animals, or people who are innocent of any wrongdoing." She thinks about those years and her friendships and muses "Funny how they all grew up and went into good jobs making good money. They became a new kind of establishment, but establishment nonetheless. They have big homes, big cars, but they are involved in political issues. I guess that's what distinguishes them from their predecessors. They are involved. That's often hard for me to be in my business. It is so insular. People in show business seem to eat and breathe 'the business.' I love my work but I refuse to get swept up in that bullshit. I never did. From the beginning producers and agents seemed to sense the casting couch wouldn't work with me. Seldom was it offered and when it was, I simply refused to sit down. A very corny philosophy has gotten me through. I don't think one needs to put out to make it in this business. Talent will eventually win. Talent is needed in Hollywood or else the industry shrivels and dies. They are all a little nuts out here. Insecurity should be the middle name of every major studio. There is still much confusion as to what kind of movie will sell. There is even more confusion as to how to depict women. Generally there are no roles written for actresses because most screenwriters are men who have no grasp of today's woman. So they write for the Redfords and Newmans. Eventually some will write for men and women equally. I don't mean each will have an equal number of lines but that as people they will be equal to one another. Can you imagine that some writers today will still have the woman stand by and watch with a horrified expression on her face as her man is slugged to a pulp in a fight! That woman ceased to exist years ago. I don't know any woman who would play the helpless, in-need-of-protection female, if it came down to that kind of nitty-gritty situation. Hollywood fails to recognize that women can and do stand shoulder to shoulder with men these days. And I'm perfectly willing to stand shoulder to shoulder with Robert Redford or, for that matter, in any other *equal* position where he is concerned."

She is laughing and obviously enjoying herself. She has yet to become so sated by interviews that she finds them boring. She soon will. Already she is rebelling against the persistent rumors spread happily by gossip columnists that there is friction between her and Penny Marshall. "Why do they do that?" she asks somewhat naively. "Penny and I have known each other long before there ever was a *Laverne and Shirley*. We've been friends for six years. For five days a week we see more of one another than most husbands and wives. And we get along a helluva lot better than most married couples. Weekends we avoid each other like the plague. Wouldn't you if you worked that closely with someone? Actually Penny and I prop each other up and keep one another going. Penny is not exactly Kid Confidence. Nor, for all my sometime bravura, am I. This sudden fame thing can be very unnerving. We are both still learning how to handle it."

Cindy is mainly ignoring it. She recently "presented" at the Emmy Awards and found it "fun" but hardly stuff of which dreams are made. Her one totally free day is not spent at pool parties with the Hollywood "Wild Bunch," but in church and with her mother with whom she now shares "an X-rated relationship. Six years ago my mother wanted to know every detail of my life and I would tell her nothing. Then when I felt both of us had let go of the apron strings, something very strange happened. She became this sixty-six-year-old person with whom I have a friendship. I talk to my mother just as I would talk to Penny or any of my girl friends."

Recently, however, her mother-the-girl-friend laid a typical "mother-trip" on her. "I ain't getting any

younger, Cindy," she said, "and I'd like to see some
grandchildren around this dump before I kick off."
Before Cindy could quite recover from that number,
her mother-the-girl-friend continued with: "Did you
pay the car insurance yet? You better, the way you
drive!"

"I hate it when she does that, but I have to admit,
I also love it," says Cindy. "I guess I never want to
get that independent where I'm not glad I've got a
mother who mothers me. I love the ole lady and I tell
her so every chance I get. I believe in that. Why wait?
Life holds no guarantees that there will be a tomorrow. So I tell the people I love that I love them. But
her knock about the grandchildren hurt because I
would love to be a mother. All my dreams are about
husband, home, and family. I'm very afraid of *not* settling down. I seem to be awfully weak at making a
relationship work over the long haul. Till recently
the men I chose didn't much help matters. I know I
will feel very incomplete if I don't marry and know
motherhood. I'd like to help some kid grow up free—
to assist a child—*my* child—in becoming her or his
own person. And by the way, my desire to marry is
not to please my mother or those crazy ole lady
friends of hers who cluck 'What? Cindy is twenty-
eight and still not married?' I want marriage because
for me it is a commitment I need to make and one I
need to hear another person make. I make no value
judgments about it—whether it is good, bad, necessary, or valueless—but *I* want it and that's all that
matters. I believe in living with a man first, however.
You really cannot be intimate with someone until you
do live with him. You really cannot see that other
person or yourself clearly until you are sharing both
bed and board. When you live with someone, you see
much more of yourself—your pettiness, your jeal-
ousies, your need to control or be protected, your craziness—than if you lived alone. I learned something
from each of my relationships. Unfortunately the de-

mise of each made me a basket case, especially one which sent me to bed for a month with the covers pulled over my head and nailed to the headboard. But you know, as painful as that was, it resulted in one big positive, as it forced me into a deeper awareness of who and what I was and why I allowed myself to be with, and stay with, certain kinds of men. It made me recognize my dependency on having a man around to protect me. What bullshit that was! It was based on my own lack of self-worth . . . of self-esteem. I think many women born in the fifties and raised in the sixties grew up in a society that contributed to our feeling like second-class citizens. It has taken some of us a long time to stand on our own feet—to realize we have our own strength.

"And it was this lack of strength—or what I *thought* was my lack of strength," continues Cindy, "that made me hang on to a relationship long after I should have hung out elsewhere. And all because I really didn't know myself—didn't see me for what and who I realize I was and am. Always after a man left, I went through terrible depressions. But the suffering was good. Without it there'd have been no growth. It forced me to evaluate why I took the treatment I did—why I would allow me to give eighty percent and accept the pitiful twenty percent the men I dated gave. Suffering made me explore my pain—made me find me. It helped me change from a clinger who thought she needed a man to make her life work to a woman with her own strength. I need no one to make my life work today. *I* make it work. *I* make me feel strong. I'm no longer grateful for the crumbs some crumb hands out. In fact all the crumbs are gone from my life. I no longer fear loneliness or being alone because I have learned how to be alone and enjoy it. What's more, I can go out alone and have a damn good time. And if I fall, guess who picks me up? Me!"

* * *

In addition to her own introspection, she received help in changing from her study of metaphysics, which she sees as "a religious kind of science or a scientific kind of religion—take your pick—which believes humanity basically travels as one person and that we all have that spark, that divinity within. All of us have that unique part of us that is successful or which can be. And it is our responsibility to nurture it. We must assume responsibility both for our successes and failures. The unhappy people in life are those who have *failed* to follow their souls—who haven't listened to what *they* wish to be but have allowed other voices to rule their lives."

The church Cindy attends, the Church of the Universal Master, is nondenominational. "It's a place where everyone gets high—not on dope—but on themselves. Years ago I wondered if I were . . . okay, a decent human being. In recent years I've examined my values, ethics, beliefs, and discovered this Cindy Williams person, is a pretty nice kid. Funny thing about this is . . . I always was but didn't know it." Her church and its philosophy seems very neo-Californian in philosophy. Whereas the Cloris Leachmans and Valerie Harpers have come to the same realizations through est as have Dyan Cannon and Carol Burnett through yoga and TM, Cindy has found hers in metaphysics. All the philosophies are united in their stress on positive thinking. "I used to be very cynical, very negative, and hypercritical. Most people who lack self-esteem are like that. But I'm not in that place anymore. My church has shown me that most people do strive to find their own happiness and that the people who are bitter or ugly are those who have become frustrated because they don't know where their own happiness lies."

But she knows. Stretching to her full five feet three inches and placing her hand over her heart, she pledges to "always be film people. Even now, despite the duress of the series, I'm writing a screenplay." She has also kept her ties with her "theater-folk." Summer hiatuses from *Laverne and Shirley* will either be spent on stage or on sound stages. Both will make her happy. She is also considering buying her first home because "I can afford it and I think it might make me feel good. One thing stops me. I hear them talk-that-talk about second mortgages with three-year liens and I say to-hell-with-this because I don't know or care what they're talking about. Nor do I wish to. It's not my bag. I would rather concentrate my energies where they are most needed. I tend to divorce myself from things that interfere with my priorities."

Right now, a live-in relationship would be an inter-ference. Yet there is a man in her life and has been for six months. She likes him very much, stating he is "creative, funny, supportive, and, most important, he likes women. A lot of men think they do but truly don't. This man truly does! But I couldn't live with him now. I feel so pushed with this *Laverne and Shir-ley* thing that I would not have the time to give. And a relationship needs a lot of giving and . . . a lot of time. Right now, the pulls on me are enormous. There is not only the show to do each week but the interviews and the appearances at various functions one has to attend for political reasons. They're all part of the game and I'm not complaining but now, more than ever, I need my space. I need to be alone . . . often. If I had to add the burden of trying to make a man-woman thing work, I think I'd go under. Happily, this man I date is not pushing for anything other than what we have, which frankly is a steady Saturday-night date. He allows me my during-the-week aloneness. Nor is he threatened by my Shirley status. A lot of men would be. It is tough being a star type. Many men feel deballed by such a lady even while they are attracted to her. Happily, I'm not a Streisand-type lady-star. Nor do I wish to be. The kind of man I am attracted to would find my success nice for me and unimportant to him. My so-called stardom and the money I earn wouldn't crush him because he would have his own thing and would not be competing with me. There *are* such men, you know."

Is she then getting further away from the goal of marriage, which she has insisted is primary? "Oh, God, don't put it that way or I might bawl," she says. "Marriage is still the priority but it will come when it is right for it to come. Right now, my life is about work. I *need* my work. I *love* my work. It isn't about money—although the loot is lovely—it's about arriving; about getting recognized for doing a job well. It's about having a job, period! That's it! It's working. If Shirley drowned in her beer at the brewery tomorrow, I'd survive because I'd go back to my little theater group and act. It's the acting that makes me happy."

She thinks about what she has said and a smile creeps slowly onto her face. Looking heavenwards, she says, "But, God, please don't let that happen—not to Shirley. Not to me. Let those Nielsen numbers and all those cards and letters keep right on coming."

CHAPTER SEVENTEEN

LABELLE

ACT I

Scene 1

Time: Late autumn 1976—the Palladium, a New York rock palace where Labelle—Sarah Dash, Nona Hendryx, and Patti Labelle, ages thirty-one, thirty-two, thirty-two respectively, are performing to an SRO audience.

Patti Labelle is strutting and screaming as she pounces on lyrics that she then pounds from the stage into the audience. Mass hysteria. Two hours of Labelle's frenzied foreplay is about to erupt in a massive, collective orgasm. The ladies of "Marmalade" fame are peaking. Nona is shaking her whip. Sarah is shaking her ass. Patti is shaking, period, quivering top to bottom as she reaches release. Suddenly she stumbles to the lip of the stage. Down on one knee, she is spent. A glitter groupie attempts to revive her by shoving a pep-producing popper (amyl nitrite) under her nose. Instinctively she pulls back. Startled, shaken, Patti Labelle staggers off stage. The audience, unsurfeited, passionately screams for more. But Patti has nothing more to give.

Scene II

Time: December 1976, shortly after the Paladium engagement. Nona and Sarah sit in a ratty publicity office overlooking Broadway, while Patti, ninety miles away, talks from her ranch house set on a suburban acre outside Philadelphia where Mrs. Armstead Edwards (Patti) lives.

Sarah Dash and Nona Hendryx are on a natural high. The following day, as part of Labelle, the most successful girls' group in America, they leave to complete a six-month tour. They are eagerly awaiting departure time. It's been a long trip for Nona Hendryx from the Trenton ghetto where she was born to the stages of the Metropolitan Opera House and the Ahmansen Theatre in Los Angeles, where Labelle has performed. She is now traveling first class, which wasn't the case in her past. Rough roads and hard times and one-way tickets to Nowhere-in-Particular were the "trips" her childhood chums took. But Nona, as Labelle's songwriter and its high priestess of pop poetry, now has position and power.

Sarah Dash, bundled in her white winter-warms, looks like a contented bunny rabbit. She is no longer the "skinny kid" (whom Nona refers to as "Inch") of her youth but a woman who has married and divorced and whose natural endowments add a sultry softness to the often knifelike edge of Labelle. She comes from a restrictive and religious upbringing. Only recently has her minister father reconciled himself to his daughter's choice of profession. Only recently, after sixteen years of her performing, has he relented and viewed his daughter's deportment—which could hardly be called religious or restrictive—on stage. He survived the shock.

And it is a shock viewing Labelle for the first time. In their feathers-and-leathers they are not exactly Girl Scout material. Their audience, also in feathers-and-leathers, is a potpourri of the more blatant and "liberated" gays, the acid-heads and pill-poppers, the bisexual chic and some "straight" young black couples who groove with the music and the action on and off stage that surrounds it. A visit to see Labelle is not unlike a trip to the zoo. Only at Labelle, the animals are not in cages.

"We've dropped the space suits and all the silver glitter from our act," says Sarah.

"The feathers are gone too," adds Nona. "That stuff served its purpose. It made people stop and look. Then they listened. That's what we care about. Maybe folks don't like what they hear but at least we are communicating."

In Philadelphia, Patti Labelle didn't like what she was hearing. Her communication was "jamming my head. Like I'm having a talk with myself for the first time in my thirty-two years. I'm asking me some heavy questions, checking out my life . . . seeing how things balance. Funny, but before, the scales never tilted in any one direction. But something is wrong now."

Her three-year-old son, Zurie, is crying, still hurting from a nosebleed. Patti was cooing to him with a tenderness sensed but never seen with Labelle. Her bags were packed for her following-day departure. Looking at them and then at Zurie, she says: "When did it stop being fun? When did it start to hurt? I always minded leaving my family but never like this. If the road was anyplace for a kid, Zurie would go with me. He cries so when I leave."

"I was married nine years ago," says Sarah. "The marriage lasted eighteen months. Few men can handle their wives being on the road nine months a year. My husband wanted me to quit. He forced me into making a choice. I made it. I love my life today. Marriage is for other folks. Me? I want to see where all this madness leads. Besides, I like my freedom."

"I feel trapped," says Patti, "caught between career and family. Do you know I was on the road when

Zurie took his first steps? That hurt me. And I was
somewhere—who knows where—when he started talking in sentences. Why? What was more important out
there than what I have here? What have I missed?
What has Zurie missed? Missed . . . missing . . .
the words alone make me feel lonely."

"We have so many friends out there that it is impossible to feel lonely," says Nona. "After sixteen
years of touring, we know folks all over this country.
I find the road exhilarating. Each city has its own energy. There's no time to be lonely. Besides, we have
each other. Funny how in every city the management
provides three separate dressing rooms. But we're so
close we crowd into one."

"Folks often ask if I don't miss having a steady
man," says Sarah. "Why, I have a steady man in every
city we visit! I'm never in want for male companionship."

"I've been married to Armstead Edwards for seven
years now. We were childhood friends," says Patti. "It
takes a strong man to deal with the Labelle image.
But Armstead is strong. He is a mini-principal in the
Philadelphia school system. He's working on his
Ph.D. now. He's ambitious. He makes a good salary,
so I don't have to work. Armstead has never suggested I do or I don't. But now, when he sees I'm not
happy—that I'm putting more into it than I am getting out—he's suggested I quit. But not because he is
jealous or insecure about my being away so much.
Not Armstead. He knows there isn't another man no-
place, nowhere, who could take his spot in my life.
Not even for a night. We got something together not
too many other folks ever share. With a love so
strong, I don't worry about some woman coming
along when I'm gone and ripping him off. But I do
worry about time, the time we might be spending to-

gether but aren't 'cause I'm off doing my Labelle thing."

"Time was when I thought marriage, a home, might be where I was at," says Nona. "But it's not my statement. I like being Labelle . . . being recognized, being a positive statement—undeniable proof to black girls everywhere that a chick can make it out of the ghetto to do her thing. I need to work. My music is as much a part of what makes me as my right arm. And that arm, through the music in me, reaches out to touch the people. And people touch back. That's what Labelle is about. You can't separate Labelle from the people. We are one. We nurture one another."

"I wish I knew when the well went dry," says Patti, her own eyes not at all dry. "I've always put every ounce of me into my work, and other than what I share with Armstead, my work has been my life . . . the greatest joy I have known apart from being with my husband, the greatest feeling of love. Night after night I have felt love pouring onto the stage like a big wave that scoops you up and carries you out to even bigger seas of emotion. But now I feel like the wave is taking me under . . . that I'm drowning. Why is it I feel I am doing all the loving and some folks are only pretending that they do? Maybe I'm tired. Maybe Labelle is tired. I just don't love it anymore. I think the business has consumed me. And I don't trust this business. I know damn well that I'm thirty-two and soon my ass will start to drag. Will the business love me then? I never thought I could quit, but now. . . . Yet to quit would kill me."

Sadness sits on her face. There is no strutting now. That's reserved for another night when Labelle does its thing. "Maybe things will get easier when we do Broadway. Nona is writing a musical and if it goes, then I'll be home every day. We're thinking of it for next year. But . . . next year seems so far off. Strange, but everything about Labelle seems far off except my leaving on tour tomorrow . . . and my saying good-bye to my men. Funny how I used to think of Labelle as a lifetime commitment. Real funny, except I don't have me the heart to laugh."

Curtain

ACT II

Scene 1

Time: The same day, several hours later. Nona Hendryx is visiting Sarah Dash's apartment, helping Sarah to pack.

"Sure we get on one another's nerves," says Nona. "Sometimes we scream: 'Get your face out of mine!' But the fact we can do that—that we can talk straight to one another—that's what counts. There is no holding back between us."

(Patti Labelle's offstage voice is heard: "Sometimes I feel I am doing all the loving and some folks are only pretending that they do.")

"The only time we get into trouble is when other people carry stories and we listen."

"Not me. I never listen," says Sarah. "There ain't no way I'm going to allow anyone to sound off about Pat or Nona. I don't need that kind of hassle."

"Lots of people are always 'advising' us on what we should be or do," says Nona. "But we are not and never have been a slick, sexy black girl's group. The Supremes we ain't. Whatever we are is what we are always going to be. Maybe our asses will start to drag from age but our minds can always stay young."

"Some minds can be old . . . and rotten at twenty," says Sarah. "People are always making as-

sumptions about us. They read things into our music.
And that's cool because part of our purpose is to help
people become aware of their own attitudes . . .
their own lives. But contrary to anything you might
hear, we've yet to record anything that's about
women loving women. If you hear that in our work,
then that's what you hear in your own head. But it's
a misinterpretation of what we are doing. I guess
people take us through that trip because we've always
attracted gays. From way back when we were Patti
Labelle and the Bluebelles, gays dug our work. They
got into our feelings. They liked our theatrics but
they loved our touching . . . our holding hands.
They heard us singing about freedom and love and
rage. They heard and they understood. So they stayed
with us. So now people think we are doing tributes to
homosexuality."

(Patti Labelle's offstage voice is heard: "I wonder
if Armstead has heard the rumors. . . . We gotta
do more John-and-Jane songs—more stuff about men
and women loving.")

"Let me tell you as the writer of our songs that I
have never written anything that was intended to be
a tribute to homosexuality," says Nona. "I think that
unnecessary. Homosexuals, like all people, should be
a tribute unto themselves. I write tributes to sexuality. And why not? That's how we all got here and in
many of our cases it was something beautiful. People
can be so damn funny about sex and sexuality . . .
so uptight. Well, that's their bag. I say sex between
any two people who love is beautiful. My music isn't
about gay rights but about your right and mine to be
whatever we wish to be with whoever we want to be
that with. People think of my work as 'gay' 'cause I
don't write the classic John/Jane love songs. I don't
divide people into men and women. To me, all
people are sexual and all people have sexuality. I

don't add labels like hetero or homo or bi to my view on sexuality."

(Patti Labelle's offstage voice is heard: "I know what I am and I don't care for people sticking any labels on me that aren't true. Now I don't care who loves who but me, personally, I sing about love between men and women because that's all I know and I wish people would quit saying otherwise.")

"Whatever you read into us," says Sarah, "it just doesn't matter. We're not changing anything about Labelle to make us more palatable. We'll change because to grow means to change. But we will always be Labelle."

"Absolutely," adds Nona. "The basic structure of the group will never change. Patti is the lead singer because she has been that for sixteen years. She is the driving energy, the generator. Now me, I'm the ignition. And Sarah . . . come to think of it, what are you, Inch?"

"The gas, honey, and don't you forget it," snaps Sarah.

"So, we are all interconnected. Sure, Patti could go out on her own. So could Sarah. So could I. But we don't and we won't because the kick is, *we're Labelle!*"

(Curtain)

ACT III

Scene 1

Autumn 1977. Another press agent's office on New York's West Side. On its walls, pictures of Sarah, Nona, and Patti as Labelle. Near it a poster-sized blowup of Nona Hendryx, fondling the tip of a large and menacing knife. In jeans, T-shirt, and zip-up jacket, she looks punk-tough. The poster is a replica of Nona's solo album released in September, two weeks after Patti Labelle's, and nine months after Labelle has broken into three very separate pieces. Suddenly the office door flies open and Nona Hendryx, followed by her mother, breezes in, apologizing for her lateness. "The act," she explains, the one she is taking to Europe for a month the following day, had a rather long dress rehearsal.

She is *all* there, this Nona Hendryx. Hers is a full, voluptuous woman's body. She is not her poster. The Hendryx eyes are warm, soft, anything but tough. As is her attitude toward her mother, who has unexpectedly dropped by to see her "baby." Although "baby" is busy, she draws her mother down to a couch, pulls her head onto her shoulder, and coos to the gray-haired woman whose lined face reveals hers has been no easy life. As Nona strokes her mother's face, her hair, the poster grows smaller in the office. It finally fades from sight.

An offstage voice—that of Nona's press agent—is saying: "I don't know if Nona will ever come out and tell you how deeply shaken she was when the split came about. It took her by surprise. She had two very bad months. Not just physically but emotionally. I think she believed Labelle was family and as such, would always be together."

"I never had a sense that we would break up," says Nona. "Sure I knew some things were wrong but aren't some things always wrong in any job? But I never thought things were *that* wrong where we would break up. Yet," she says, sipping iced champagne, "we were feeling strongly as individuals . . . growing up, I guess, and growing apart. We had so many chronological years together. It never seemed that we would grow into different people. I guess we each needed our own individual persona rather than a collective identity."

But Nona, how did you feel when the group broke up?

She slowly sips her champagne, draining the glass as color drains from her face.

"When we split, I wondered what I would do with the rest of my life—where I would go, how I would live. For two months, I was someplace else . . . lost, gone. I just couldn't imagine doing anything without Sarah and Pat. I was in shock. And the depressions! You can't imagine how unusual it is for me not to move—not to be doing something with my life. Each day I'd try to get up energy. Each day I seemed to slide further and further away. I loved Labelle— what I was to it and who I was in it. I always felt so interconnected. It was Pat who was someplace else. She wanted out. It wasn't over a specific thing. There was no straw that broke the camel's back. Just one day it was over. Time to move on. I couldn't stop that . . . couldn't stop Patti. And I wouldn't want to. When you love somebody, you don't stop them from doing what they need to do. Loving someone is allowing them their space . . . their freedom.

"But it was hard for me to adjust to a new life. I took two months and went away. Far away. It didn't feel like it would ever be natural for me to go it alone. I had known such highs performing with Pat and Sarah. Could I know such highs again? My head said yes but it was strictly a head trip. Emotionally I had my doubts. But here I am, giving it my best shot. You see, when I did come out of my depression, it was with a sureness of not only what I wanted to do but *had* to do. I need to write my music. I need to perform it. What's more, I want and need to broaden my own definitions of me. Tomorrow I take off on a European tour. Today I did my first dress rehearsal. It was hard. I kept wanting to go places musically I couldn't reach without Pat and Sarah. And at first it just didn't feel natural being out there alone. But I am discovering where I can go musically as Nona. I am finding out I don't need two people to hold onto—to coddle me—to say, 'Hey, it's okay.' There is this excitement about me stepping out there alone. It feels good because it's me *in* my music. And *me* wants to be something more than I was. I'm going to make it work."

She looks up and her face is radiant. Her words have been strong but her voice has remained soft.

"Sure I'm scared at times," she almost whispers. "I want to be good—the best I can be. But I'm not afraid of failing because I haven't known success yet. Not as Nona. But there's no doubt in my mind I'll make it. I have to. I must. It's my number-two priority in life. Number one being . . . living my life and enjoying every second of it. Should I make it as a performer, that'll be the icing on an already delicious cake. It'll be wonderful if I do and wonderful if I don't because I'll have had a wonderful time just trying.

"Failure is just a word. If I don't make it as a performer that has little to do with me as a person. I'll still be me. My work is mainly about what I write. I'm not a great singer. I don't have that gift. The best of what I have to share is in my music. Nobody can take that away from me. Nobody can say it isn't good, because someone's *feelings* can never be judged as good or bad. They're just feelings and I'm going out there as a songwriter who feels certain things and wants you to feel them too.

"I need to reach people . . . move them. I want to free them . . . hit them where they live. Make them feel things they have perhaps never felt before. My statement is simple. It says: 'Live! Get your thing together, your ass off the ground, and do it! Live. Go past the bullshit in this life, the bullshit in the system, on your job, and do you! Get off on you because that is the best getting off of all.'"

She looks at her mother nestling on her shoulder and she says: "It all stems from when I was born and where I was raised. I came from a real ghetto and I lived hard and I can't forget that. Yes I wrote poetry even then, but I was on-the-street. I could've gone a whole other route. But I didn't. Today I own two houses in Jersey but I live in neither. They're reserved for my family. I don't need houses or yachts or diamonds. I'm not into things. Nor am I a homebody. I make home wherever I am. The roots are inside me.

"I have great love for my family. I hate to see either my mother or my father hurt. When that happens, the hairs on my back—and I've only got a couple—rise up to do battle. Although I'll always be their baby, I'm now the parent in the relationship. I support them willingly, gladly, just as they did me when I needed their support. They still support me emotionally. Although we are worlds apart as people, they *allow* me. I live my life as I choose to live it and they don't challenge my space. They make me glad to be alive. They make me feel good about me."

Carefully she removes her mother from the room so that she may talk more freely.

"One of the things that keeps me in this business is keeping them—my parents—out of poverty. God, how poverty hurts. It cripples people. I *need* to be a positive image for black girls from ghettos. A lot of the girls I grew up with didn't make it—are dead or might as well be what with all the junk they're strung out on, but I am proof that a girl can get out, can make it. I had me the dream and I made it happen. A girl can. She really can. Everyone has the chance. I keep wanting to scream: Take it! Take it!"

"The Revolution Will not Be Televised" is one of Nona and Labelle's more brilliant numbers. It encapsulates the feelings of all oppressed people. Nona Hendryx admits she has fought—"and won"—to be free of her own oppression. "It took me years, but today I have my freedom. I don't do one damn thing I don't want to do. Not ever. Not for you. Not for 'them.' Not for anyone. I live as I choose and I love who I choose. I have but this life that I know of. You can't live it for me. Even if you wanted to, I won't let you. It's mine and I claim responsibility for it."

It is strength and not bravado that halos her words. "It is often difficult living and loving as you choose," she continues. "Not everyone understands. And often the person closest to you—your lover—doesn't understand, can't fathom why you should need others. But I do. I cannot practice fidelity. I do not believe in it, at least not for me. I am fully alive and thus no one person can satisfy my needs, be they sexual or otherwise. No one can be it all for me. My body changes from day to day and I need different things for it at different times. I cannot be tied down in the conventional sense. I cannot be owned. But it is not a fear of commitment. I have been in love for nine years now, which is a very long time. We have lived together and we have not. It will last for however long it is meant to last. It is a lovely relationship and it adds security to my life and . . . fantastic sex. There can only *be* fantastic sex when there is love. So I love and I am loved. Yet as a total being I need others. I need the physical, emotional, and sexual stimulation of others. And yes, it can be either a man or a woman. I don't differentiate between the two. I have experienced how love is possible in all ways. I *know* love is possible between two women . . . possible and beautiful. Love between any two people is possible . . . and beautiful. Love itself is asexual, in that when you love, the emotion itself doesn't recognize the sex of the other person. Just the person. But one must be free within oneself before one can love freely."

She is aware many will chastise her open expression of sexuality. "But I must be me!" she explains. "At any possible cost I must be that first. I cannot hide what is me so that others might approve. I cannot worry that I might lose work because some people's minds are limited. People who are blocked in their own feelings will not understand. Others will feel my words. Still others will not understand but will allow me to be. But the bottom line is . . . *I* must allow me to be. I cannot withdraw from the place where I have moved. I love a person and not the sex of that person. Thus it is neither more nor less comfortable for me if that person be male or female.

"I guess my idea of a fulfilled life is far different from that of most women. I'm not into the female 'thing.' Bearing babies is not where I am at. Yet I feel we are all children and thus we are all brother and sister. I am everyone's baby just as everyone is mine. And that's what my work is about—being brother and sister, mother and father, to people who will let me. I need to touch people. I need to hear you and I must have you hear me.

"That was what was so shocking about Labelle. I had so thought that we had all heard one another . . . always. I thought we were always on the receiving line when now it seems we weren't giving. That is what hurt. Oh, God, how it hurt! It still does, only less so with each passing day. But it's a new day. I'm grateful for that, grateful for life itself. We have gone our separate ways, but the feelings of closeness will always be there even though the physical closeness is not. It cannot be. When we called it a day on Labelle, we seemed to have called it a day in so many other ways. Which is sad. Sarah and Pat will always have a touch on my life. Too many years passed for that not to be true. Love doesn't go away. It just seems sometimes to do that because to feel it would be too painful."

Scene II

Autumn in New York finds the one they call Inch every inch the beauty, as she performs her first solo engagement at Reno Sweeney, an elegant cabaret. Someone from the mainly male audience suggests she remove the little she is wearing and Sarah Dash responds: "Honey, the contract hasn't been written yet."

She moves to soft and sexy blues, undulating about the stage, making love to her microphone. Her every nuance is suggestive. She is using her sex to sell her songs. It is body-sans-soul except for too few moments when Sarah Dash sings from within and incredible sounds come out. It is her first engagement and it shows. Although the audience knows how good she could be, she does not.

Fade out. Fade in on her Upper West Side apartment belonging to her manager. Sarah Dash, her hair combed simply, her dress unmannered, is someplace beyond beautiful. Girlishly so. The onstage sex image is gone and, like the song says: "Ain't Nothing Like the Real Thing Baby."

"It still seems unreal to me," says Sarah. "Do you know I cannot remember my first or second shows? Total blanks. I remember asking someone for a cigarette just before going on. I remember someone lighting it. And I remember thinking . . . But I don't smoke! . . . and that's it. Oh, my nerves! I don't think I came to until my third night. They want me back but first we are going to Studio One in L.A. and the Bijou in Philly. Maybe there I'll loosen up. I still am not taking enough chances on stage. I'm not loose. But when I think that only a few months ago the very idea of going out solo panicked me, I gotta feel good. Here we are, a day after my closing, and all I can think to say is I did it! I truly did it. Me. All by my-self, alone. I did it!

"Some nights after a show I'd start giggling. The staff thought I was nuts. But I couldn't help laugh-ing. I was doing it—doing my Sarah Dash 'thing' and I didn't believe it. It took talking to me—words like, 'Hey, Sarah, you've got sixteen years of experience be-hind you,' to get me out there. Sixteen years. That thought sobered me."

She becomes sober now . . . sober-going-on-som-ber. The "sixteen years" have done it.

"I didn't know we were about to bust open at the seams," she says of Labelle's breakup. "I knew a ten-sion was building, but I thought we were just tired. Too many tours to too many cities for too many years. Yet although I couldn't admit it then, I knew something was going wrong with us. The excitement was missing in us, and thus in our work. Our sound was flattening.

"It wasn't until much later—after the split—that I was able to face the fact that what had happened was about *us*. Somehow the train had jumped the tracks. Yes, we sat down and we talked. And we talked some more. We were talking all the time we should have been recording our new album.

"When I realized it was over—that all the talk in the world couldn't bring it back—I was shocked. Thank God I was home in New York and not in Peo-ria. If you gotta be devastated, better to have your own bed in your own home to go running to. The shock was tremendous and the aftershocks weren't ex-actly easy either. It's like a marriage that is over, only you didn't know until he has gone and the lawyers are dividing you up into little pieces. Just as no one is ever really prepared for a divorce, I wasn't prepared for the breakup of the group."

She never allowed herself a mourning period. In-stantly, she began writing music and thinking about a return to acting. She had studied with the Negro Ensemble Company. "I made lots of decisions and acted on almost none. I was certain of only one thing: I had to do something. Stepping out as a solo singer just sort of happened. First I was asked to sing at the Women's House of Detention and next thing I knew ...Reno Sweeney's. It sounds simple, but seven months went by before I could group my energies together. Then when I did, things happened so fast that I never had time to think about being alone on stage. I think when I begin touring, I'll feel the aloneness. I'll suddenly wake up and realize there isn't any Patti or Nona to have breakfast with. I think then it'll get heavy again."

Her "heaviness" occurred last summer when so-called friends carried stories of what this "one" was saying and that "one" was doing. Still other friends were free with advice. It was called: "How to Live Sarah's Life for Sarah." She changed her phone number, her friends, and her life-style. "I cut everything by half. I took buses instead of cabs; shopped supermarkets instead of specialty stores. I learned to economize . . . with money and with myself. And I got through by holding Nona's hand . . . often, frequently. She needed it. She was devastated by the split. Not that I wasn't affected but . . . I have always been the balance of the group. On stage it seemed like Patti who was Mother Earth. In truth, when Patti and Nona would go off into their thing, it was me who held things together. I was able to. Labelle gave me a lot of love. I was filled with it. So when the split occurred, I had a surplus. I was able to help Nona. Even when she was on tour in Europe, we spoke frequently. We are still very close."

And Patti?

"Patti?" she echoes. "I haven't seen or spoken to Patti in nine months. But she is my sister. I grew up with her. Here, there, everywhere, it was Pat and Nona. Even on stage at Reno's, I felt them there. I did. I have no bitterness, just a hurting kind of love. Bitterness is such a negative trip. I can't afford that. I must follow the voice inside me that says to do what I must do—to follow my heart and mind. The mind, after all, is the most powerful force each of us has."

She is a graduate of the Science of the Mind philosophy. She came to its church six years ago when "I was in emotional turmoil. My marriage had ended and I was floating in and out of bad relationships, staying longer than I should but not feeling good enough about me to say: 'Hey! No more.' My marriage turned my head around. It was a bad one. Not that he wasn't a nice man, but we were both in the business and I started happening and he . . . Well, the ole ego-devil took over. I'd go on tour for a month or a week and come back to a stranger, an angry one. He wanted *his* woman to quit. But this woman, *my* woman, wasn't having that.

"So we both walked. And that's why I sometimes flip when people ask about me and marriage. It is just too painful to remember what was. Now things are good. I stay in relationships for as long as it feels good. Once they are over, I'm strong enough to move on. I got that from Science of the Mind. I stumbled into it when everything about me was a question mark. There was little *me* left. And I was so confused about my place with God, if I indeed had a place at all. Through my church I found a God, a beautiful God who lives within us all. He is very different from the God with which I was raised by my preacher father. This God is always there, inside, rewarding you as you allow it. Ninety percent of the time I feel centered in life today . . . strong, secure, and optimistic. There isn't a doubt in my mind that my religion got me through the breakup. What's done is done. My life is about now. I'm thinking only of Sarah Dash and she has the most wonderful feeling that she is going to do all sorts of good things. But don't ask me where. Maybe Broadway, maybe nightclubs. But somewhere. I *must* work. I've got a mile-high need to communicate, to express what I feel. On stage I can be all of me . . . the little girl, the woman, the strumpet. I put all of me into that little devil on stage. Once my motor gets going, I'm very single-minded where my energies are concerned. Labelle absorbed me totally. Traveling the world, we saw all kinds of people in all sorts of situations. I learned about life. It gave me tolerance. Like maybe Patti was bothered by the image of the group. Not me. Some of our fans were gay; others straight; many black; still more white. So? I chose companions from those that I liked. If someone is gay, that's not my business. I know where my head is at. Actually having gay friends has opened my head. I see where gays are persons too, just like me. With morals, ethics, values. What they do is what they do, and it has nothing to do with me, just as what I do with the man-of-my-moment has nothing to do with them. I don't make hassles where none exist. Work should be fun. I make it that. If the fun should go, I'll go—find me something else to do in life. 'Cause there just ain't no way this child is going to get pushed into a hole and not get out.

"And marriage, right now, would be a hole," she continues. "It might not be a year from now, but today I'm into me. And me is all I can handle. Sarah here is learning to take care of Sarah. She likes being single. Years ago I discovered I couldn't be a mother for medical reasons. I felt then and now no sense of deprivation. I do not have the need to be a mother but I do have the need to be a woman to some man. I may be saying later to marriage but I'm saying 'Now!' to a man. Busy as I am, there's always time for that.

"But he's got to allow me my thing. Sarah here likes 'things'—pretty things. I don't mind if he wants to buy them for me but . . . I give nothing back. Not ever. If he goes, his stuff stays. Once you give something to me, it's mine! Now I'd like a few er-

mines, rubies, and diamonds hanging around my
house and if things go as planned, I can see me arriving for my next big interview in a chauffeured-driven
Rolls, wearing a wraparound mink and a diamond on
my finger that would knock you out if the man on my
arm hadn't already done that. Yes, sir. I can see this
here child doing that and finding it fine. Real fine."

Scene III

Halloween 1977 at Avery Fisher Hall in Lincoln Center. On stage, Patti Labelle. In the audience an SRO
audience composed predominently of young black
couples with a large handful of gay white males.

The moment she struts on stage, doing that Funky
Chicken walk of hers, the audience rises in a roar to
its feet. The standing ovation lasts a full five minutes.
Patti Labelle stands speechless. At first she seems confused. But finally she stands motionless and drinks in
the tribute.

Bango! From the opening number she soars. Her voice
has improved. It is yet stronger than it was. If she is
nervous in her New York debut, it is unnoticable.
Patti Labelle is "working out," and making the folks
happy.

Fade Out

Fade In

A small but nicely tailored room with but one double
bed in the elegant Park Lane Hotel overlooking Central Park. On the bed, very laid back in *all* senses of
the word, is the unexpected Armstead Edwards. He is
young, handsome, and instantly likable.

He has been the rumored behind-the-scenes "villain"
in the breakup; the husband who wants to control his
show-business wife for his own greedy purposes.

The other "villain" trips out of the bathroom with a shiny face and a smile that shines. Patti Labelle is radiating warmth and affection. There is not one sign of guilt hovering about her new slim self.

"Betcha think that I broke up the group," she says, going right to where it's at. "Most people think that. But I didn't. I was just first to voice what we were all feeling. We broke up because we had gone as far as we could. If we had continued, it would have been like trying to sell day-old bread. The act, us, just wasn't fresh anymore. We weren't working together. We weren't happy. Certainly I wasn't. But to admit that . . . well, for the longest while I couldn't. But when it started tearing at me, I had to. But I didn't break it up. We all did. Time had marched on and we had to march on with it. To other things.

"But it was never in my head to go it alone. Not ever. When the group broke up, once I was able to get my head screwed on straight again, I knew only one thing. I had to sing. I've always had to sing. I couldn't see myself going with two new girls in a new group because I had been with the two best. So I decided to go it alone. And even in that there's a story.

"I was so messed up in the head before and after we split that I didn't know where to turn. I was tired . . . depressed, and scared. I was imagining all sorts of things and not able to distinguish between what was and what wasn't true. And Armstead here, all he ever said was: 'Do what you need to do.' And when I couldn't get to that, it was he who suggested I see a psychiatrist. Which I did and I'm not the least bit ashamed of it. I couldn't make decisions before the shrink. And Armstead sure wouldn't make them for me. I couldn't see me on my own. I couldn't see me on stage or in a recording studio doing it for and by myself. I had to work that through.

"Funny, but without knowing it, throughout that three-month period I was wearing black almost al-

ways. I was in mourning and didn't know it. I was so
down. Like, from winter of '76 to spring of '77, I was
more down than up. I had suffered a real loss in my
life. I didn't know then that in giving it up, I'd gain
so much. And I have. Last night on stage I felt such
devotion and dedication to my audience. Their love
made me cry. I love performing. Forget everything
else I might have told you a year ago about quitting.
I couldn't. I need to sing. I need to be with the
people. I love performing. I wish last night could
have gone on and on.

"It's easier for me to love performing today 'cause
I'm less hassled. Labelle was located in New York and
I had to travel in each day to rehearse or sign papers
or discuss tours, albums. But now everything is
concentrated near where we live in Philadelphia. I'm
home evenings for dinner with Armstead and Zurie. I
can even take Zurie to rehearsals if I don't mind him
busting up the place. That kid is some kind of four-
year-old monster! But I wouldn't want him any other
way.

"There's just no more pulls on me. I don't feel like
my career and my home life are bumping head-on. I
no longer feel torn."

And it shows. Patti Labelle, slimmer than she has
ever been, her hair pulled back Diana Ross–style in a
bun at the back, looks relaxed and happy. Her near
breakdown and the physical exhaustion she experienced are traumas of the past. This is, if not a new,
then a changed woman.

"True!" agrees Patti. "With Labelle I always
needed Nona and Sarah's reassurance. I was insecure, always falling apart over something. I never felt
I was particularly special as a talent. I shied away
from any responsibility. Today I'm the boss. I carry
my own life. I carry *me* on stage. I'm not that fragile
chil' of a year ago. I can still be hurt but now I know
a little hurt ain't going kill nobody. Before, I was
naive going on stupid. I've now shaken hands with re-

ality. I can make decisions regarding my professional life.

"Yet, before I get myself too cocky, let me tell you about my first time on stage alone. In London last summer at the CBS Records affiliates meeting. I damn near wet my pants. Talk about scared! But once I was introduced and the applause started, I felt just fine. I mean I stood there as folks cheered and thought: 'Hey, girl, this stuff ain't bad.' So I started working the stage and here's what's weird. I started looking for Nona and Sarah but they weren't anywhere. I wanted to cry. But that didn't happen last night. I was comfortable. I was alone and I knew it. But it was cool. I've moved to higher ground. I'm not *that* Labelle anymore. People are coming today to see me and I like that.

"I like lots of things, actually just about *everything* these days," she laughs. "Armstead and I are moving soon to this cute little French country house just outside Philly. We can't afford it. [Armstead groans.] But we is buying it. Armstead? You is just going to have to work your face off to meet those payments!"

Armstead Edwards smiles and shakes his head knowingly. He is low-keyed and seemingly very secure in his own identity. He is a year away from obtaining his Ph.D. in psychology. One of his reasons for seeking yet a higher degree is about "No one ever thinking I'm Mr. Patti Labelle. I do well in the Philadelphia school system as a mini-principal. I intend to do better. I'll meet the mortgage payments. I met them before when Labelle was first getting started and didn't have loose change. I've always supported my wife. I've always been *Mr.* Edwards. I don't think I'd like being called Mr. Labelle, even by accident. I'm me; Patti's Patti. I accept her professional existence. She was working when I met her so why should I expect she would not be working now. I like her needing to express herself. At home her public persona never comes through the front door. Till a month ago we never even had a maid for a day."

"Why should we when nobody does it better than me," says Patti. "Besides, I like to cook and clean."

"Our life-style suits me 'cause I've never known another," says Edwards. "Yes, Patti's away a lot. Frankly, I like that. I'm the type of person who needs time to be alone. Our marriage gives us both a lot of space."

"And that works for us," adds Patti. "Like when we quarrel—and, honey, we do quarrel something fierce sometimes—I'm not able to talk about it immediately. I need to get away, think things out and then talk. Armstead understands this. The road has helped, not hindered, our marriage in that respect. Also Armstead having work he loves so strong has also helped. He is not a show-business husband. Amen and thank the Lord! Actually he couldn't care less about the business, but he cares about me. Which suits me just fine!

"Actually we are total opposites. He's always got his face buried in some book. Now me, I begin reading and by the end of page one, I'm sound asleep. And he's not into music. But what we do share is a deep respect for marriage and children. Our values are very similar. We have something good going in our marriage. Maybe it's about my not telling him how to run his school and him not telling me how to sing. But the truth is, I'm blessed. My husband knows what I do is what I must do. But he also knows that although I now intend to make all aspects of my life work, my marriage and family come first. 'Cause, honey, let me tell you about this business called show. If your wax ain't hot, nobody stops to chit-chat. But with Armstead and Zurie, it's never about whether I hit the charts or not. Their love is constant. The business is basically bullshit. I gotta have the constant. I couldn't live without my men's love. Yes, indeed, I'd like to be a superstar but not if it means sacrificing the real things in my life to get it. From here on, whenever possible, the family joins me on the road. And I work only when I choose to. I don't have to ask permission anymore to take off Christmas. I can just take it.

"Not that Nona or Sarah ever said no to something I felt I needed. But I felt bad . . . selfish in asking them. I don't take that guilt trip anymore because it's just me."

And now that it is just her, there are other "trips" she refuses to take or to allow others to take her on. This very day, for perhaps the first time, she admits she hated the assumptions people were making about Labelle. "When these rumors reached Armstead at school—when he heard them from so-called friends—I was sick. It's okay to say . . . well, I know where I'm at so who cares what people say. It's okay but . . . it doesn't work for me. I'm not that together. It bothered me a lot that some folks thought I was into drugs. Actually, the business knows me as 'Miss Tuinal' 'cause I'm such a downer where drugs are concerned. I don't want them around me. Once I tried a reefer and I damn near went up in smoke. I'm so high most of the time on my own energy that the last thing I need is to go higher. But if you want to dope yourself up, that's your business. But don't lay your trip on me.

"What bothered me even more were the people who were assuming that Nona, Sarah, and I were all loving each other. Well, we were. Lots of loving but not the kind they were inferring. I loved them as friends, as sisters, as women. But that was it. I was proud of that love . . . still am. And frankly I don't see anything wrong in women physically loving women, but that's not where I'm at. I'm not saying mine is better than theirs. No . . . I'm just saying, 'Hey, the only loving I know is between me and my man and even that ain't none of your business. That part of my life belongs to no one but me.' "

And how did Armstead Edwards react when these

rumors were brought to him? "They bothered me," he says. "I guess that makes me human. Frankly, I can't think of a man who wouldn't be bothered by such rumors. I knew they weren't true but it bothered me that some small-minded people were making something ugly out of something that might have been beautiful had it been true, which it wasn't. People's heads get funny where sex is concerned. Yet I think I handled it better than Patti did. She was sorely affected."

She is sorely affected now. Staring out the window, motionless, speechless, she is on yet another trip. When she returns, she says softly. "I still love Sarah and Nona. I still sing Nona's beautiful music. I think about them often. I don't have any friends today. The ones I thought I had, split when Labelle split. They weren't real. Actually no friends have ever been real in my life other than Sarah and Nona."

She is near tears as she whispers: "I'm glad they weren't in the audience last night. Although the night before I dreamed Nona was in the wings giving me a sign that said 'All right!' It broke me up. Which is why I'm glad they weren't there last night. I would have cried if I had seen them. I mean . . . they could come to the show but . . . don't tell me. Don't let me know it. I'm still facing the fact that we just ain't no more. Not in any way.

"And I wish that weren't so. I wish we could be reconciled. Oh, God, how I wish for that! Whatever good stuff I wish me, I want the same for them. Everything in my life today feels so good other than this ache. Sixteen years and now, no Nona, no Sarah. I know I love those girls. I know I always will. Yet we haven't spoken in eleven months. They haven't called. Nor have I. I would like to but I wait for them. Suppose I called and their voices told me they weren't happy to hear from me. That would kill me. It surely would."

Curtain

CHAPTER EIGHTEEN

ARETHA FRANKLIN

The voice is soft, the speaker quietly at ease and composed—Aretha. She is so much smaller than she appears on stage, sounds on records. Aretha, the Mixmaster of joy and pain, who in her singing "hangs out" emotions like so much laundry on a line is, if not different or separate, removed from the Aretha who lives apart from her music. Her words are weighed carefully before spoken, her emotions controlled and preserved. Aretha Franklin, woman, is not about to get caught up by her image. And remembering how many before her succumbed to the image, died *for* and *from* it, one can hardly blame her. She is seemingly determined to "beat the rap," publicly giving her music—that part of her that no one can hurt—while sharing that which is vulnerable, that which is unsung and unspoken to only a very chosen few.

Ruth Bowen, president of Queen Booking (the oldest and largest black booking agency), Aretha's manager and friend, is one of those few.

"I met Aretha through Dinah Washington who, in addition to being my client, was my closest friend. She introduced us, saying, 'Ruthie, keep your eye on this child; she's going to do it.' And then one day Dinah was dead and I could neither believe nor accept it. It was a very bad time for me, and Aretha, young as she was, sensing it, stayed in touch; let me know someone was there. When suddenly, she was *really* there. She entered my office and said: 'How

would you like to do for me?' I saw it as the workings
of God—that He had sent someone wonderful to replace the friend I had lost.

"She was still a child then," remembers Ruth. "Not
so much in years as in maturity. Her mother had died
when she was young, and she needed an older woman
to turn to. I was that woman. So we both gave to and
took from each other."

"Aretha was ten when I realized she was special,"
says her father, the Reverend C. L. Franklin. "Because it was my plan that she be a star, I wasn't too
upset when she dropped out of high school at thirteen to tour with me as a gospel singer. On the road
Aretha grew up with Mahalia, Clara Ward, the Davis
Sisters, always hearing the best in gospel. I think that
even then Aretha was taking what she heard, synthe-
sizing and rolling it into her own thing.

"When I felt she was ready, I took her to New
York and she made a fistful of demonstration records.
Then we made the rounds. A lot of big-time executives are still kicking themselves for having turned us
down. Eventually Columbia Records nibbled. . . . I
had them come to Detroit, where we lived, to do
business rather than us go to New York. I wanted
them to see that Aretha was no starving black girl who
would do anything to get a break. Not my Aretha.
She would make it on ability alone."

"The years with Columbia were very hard on Aretha," says Carolyn Franklin, another of the chosen
few and Aretha's two years younger sister. "I remember when I decided I wanted the business, Aretha sat
me down and read out the facts.

"She had trouble then. Columbia didn't understand
her or her music, and worse, she had a manager [not
Ruth Bowen] who worked her too hard, too often,
and too much. Aretha was half dead most of the time.
To keep her going, to keep making her commissions,
the manager fed Aretha pep pills. And sometimes
pep pills with No Doz. When Daddy found out about

that, he flew to New York, busted Aretha's contract, and took her home. And that's where she stayed until she got it together."

"Yes, I worried plenty about Aretha in those days," admits Reverend Franklin. "Every couple weeks I'd fly into New York to be with her. Aretha was inclined to be lonely, particularly in a strange city. She was different than my other children in that she was not outgoing. She was always a lonely child and tremendously sensitive. I think both are part of her artistry."

"There is something about the Franklin family no one can understand unless they've been there with them," says Ruth Bowen. "There is a closeness, a bond. If you could just sit in and hear them when they get together around a piano, each one doing his or her thing. The music they make! You might expect her sisters and brothers to be jealous of Aretha's success. But not so. It's just the opposite. They all enjoy it."

And today, so it would seem, so does Aretha. She is vastly different than she was. She has bloomed, become graceful, slender. A substantial weight loss contributes to the difference.

"I feel better about myself," says Aretha. "In fact, I feel good. I guess I reached a point in my life where it became important to me to look good, to feel attractive. I like being thin, and I must admit, I feel pretty. People speak of this sexuality they see coming from me on stage and I like that. I also think it's true. I've grown, mainly as a woman, although I don't think I've basically changed. But even though I'm the same me I was as a child, there is nonetheless something new. That thing that was bottled up within me is coming out. What is it? Joy . . . womanhood . . . I'm not really certain. But I talk more now. I am trying to communicate with words as well as with music. That's a big change for me. I've never been much of a talker. I was afraid to talk, afraid people wouldn't listen, and if they did, that they would laugh. I guess I felt I never had anything of interest to say or that what I would say would be wrong. Somewhere along the line I have found the confidence that was always lacking in me. As I learned to trust and depend on me more and others less, I grew. I no longer feel, as I did when a child, that the first thing people notice is my big feet."

"It's true Aretha has always lacked confidence," says Reverend Franklin, "and she was so shy. Today people mistake her shyness for big-headedness. They think she's aloof because she's such a big star, and that's not it at all. When Aretha feels people moving in on her, she moves back . . . withdraws. That child is just plain shy."

Ruth Bowen concurs. "Funny thing about Aretha's shyness, though. Once she knows you, relaxes with you, it goes. Sometimes you wish it hadn't. The girl is a prankster, the kind who will call you at four A.M. from China and begin her conversation with, 'I bet you were sitting up waiting for my call.' "

"I could have killed Aretha sometimes," laughs Carolyn. "Oh, that girl could be mean! When I was a child, she would take me to the rabbit field across the street from our house, place me in the middle, and hide. I'd scream my head off in fright, darn near had a stroke screaming and crying, while I'd hear Aretha laughing her fool head off behind some bush. Always laughing and all the time funny.

"We had a hamburger joint we used to frequent called the Tip-Top. Aretha used to eat down that whole place, sassing everybody who tried to outeat her. She was very popular. But even then all she lived and breathed was music. She formed a trio, a gospel group—me, her, and this other girl, Yvonne Parker. We actually picked up pocket money playing some churches. We had this routine we did to 'Drink from the Fountain.' Aretha would be at the piano, playing her fingers to death, while Yvonne and I danced the little number we choreographed. As we'd sing, we'd keep dancing back toward the fountain. I used to really get into it and become oblivious to everything. One time I'm singing away and all of a sudden, I hear this giggle. Aretha falling apart at the piano, laughing and carrying on. It seems Yvonne got carried away too, fell off the platform, and damn near landed in the fountain. And I'm just singing, feeling the spirit, while people are falling out all over the place. Aretha never let me forget that.

"Aretha had no sadness as a child. Even when Mommy and Daddy separated, she handled it. We'd spend summers with our mother, and our mama had a way of making us feel loved.

"Aretha was my 'big sister,' " smiles Carolyn. "She was like a mama lion with me. If anyone messed with me at school, they had Aretha to deal with. She had a way of being angry that was terrifying. She wouldn't say anything, not a word. No screaming. No yelling. Just this look. That girl used to scare the life out of me when she'd throw one of those. And could that girl fight! Why I remember when Aretha was only twelve or thirteen, some older girl punched her for no reason. Well, Aretha waited until she could get behind that girl and I think they still are picking up pieces of that chick all over Detroit."

"My childhood was pretty much a happy one," recalls Aretha. "I was always falling out of trees, scraping my knees. A real tomboy. I liked school, and even though I dropped out, I was a pretty good student. But it was always music. That's what I remember most about my childhood. Music at home; music in church. The back-porch singing we Franklins did. Oh, lord, could we sing!"

The neighborhood in which the Franklins lived was racially mixed and mainly middle and upper middle class. The school, however, was predominantly black, and the church was pure Soul. Aretha remembers the church and religion, then as now, "being my strength. Religion is my guide to everyday living. I've never wavered in my faith. Never. It's the foundation upon which all else has been built. I think there is a movement back to God in our country and I'm glad of that. I think there is also the beginnings of a movement back to the family and I think that is good because my family has been my other strength.

"I'll never forget the two years spent on tour with my father. I loved his preaching, the hymns he'd sing after the sermon for which I'd accompany him on the piano. I loved his honesty and sincerity. I remember, as though it were yesterday, his vocal ability and his style, that special talent of his to make things plain. I would be pleased to have my singing described as such. His way was very much mine and it still is."

"Aretha and her father have a unique relationship," says Ruth Bowen. "Aretha respects her father and listens to him. Aretha knows he is one of two men who talk straight to her, who isn't about to rip her off. Aretha is constantly in touch with her father. She doesn't take his love for granted. In some ways she is still his little girl and I think she may always be. Deep inside, she knows that if the going ever gets too rough, if all else fails, Daddy will be there."

"I suppose my relationship with my father is unique," says Aretha. "People tell me it is because few children like their fathers as I like mine. My father is so honest. He loves his family and his work. He is a beautiful man. As a child I thought of him as a modern man, a modern father, just as I think of him now.

"My mother died in 1952. I was young, but I remember how warm and beautiful she was. I was very close to her and I can't say which, if either of my parents, was the greater influence of my life. Both gave me something, as has each member of my family, which is why it has not been difficult remaining close to them. It's not the Franklin way to be separate."

"Aretha doesn't need her 'daddy-love' like she used to," says Reverend Franklin, "and no one need think she does. She's made it today, happier than she has ever been as an adult. Once I worried about Aretha, and in particular her family life. But no more. Yes, I still speak with her often, but now I'm speaking to a grown woman and not my 'little girl.' "

"We used to speak two, three times a week," says Carolyn. "Although it's harder now with me in Detroit and Aretha in New York, the closeness hasn't changed. It never can. Aretha is someone I *still* worry about. She is still not the happy person she was many years back. But she is a lot happier than she was when her marriage was ending. That man [Ted White] hurt her. He really did."

"Aretha had her share of misery," says Reverend Franklin. "You know the old story—the bigger you get, the more you're a target for those who feed off other people. She had an unfortunate marriage. He was not her friend; his motivation was not sincere."

"Five years ago Aretha wasn't happy," says Ruth Bowen, "and it showed. Her personal problems often affected her health. She kept getting sick. Eventually when she thought her performances were less than what she was capable of, we canceled an entire year's bookings. And why not. It takes a while to get over loving a man. Frequently a woman is controlled by the man in her life, and Aretha is no different from the rest of us. She had her stormy period, but she weathered it. She cured the hole in her heart."

"I used to cry about things I couldn't do anything about," says Aretha, "but no more. What difference *what* things. I don't cry easily today. Maybe that's due to maturity and maybe it's due to acceptance. But no more crying over what was, or what might have been.

"People seem to like to conjecture about the deep sadness within me. Well, there isn't any. Oh, I've had my bad times, but they're the same problems, aches; and pains other people have: relationships that don't work and relationships that begin not to work. Okay. That causes pain but when I think back on my marriage, I only think of how beautiful it was . . . and then there came the time when it wasn't."

She will not speak further of those years. "I'm a private person," she explains. "Why should I share my disappointments, my hurts? I try *not* to look back, only ahead. I try to remember the beautiful and seldom the bad. Yes, I know the bad is there to be looked at and learned from. And I have done this. Now it is where it belongs . . . in the past. There is nothing in my life today that I would change, nothing that has not contained some good. My life is not filled with regret or revenge."

"Don't be fooled," says Reverend Franklin. "Heartache is one of life's built-in guarantees and Aretha has had hers."

"Heartache is part of being a woman, and in particular being a black woman," says Ruth Bowen. "There are a lot of professional things Aretha should have had by now. And she knows it."

"I've been in the business for eighteen years and I've been lucky," says Aretha. "I've not met discrimination face to face. But it's been there and it is still. Timing helped me not to feel the hate. I've never been to the door only to find it closed or opened just a crack and then slammed. I have Lena and Ella and Sarah to thank for that. Except for television. That situation is racial and political. It often boils down to whites getting preference to blacks. Does that make me angry? I would rather not discuss that."

"All black artists are angry," says Ruth Bowen, answering for Aretha. "And Aretha is no different but she won't shoot her mouth off publicly. She would just rather keep her views to herself. Also she negates negatives. She doesn't acknowledge the ugly, only the pretty. To express black rage is just not Aretha's way. Many organizations would like to involve her but Aretha has no eyes for that. She was very close to Martin [Luther King, Jr.] and she ran whenever he called for her. But I don't think Aretha is about to pick up the cudgel today."

"People do try to place demands on me," says Aretha, "but that doesn't mean I do what they demand. It would be foolish for anyone to think I could be a spokesperson because I can't and I don't wish to do that. I don't think of myself as having any special power over people. I am aware that many like my music but I don't think of using that in a manipulative way. I'm not interested. I just want to have my life, *be* me."

Being Aretha is not always easy. She is often the subject of conjecture, as she has said. Like most black women singers, she has been victimized by those who seek to destroy what others have helped to build. Rumors abound and rumors persist, running the gamut from drugs and alcohol to emotional disorders. Ruth Bowen shrugs off the talk. "It's part of the price. Then, too, there was that year Aretha took off to have her last child. What people made of that! Even the proof, the baby, didn't stop the speculation."

"Rumors are started by people who don't know anything but who pretend they do, so they can look important to others," says Aretha. "No, I hadn't heard that some people were saying I had a drinking problem. Well, I can't do anything about people's talk or malicious thoughts. And I don't care that much. I care about what I know of myself and what I know is more important than what others think they know. Yes, things like that hurt, but I move past them to what's real, to what's true. And I refuse to think it is more than a handful of jealous people who start those stories. It isn't everyone who hates, only a few. People are basically good."

"Aretha is exceptionally kind and . . . naive," says Carolyn. "That's why she gets hurt as often as she does. She's inclined to trust people. She'll give you the last thing she has if you ask and she'll never ask for anything back. She's not one to hold grudges and she is forever helping all kinds of people who don't deserve to be helped."

"No kind of talk can change that part of Aretha that is so special," says her father. "She has a heart as big as all outdoors. She is just a beautiful child."

"Aretha is about as untouched by success—its pitfalls and its joys—as anyone can be," says Ruth Bowen. "Basically she is the same girl who came to New York eighteen years ago. She is a homebody. I think sometimes she would rather stay home, watch the soaps, and be a housewife than be the public Aretha Franklin."

There was that conflict—career vs. family—but no more. She has limited her road work—the distance and time spent away from her family—by half. "I was constantly being torn previously," she explains. "The kids were at home needing me, and I was elsewhere being needed in another way. It just created too much stress."

There are four sons—Clarence, seventeen; Edward, fifteen; Teddie, ten; and Kecalf, three. Home for the Franklin family is New York, despite Aretha's misgivings about the city being the ideal place to raise children. "I'd rather there be a big backyard with trees and horses but my work now demands I be in New York. Happily, they have the outdoors in Detroit with my father where they spend a lot of their time."

She changes as she discusses her children. The attitude becomes the same as when she spoke of her music. It's her "here-I-am" look. She is comfortable.

"My children mean everything to me. *Everything!*" she reiterates. "They are given to me through God. Gifts. Not for me to impose upon them those things I might want or like but to help them emerge as persons with personalities of their own. They are beautiful boys—or should I say men. They are all musical and I think with their talent, if they decide to be entertainers, I'll encourage them. But I do want them to finish school first. I've always regretted not having gone past the tenth grade.

"If I have given them anything, I hope it has been courage and direction. My hope is that each will find the real thing in life . . . himself. Let them just be together with who and what they are, and they'll come to whatever it is they wish to do with their lives with grace. I've raised my children with love—not just my own but that which I feel is in all people. I have stressed the love rather than the hate. I believe one moves us ahead and the other turns us back. I hope my men have my optimism about life and, in particular, life for blacks in America. I do believe that on some levels we continue to move forward. I am not for the giving or taking of advice, but I think blacks must learn to think positively, *must* get involved with themselves first, then the family, the community, and so on. And we must listen. So few people know how to listen.

"By traveling throughout the country with my work, I know what many people are saying. They want to feel good about themselves and about the future. They feel the need, as I do, to do it together. Unity! We need ourselves, yes, but at the same time we need others—the brothers and sisters who help to move it along with you."

"It is her blackness you hear when Aretha sings," says Reverend Franklin. "Musicianship is only a word. Aretha has that, that ability to hear each note perfectly in her head. More important, she feels what's in the music. Her soul is being black and liking it."

"Being black means being beautiful," says Aretha. "It also means struggles and it also means pain. And every black woman knows of that struggle, that pain, and she feels it whenever she looks at her man and her sons. Being black also means searching for oneself and one's place among others. There is so much we need to find. Like more purpose in life and more self-love. That must come first. It certainly had to come first for me."

"Yes," says Reverend Franklin, "it has come for Aretha. She has made it. She can stand up and be Aretha anyplace without hanging her head."

"She's matured," adds Ruth Bowen. "The time when I would have to sit in with Aretha on her interviews, protect her from questions and attitudes that upset her, is over. Today Aretha is fully capable of doing her own stopping and starting. She's her own woman. A good man in her corner has changed her. It would change most any woman. I think what Aretha has always sought from life, in part, is a little happiness with a man, *her* man, and at last she has found it."

"Without a doubt," says Carolyn, "Aretha has herself a man she trusts, a man who gives to her as she gives to him. And that is what she never had before and that's what has made the difference in her."

Aretha will not discuss him by name. That is too personal. She speaks only of herself and him in generalities. The intimacies of the relationship remain just that, intimate to the parties involved.

"I need a relationship with a man. Understanding and communication, exchange. These are the qualities I most need," says Aretha. "And direction. A man who knows where he is and where he is going and can make me feel both. That's security for me. I also need for a man to be sensitive to me; a man who makes me feel he knows me and wants to know me and who wants me to be the same to him and makes me feel that I can be. A man who is genuinely interested in me, in him, in us, past the point of just saying 'I love you.' I have that kind of man and that kind of relationship now. It has been five years, five *good* years. A woman knows when a man has given some thought to her, has really dug into her to find out who she is and why."

Her man is young, ambitious, and talented. Those

who know insist he will never be a Mr. Aretha Franklin. He is a black man seeking to break into film production. Doors will not open easily for him, the profession not welcoming newcomers, particularly black ones.

"It is the nature of the black woman's role with her black man to be encouraging, to be the things he needs without losing her own identity. For some women it is a natural course and for others it is something that must be learned. It was a little of both for me. It took me time to realize that in a relationship the black woman must know she is the one who must give more. Now, more than ever, is a difficult time for the black man. I think it makes the black woman's role very exciting. Just think of what we can mean to our men! Of course it is not all exciting. Sometimes watching what can happen to her black man and being powerless to change it is painful . . . very painful."

She worries about a possible collision between her career and her relationship. She is trying to make both work and thinks she can. But "if I find the relationship suffering because of my work, then my work goes. To be with my man—that is now *my* priority. Nothing is more important to and for me than the love that can exist between two people and preserving that love.

"Not that my work isn't love, because it is," she continues. "I have known total fulfillment in my work. I've been able to look at it objectively and say, 'It is good, girl.' I can feel an audience, feel when they are with me. And they, in turn, can feel when I am feeling them. It is like a game of catch but here the ball is called love. But if I had to, I could leave it. I have a good man now, a good family, and I believe that is what most women want. At least it's what *this* woman wants. Yet I can't imagine the day coming when I will not want to sing."

CHAPTER NINETEEN

CLORIS LEACHMAN

Cloris Leachman is giving her usual dazzling performance. Wearing a lemon-yellow silk robe, Oscar- and Emmy-winner Leachman is standing . . . no, sitting, no . . . jumping . . . now sitting again on her king-sized bed in her king-sized suite at the Plaza Hotel. She is proclaiming, exclaiming, declaiming, or, as mentioned, giving her usual dazzling performance. All springtime and gaiety, laughing and joking, talking nonstop but saying very little, she is playing the Good Sport role, the scorned but unscorched "little woman." Bette Davis never played it any better.

She prattles on and on. Her house in Mandeville Canyon, after a six-year restoration period, is finally completed. Which is why we are about to see so much of Ms. Leachman. First there is *North Street Irregulars,* a dash of Disney for the family audiences, to be followed by *Fooling Around* (the title speaks for itself), and *The Muppet Movie.* TV viewers will see her in *Willa* once she fades from the screens in *Backstairs at the White House.*

"Don't use the word *busy,*" says Cloris. "Busy is such an awful word. It sounds like I've been flitting about and I don't flit. Say I've been 'active'—hard at work to pay off the debts of redesigning and redecorating *la maison.* After all, if I don't who will? I mean . . . there is no one but me to take care of me," she says brightly, about to bounce on the bed again.

Asked to repeat what she has just said, Cloris Leachman does. "There is no one to take care of me but me," she says. This time there is no laughter. Just a sharp intake of breath and then. "My divorce became final just this week. Isn't it wonderful?" she asks, again resuming the character of whatever role she has decided to play this day. "I mean *what* a wonderful divorce! As soon as I get home, George and I [George being George Englund, Cloris's husband of twenty-five years] are going out on a date. So nothing's really changed except we're not married. And," she adds after a long pause for a thought to emerge, "he is living with someone else. A lovely girl. Truly a lovely girl. Bonnie is her name and I *really do* like her."

Cloris Leachman's life has always been right out of a soap opera—a not so *Secret Storm*. She and her George have been Hollywood's most open marriage. For years they have maintained separate residences and separate identities. For years Cloris has maintained "I think people *should* live separately. It makes you and the relationship so much more interesting." Of course few people have taken Cloris seriously. In her industry, where she is highly regarded as an actress, she is also regarded as somewhat of a "ditz." Many believe she and Phyllis, her most famous TV role, were and are one and the same. Everyone loves the "madcap," "slightly batty" Cloris, but few take her seriously.

At the moment our "madcap" is proclaiming, still, how "nothing has changed. Really, it hasn't. We—George and I—have lived apart for years and together only when we felt we wished to. Ours was never the usual marriage. Nor was ours the usual family. The 'ties that bind' were something we wouldn't use. We don't believe in 'ties' or in 'binding' one another. People come and go in our home. We are all free spirits."

"All" besides George and Cloris are five children ranging in age from twenty-five (Adam) to thirteen (Dinah). Morgan (fifteen) lives with both his

mother and his father. "Wherever his spirit takes
him," explains Cloris. George, Jr., now at college after his dropout years, flows equally freely through
Cloris's front door and life whenever he chooses.
"Frankly," says Cloris, "I never know who is living
where and at what time. But I'm never alone," she
adds quickly. And then equally quickly she insists,
"How I wish that I were.

"You know what is one of the biggest myths in this
country?" asks Cloris, pouncing, as only Cloris can, on
a subject. "Aloneness. Particularly where women are
concerned. Divorced women. The culture would have
you believe a divorced woman is miserable—that she
is dying from her aloneness. What a crock! I *love*
being alone. It's a relief. Cooking for one, cleaning
for one, they're joyous events after years of doing it—
with little thanks—for two. Another marriage? Not
me. No, thanks. Besides, what for? Who needs it when
George and I are closer than ever."

Closer than ever but divorced. This, Cloris Leachman would have us believe. Cloris, fifty-two years old
but a little girl playacting her way through real-life
situations. Cloris, really a rather endearing and bright
child who was at her most real and at her most vulnerable when she admitted, "All I have ever wanted
was to be George's onliest little darling." Over the
years and into today, Cloris always talked of George.
With a divorce that is final, she still speaks more of
George, of his work, than of herself and her own.

"Well, why not?" she asks good-naturedly. "I'm still
very close to George. It's just that some things have
changed. Bonnie—his girl—is really a darling. Of
course she is much younger than I, but I have no
feelings of jealousy or competition. Really I don't."
She is smiling eagerly, winningly. She is reminded
that a "much younger" (her words) woman has far
fewer lines, wrinkles . . . stretch marks. "I don't
have stretch marks," she snaps. "And I'm not jealous.
Oh, I have a few little nagging thoughts but they're

unrealistic. Bonnie honors and respects me. She even laughs at my jokes more than George does."

Cloris Leachman is biting her lip. "She can never replace me—never replace what I was to George," she spits out. "Not ever. And she knows that, which is what makes her special. But then we're all special, aren't we," she says, jumping off her point again. "You should see my Dinah. If anyone ever had a shot at life, it's Dinah. She is totally in charge of her life, knows exactly what she wants and doesn't want. As do I. I *know* I do not have time for a relationship now. I scarcely have time for friends. Why I haven't seen Valerie [Harper] in months! And she is so dear to me. But we're both so . . . *busy*." Valerie too is recently divorced.

"Do you know I used to think when I turned forty-five I'd be alone and sad and take up painting," says Cloris. "Well, forty-five is long gone—went by in a blur—and I'm not alone or sad and I've yet to pick up a paintbrush. Actually I am alone but I like it. I'm not afraid of being 'a woman alone' or of growing older or of sleeping alone. Actually, it's delicious to sleep alone *if* I choose to sleep alone. My life is full. I'm never lonely.

"How can I be lonely or sad?" she asks of no one in particular. "Do you know if I were in need, George would be the first one there. My husband has *always* been there when I've needed him."

Your *ex*-husband, she is corrected.

"I hate that. How do you X out a husband? I refuse to do that. We are not married anymore, but that doesn't mean all we had—that we *still* have—should be X-ed. And we do still have it. We do."

"Cloris, you don't. You are divorced," she is reminded.

"I was always George's onliest and I still am. No one can take that away," she says defiantly. "I am. I am. I am. But what is so ironic is that when I truly was his onliest, I didn't believe—couldn't accept it. I wanted it to be something other—something more than it was. George gave what he could, but it wasn't enough . . . for me. We kept colliding—he not allowing himself to be understood, and me, a woman who felt she was basically unlovable. What a pair. Send in the clowns."

She is off stage now. Shorn of her makeup and her pretensions, Cloris Leachman looks painfully small, so very different from her phony larger-than-life image.

"My life hasn't worked out the way I hoped it would," she says softly. "No, it really hasn't. Not at all. I loved George so much. Now I have to be my own onliest little darling and perhaps that's best. Perhaps it's wrong to want so much from one person. I made George my everything—a father figure, a knight in shining armor . . . everything. What man wouldn't buckle under such weight.

"What I really feel about the divorce, what I have *ever* really felt about anything, is no one's business," she says. "It was easy for me to slip into the Phyllis characterization in interviews. It still is. Phyllis can be zany, madcap, throw out meaningful yet meaningless answers. Why should I *bare my soul?* Who cares? I mean beyond the titillation of gossip, who really cares? My life with George has overtones of melodrama. But it was my life and . . . my pain. My God, how it hurt sometimes. Always having to leave the door open to both my home and my heart, hoping, praying, believing he would one day walk through one or the other or both. It's not something he asked me to do but something I *had* to do. And it was killing. Often I was in anguish.

"But it's over . . . done with. Life goes on and all that. Right? So there's pain. So I could cry right now. So what?"

Cloris Leachman asks for a hug. She tightly winds herself into and around your body seeking warmth . . . comfort. When she breaks away, she walks to her window overlooking Central Park and with a wry laugh, but she isn't laughing, says: "People say divorce is tough. They're wrong. Divorce is easy. It's marriage that's a bitch."

CHAPTER TWENTY

NANCY WALKER

"Let me tell you about bad times," says Nancy Walker, who considers herself an expert on the subject. "Without them, I wouldn't be where I am today and where that is ain't bad!"

It sure "ain't." After thirty-four years of bouncing between Broadway and Hollywood and from one bad time to another, Nancy Walker has become a star. But Nancy Walker doesn't quite trust her success. "Let's not go overboard with the terrifics," she cautions half-seriously. "I doubt if it'll last the week, if you want the truth." At her worst Nancy is a compulsive worrier about being "too clutchy, too possessive, too angry, too unattractive, and not too bright." At her best Nancy refuses to give in to the bad times, which she admits she herself often creates. Of those she went through in the sixties, she says, "I always knew either they would end or I would and *I* wasn't about to. Not this lady! Something inside me always prevents my ever giving up."

At the root of all Nancy Walker fears is that "Everyone I love will leave me." It's a fear founded in some fact. In her past some did leave. But in her present no one does. She and David Craig have been married twenty-five years. In Hollywood not only is that a rarity but so is an actress with real friendships, which Nancy has. It's impossible not to respond positively to her warmth, her honesty, and her on-and-off wit. Her friends and coworkers seem to appreciate her more than she appreciates herself. They refuse to take her fears seriously, although they know that those fears are very real to her. Valerie Harper insists: "Regardless of Nancy's feeling to the contrary, she has a strong sense of who she is and what she can be." Says Rock Hudson: "She'll be bailing water while she paddles her own canoe to the very end." Hudson is one of the few who has seen what Nancy calls her "Irish melancholia" but which Hudson and her husband refer to as her "dark side." "She becomes quiet, too quiet for a normally effervescent person. She becomes almost unreachable," says Hudson, who is also one of few to have seen the rage Nancy claims to feel most of the time.

It's probable that many childhood experiences are at the root of Nancy's fears and foibles. Her parents, Dewey and Myrtle Barto, were traveling vaudevillians and home for the family was anyplace they could hang their names on a marquee. Nancy's schooling was thus sporadic and incomplete. "But I had something better as a child . . . love. We were a very close family," she explains. Then when she was eight, her mother, whom she "adored," suddenly died. Like so many children she interpreted her parent's death as a rejection, and "I felt it was because I had done something wrong." Her father booked a European tour, thinking that might ease their suffering. "Suddenly my baby-sitters were Josephine Baker and Nick the Greek. I remember picking up a bit of philosophy from Nick that has stayed with me all my life. He would bet on anything and on Sunday mornings when he would take me for a walk, he would make a wager on every street corner. When he lost, I'd cry. He'd comfort me saying, 'Don't worry, kid. We'll pick it up again on the next street.' Later whenever I lost something I wanted—personal or professional—I'd say to myself, 'Don't worry, kid. You'll pick it up again on the next street.' And usually I did."

When she was thirteen, her father plunked her down into middle-class conventionality by sending her to live with her grandmother. But she was bored. At ten she had decided she wanted to be a song-and-dance woman, "and I was too grown-up to suddenly be a kid among other kids. I was itchy to get on with life." So much so that she got herself engaged at fourteen, but decided against marriage when it became obvious that it would interfere with her work. Instead, under her father's guidance, she studied. She even took up sculpturing. " 'An actress must know what to do with her hands,' my father said. Years later Noel Coward, after one of my performances, came backstage loudly proclaiming, 'But I *must* buy your hands!' My father was very proud."

She finds it hard to talk about her father, who died two years ago. Reluctantly she admits that in later years their relationship altered for the worse. "My father thought everything he ever taught me belonged to him. He felt I owed him something. Did I? I don't feel my daughter owes me anything. He was very proud of me and yet he resented what I had become. He tried to dominate my life. I loved him so very much as a child but later . . . well, my feelings became ambivalent. He taught me never to hurt people and yet by his inability to let go of me and let me live my own life, he hurt me."

She doesn't really feel she had a childhood. "I was never young. I was born old. But I saw the world long before other children my age knew it existed. There was always excitement in my life." There was also loneliness. "I've always missed my mother. A part of me has always been lonely."

She was nineteen when she walked on a Broadway stage in *Best Foot Forward,* portraying the blind date, and became an instant celebrity. MGM signed her to a seven-year contract and life should have been merry, but it wasn't. She hadn't planned to attain success as a clown. "It killed me when people laughed. No one ever laughed at pretty girls."

Her looks remained a problem for many years. At

MGM the studio's "pretties"—its Lana Turners and Elizabeth Taylors—were at the top of the caste system while the "second bananas" lagged far behind. "In Hollywood, to be beautiful was to be loved," recalls Nancy. "I quickly learned that Pretty People are not always pretty people, yet I was miserable. I was also confused. I never understood why in a town with so many beautiful women, I was never without a date. And it wasn't because I was a bundle of laughs off stage. I was always *me*."

Her conflict was partially solved when her friend, set-and-scene designer, Oliver Smith, told her, "Nancy, people aren't laughing *at* you, but *with* you!"

Today, to Nancy, getting laughs is "like heaven and money in the bank. In that order!" But her pretty-problem has never been totally solved. Interestingly her husband, David Craig, besides being a formally educated and scholarly man, is matinee-idol handsome. Asked if marriage to a good-looking man poses problems for a woman who doubts her own attractiveness, she replied, "You're damn right it does! A lot of days when I'm not feeling so hot, I look at his gorgeous puss and think, 'What is he doing here? Why hasn't he left yet?' Some days the answer—that he loves me—is clearer than others."

When the David Craigs first met, bells didn't ring and trumpets didn't blare. Nancy began studying with David, who's one of the best voice coaches in the business, because she was having vocal problems. Within weeks she was hooked. "He was kind. He was compassionate. And he was bright. I used to run home and look up what he said in the dictionary." One afternoon, as she was arriving at his studio, a friend who was leaving clasped her hand and offered his congratulations. Perplexed, she asked David, "Are we celebrating something?" To which he said confusedly, "Didn't I *tell* you?" As she shook her head no, he asked "Will you marry me?" To which she re-

sponded "Oh, yeah . . . sure . . . thanks a lot
. . . Something brilliant like that," she adds, laughing
at the memory.

Nancy's marriage has caused her great joy but it
has also caused her pain. The pain is because she
persists in disbelieving that anyone—least of all
David—will be there over the long haul. This fear
found her choking both David and the marriage. She
has fought constantly, and now seemingly successfully,
to loosen her reins on David and hold on tighter to
herself. Bouts—"and that's what they have been"—of
therapy have helped. The marriage today is very
solid. "It gives me a place to put my deep need to
have someone who needs me," says Nancy. "And
. . . I always wanted to love somebody very much."

Her "somebody," David Craig, understands his
wife. Although he appears to be crisp, even sharp at
times, he is, as Nancy has claimed, a sentimental man.
He's also a loving man, one who casually will touch
his wife's hair or clasp her shoulder upon entering or
leaving the room. His spontaneous affection is
matched by hers. Yet he's the first to admit that their
marriage has not been an easy one. "The dark side of
Nancy makes *anything* easy impossible. Like most
great clowns, she's a brooder. But she's also a very
good person and a woman who has kept home and
hearth in one part of her forest and career in another.
I have enormous respect for her as an artist and as a
person. But I have learned that when she is in the
pits, to leave her be. Nancy will knock herself down,
punch herself out, bury herself even, but then without
any help at all she'll pick herself up."

"I just don't accept defeat," Nancy says. "I was
married before David—for a year, to an actor whom I
loved very much. When it failed, I was hurt but instead of saying, 'Never again!' I couldn't wait to re-
marry. I knew marriage could be wonderful if it were
to the right person. And were the angels ever sitting
on my shoulder when I met my ole man!"

The early years of the Craig marriage were lived in New York City, where she was successfully combining career and marriage. Her first and only child, Miranda, was born June 30, 1953, and "I viewed her then as I do now—a miracle." Nancy never wanted a large family because "I'm not particularly good with children" but did "always dream of the daughter I might one day have." Miranda once asked her mother why she was an only child and Nancy responded, "Because you fill my life." It was David, Nancy says, who recognized Miranda's intellectual potential and insisted on her formal education. "By four Miranda was reading. Today she has advanced degrees in psychology. More important, she's so sane . . . so sensible."

Miranda is one of the rare subjects that raises only positive thoughts and feelings in Nancy. "I was always honest with her," she says. "When she was still a child, I sat her on my lap and told her if she would allow me my work, whatever time I gave her would be very full. I tried to explain what my work means to me and how without it I would be half a person and half a mother. I also told her that when my door was closed, it was because of me, *my* moods, and not because of anything she might have done. And Miranda understood. Even at that age she was a terrific dame."

It wasn't until the 1960's that the "bad times" arrived. For six years Nancy was unemployed as an actress. It was an abrupt change, one she could not adjust to. She was confused and hurt by her sudden career reversal. As the weeks, months, and finally years went by, she withdrew into herself. "I was terribly depressed. The me that had worked since I was nineteen felt as though nothing I had achieved in the past had meant anything."

It was then that she became overly possessive and "clutchy" with David. "He was the only thing holding me up at that point. I clung to him the way a drowning person clings to the lifeguard and in the clinging I nearly drowned my marriage."

At that time she had the chance to do television commercials, and she took it. "I didn't see that as a comedown and I still don't. Work is work and a job well done is just that!" The proof is in the paper towel. Through TV saturation, she gained national recognition. She also gained self-respect. "Even I, negative ole me, couldn't deny that no one other than myself had pushed me out of the house and back in the business." Concurrently she pushed herself into psychotherapy, a decision prompted by no other voice than her own.

Today, because of her own efforts in therapy and out, Nancy Walker lives very differently. First she left New York—"a hostile city that brings out my own hostility"—and moved to Los Angeles—"where the sun shines and everything looks pretty." Second, she knocked on California's Golden Gates until someone finally heard her. "They didn't exactly throw open their doors for me," she admits, "but I inched my way in through *McMillan* and *The Mary Tyler Moore Show*." Third, instead of living in an apartment, as she had in Manhattan, she now lives in a sprawling home perched on a hill in Studio City, a Los Angeles suburb.

"It ain't bad, ain't bad at all," she says of her life, which is as close to a joyous statement as Nancy Walker is about to make. "You know, they made an awful mistake all those years," she remarks, referring to all those who denied her work during the sixties. "But," she says philosophically, "as I said, the bad times brought me where I am today. Not that I got it made," she adds cautiously. "I have to fight every day and that's good—not bad. You should fight for those things that are important."

That includes her marriage. She and her husband both "fought like hell" and two years ago, after twenty-three years of marriage, they separated for two months, the only time they'd been apart from one another in twenty-three years! "The separation was awful, but David and I felt we had to let go of one another for a while. We needed to separate identities and lives in order to come together again.

"I realized I had to sort out who-and-what is Nancy Walker and why does she feel that she can't make it on her own. I discovered that although I am not sophisticated or well educated, I'm no dummy. And so I don't look like Ann-Margret. Who does, besides Ann-Margret?

"Once I wondered if I were a nice person. Today I think I'm pretty okay. So I have a lot of rage within me. It keeps me warm at least. I still worry about losing people I love, but I don't clutch so much anymore. The two-month separation from David cured me of that. During those two months I discovered I could live alone. I *didn't* fall apart and I wasn't going to because I have my *own* strength. I can be my own anchor and lifejacket. What a difference that's made in my life. To live with someone because you *want* to rather than *have* to is what makes my marriage beautiful today. I live with David because I like him and he likes me. We also love each other. Why, I've relaxed so much I can finally admit that opera bores me and let David go there with another woman as long as *she* doesn't look like Ann-Margret."

She laughs. She is actually cheerful. "Don't spread that news around or it might ruin my image," she jokes. Then she says soberly, "There've been a lot of changes. But I wouldn't trade one moment of what was in my life and not one second of what is. There was a time when it was just enough to survive. No more. Now that I know I can 'make it,' just making it isn't enough. I have always known life could be beautiful and, whaddya know, at long last, it darn near is."

CHAPTER TWENTY-ONE

LESLIE UGGAMS

What?

"Twenty-eight years!" yells Leslie Uggams over the din of dinner dishes rattling as they are removed by room service, and the noise of a nosy two-year-old determined to see what is *in* rather than on the television that his father, Grahame Pratt, is watching.

"Twenty-eight l-o-n-g years. I'm an oldie-but-goodie," laughs Leslie.

Impossible. "Little Leslie Uggams" a show-business veteran of twenty-eight years? No way. Why it was just yesterday . . . wasn't it?

"I am thirty-four," she says, looking perhaps half that in her faded jeans and peasant blouse. "No one believes me. People think I'm either 'little Leslie' or some old broad trying to look like her daughter." She laughs again. Leslie Uggams laughs a lot.

Some people think Leslie Uggams has always laughed . . . a lot, even when it wasn't appropriate. Many believe she has laughed her way through three decades, life, issues, and answers. That "little black white girl," they call her. She was thought to be *a*political and unconcerned, the product of "a white, middle-class upbringing." When she married Grahame Pratt, a white Australian, it was not liked by the black community but it was not unexpected.

What has been unexpected is the change—her own and that of her image among her own. In the past year her portrayal of Kizzie in *Roots* earned her an Emmy nomination and . . . a new *feeling* among blacks. Among whites, "little Leslie" lost her virginity, so to speak, when she came on hot . . . smoldering in a Sinatra special, very definitely *not* the girl-next-door but more likely the woman-down-the-street who throws her own block parties. This past summer-into-early-autumn, Leslie toured with Richard Roundtree in an all-black version of *Guys and Dolls*. This day, in a hotel suite that does not stock Pampers, causing husband Grahame to scour the neighborhood and on a Sunday yet, she is attempting to pack, be mother to Jason, and be interviewed. In an hour the car will arrive to move the Uggams /Pratt ménage to the next town and still another week of performances. Yet Leslie Uggams is unruffled. "I'm too tired to be," she says collapsing onto a couch, her feet up on a near-by chair. Catching sight of her face in a nearby mirror, she groans.

"Aren't I something?" she says of her "Sunday best." She checks out the hair that just sort of hangs without doing much of anything, and laughs. "People expect me to enter a room looking like Loretta Young—floating about in chiffon, looking grand and beautiful . . . every hair in place. I don't quite make it, do I? Then there are those who expect me to be in pink . . . in a pink prom dress. 'Little Leslie' . . . shy and sexless. Ugh!

"Well, I was never Loretta Young but . . . I did have my Rhonda Fleming period. Remember Rhonda? A gorgeous redhead in films in the fifties? I was working with Mitch Miller on *Sing Along* and thought a little red rinse would look just terrific. Just a little. Only how much is a little to a seventeen-year-old? I was fire-engine red for weeks and wore lots of kerchiefs to hide my mistake." Again she is laughing, having a wonderful time on her trip back to the past.

Has life always been easy for you, Leslie?

She hears the question and laughs. A big phony hoot, which says it all. "Oh, yes. Very easy. Sure, it has." Again she hoots. "The truth is I've been fighting all my life to do what I have wanted to do. All my life. Twenty-eight years of trying to be me—which is black—in a white world. Twenty-eight years of growing up in the public eye. Sometimes—not always, mind you—but sometimes it was horrible. And years ago I couldn't show my anger. You had to back me into a corner before I'd explode. And even then I'd think twice. It was the fifties and blacks were not *supposed* to explode. What's more, we weren't allowed.

"But let me tell you about 'easy.' When I was just a kid, I was a contestant on a TV game show, one in which talented kids competed for prizes. I had a big voice for my age. A good one too. The previous week I cleaned them out, winning all kinds of kitchen appliances that we couldn't use because our tenement on One Hundred Sixty-fourth Street in Manhattan didn't have enough power. The prize this week was a car. Now, I couldn't drive and neither could my parents, but oh, how I wanted to win. And I did, only I didn't. They tied the applause meter on me. I saw them do it. And they had the nerve to explain why. It seemed a black child had already won the grand prize within the past month of shows and that . . . fulfilled their black quota. But I didn't understand about 'quotas' at that age. I only knew I had been better than but had lost—lost because I was black. I cried. I mean, that child cried as though her heart would break. And I can remember asking my mama what's wrong with being black. Only I didn't need an answer. I knew there was nothing wrong with being black unless . . . you were white.

"And I was never white," she continues nonstop now that she is *finally* talking, breaking a silence of many years. "Let's talk about my so-called 'white, middle-class upbringing.' Only there is nothing to say 'cause I didn't have one. I was raised with a very great sense of black pride . . . black heritage. My grandparents, uncles, aunts, too had been doctors, dentists, lawyers, and educators. We were proud of their accomplishments. But I was also proud of my father, who waxed floors for a living and who simultaneously operated elevators. He was a man to be proud of. When it became evident early on that I had talent, he worked two and sometimes three jobs so I could attend Professional Children's School. And my mama worked too to make ends meet. We struggled, but never for our pride or our sense of blackness. I was fed and dressed and given a sense of self that has never left me. And I never got confused. Each day I'd travel downtown and went to school with mainly white kids. But each day I traveled back uptown and played where I lived, on the streets of Washington Heights, which is often ironically referred to as a suburb of Harlem. I always knew I was black. I grew up with a positive identity—black and otherwise. My parents gave me that."

That and much more. At six "Little Leslie" was starring with Ethel Waters on *Beulah*. Over the next decade she appeared with Milton Berle, Sid Caesar, and scores of others on their respective television shows. At the same time her "roots" included numerous appearances at the Apollo Theatre in Harlem. Another child could have had her head turned by so much so soon. "But my parents wouldn't allow my head to swell. They never permitted me to think I was 'better than' just because I went to school downtown and appeared on television. My folks weren't impressed by my fame and they sure weren't going to let me be impressed by it either. The only thing that knocked me out was recognition. I liked it when people said 'Hiya, Leslie.' It made me feel special. It still makes me feel special. But . . . the idea is to use that feeling rather than misuse it. I never did a 'star trip.' My parents prevented that, and so did the work itself. I was always studying . . . preparing. You may not like what I do on stage, in film, but you can never say I wasn't prepared. Right down to the shoes. Which is how that whole 'Isn't-she-lovely?' got started. I was trained never to appear in public without being 'done up.' So I was. But I never felt beautiful. I always thought I was kind of skinny but sort of cute. I never made a big deal out of beauty. I still don't. Sometimes the old clichés say it best: beauty is skin deep. What I mean by that is . . . if you don't feel beautiful inside . . . about you, life, *your* life, you haven't any beauty. To me, beauty isn't about clothes or faces without lines but it is about living. Doing it right here and now! I don't worry about 'beauty' per se but I sure do worry about what I think and feel *now* and . . . not about what others think and feel about me."

Was she and is she then immune to the "black white girl" label?

"No one is ever immune from that kind of hurt," she says very simply. "But if you know it isn't true, it makes you more angry than it does hurt. And I knew it wasn't true. Why didn't others know? Because I'm a doer and not a talker. Like, several years ago, Jesse [Jackson] said to me after I played one of his benefits: 'Leslie, the trouble with you is you don't allow any publicity about what you're doing when everyone else does.' Well, I thought about what Jesse said, but I still had to go my way. I was busy 'doing it' and I felt exploiting what I was doing would have taken something away from *me*. Even today, talking to you, it sounds like I'm blowing my own horn. I don't like that. I don't need that. Yet I have to admit to a human failing. I'd like a little credit. I was always involved. I was a pioneer and nobody knew it. And now, suddenly, it bothers me that I got what I *didn't* deserve and never got what I *did*."

Her "pioneering" took place in the sixties on *Sing Along with Mitch,* which was then one of television's most popular programs. She was the only black on a show that featured an unusually large cast—chorus members mainly. Had it not been for Mitch Miller's insistence, Leslie Uggams would not have appeared on the network show. Southern NBC affiliates threatened not to carry *Sing Along* because of Leslie's presence. They demanded her removal. Miller said if-she-goes-I-go, and the Miller magic was such then that his power was greater than the affiliates'. Leslie stayed and the hate mail began, as did the never publicized bomb threats. Periodically the *Sing Along* crew had to vacate the Brooklyn studio where they taped because some "nut" threatened to demolish it because of one black teen-ager . . . Leslie Uggams.

"Oh, yes," says Leslie, "my life has *always* been 'easy.' Tell a kid that when an entire studio is being cleared because of her blackness being offensive to some potential bomber. Tell that same kid how 'easy' her life is when she looks around at the *Sing Along* crew and sees she is the only black on the show. And tell her that as she is dressed and combed in an *acceptable*-to-whites style. And continue to tell her as she is instructed to sing white rather than black. In other words, Aretha could not have gotten a job on this show . . . not unless she whitened up. Now, I never was a soul singer, but I did do lots of church music. But on *Sing Along* even the spirituals I was allowed to sing had to have a 'white sound.' So that wasn't easy . . . not for me. But I was there, breaking through. I—a black girl—won favorite TV vocalist titles several years running. At the same time, I 'won' the black/white girl label with my own people 'cause they didn't understand what I was doing and why. It hurt. It was unfair."

By 1969 Leslie Uggams was making waves, practically spitting in the CBS eye . . . but very quietly, when she was signed to star in her own weekly TV show. Not that she was able to control her own situation . . . hardly, but she did make several demands, many of which were honored. As she sits in her hotel suite, many years removed from '69, she allows her anger to grow. "Do you know they spent two entire weeks just styling my hair so that I would look 'acceptable.' Today we would say, bug off! But then you did it *their* way in order to eventually score it your way. I wanted to wear an Afro. They said absolutely not! I wanted Stevie Wonder as a guest. They said . . . Andy Griffith. They also said . . . Stevie and Aretha and the Temptations and Smokey Robinson were 'unavailable' when I asked that they be guests. But I knew they weren't unavailable, just unacceptable. Yet, I fought and I opened my season with Sly and the Family Stone. I also sneaked in my Afro. They, in turn, sneaked in Andy Griffith. Back and forth we went. I won the right to have a black conductor on my *own* show and in exchange I gave them the bulk of my hairstyles. It sounds funny now but it wasn't funny then. Nor was it funny to me that up-and-down-the-line my people were thinking . . . 'she's not concerned.' I was always concerned. I was never apolitical. I'm just not a shouter. But I have been out there fighting all my life. Fighting and winning!"

Part of that "fight," Grahame Pratt, reenters the room successful in his "treasure hunt." Jason, their two-year-old, is taken for much needed "repairs" into the bedroom. Pratt, other than saying hello and good-bye, is an unseen presence throughout the interview. But when seen he can best be described as . . . Hollywood handsome with his blond curly hair and medium-tall, slender body. The couple met when Leslie was in the process of winning her Tony award as Best Actress in a Broadway Musical in *Hallelujah Baby*. Their marriage was duly noted by both blacks and whites. Its "reviews" were not as good as those Leslie won on Broadway.

"I was marrying 'white,' " she explains, "and what could be worse then. It fed right into the image. There I was being 'white' again. Blacks folks don't want you marrying anyone other than your own. But love doesn't recognize color. At least it didn't for me. Besides, I didn't give a damn whether people understood or not. My marriage was *my* marriage. Nobody's business but mine. And that remains true today. My private life belongs to me. I'm the one who has to be happy. What I give at the office, so to speak, is in the public domain. What occurs at home belongs to no one other than me and mine. Long ago I stopped worrying about what others think. If you try to please anyone but yourself, you can get sick. So I pleased myself. We got married. Right on Fifth Avenue in a big church with big police protection because someone rsvp'd with a death threat. I remember as the limousine pulled up in front of the church, my looking out at the crowd of two thousand and wondering . . . Is this it? Is someone going to blow me out of my white dress and out of this life with a bomb or a bullet? But I stepped out of those thoughts and that limousine to get married to the man I loved. I acted unafraid. But I wasn't."

When asked how long she has been married, Leslie Uggams Pratt responds: "For*ever!* Maybe even longer." And again she laughs. Which is interesting, considering how rumor persists that the Pratt marriage is about to fall on its pratt. She doesn't deny they have had their troubles over the twelve years they have been married. Recently their relationship was further complicated by his pleading bankruptcy after years of his being rumored to be a millionaire. Today Pratt is Leslie's manager, in itself a job laden with potential marital difficulties. She knows it. "It can be a hassle *if* you allow it. But then all of marriage is a hassle if you allow it. Don't ask me how or why ours has survived 'cause I couldn't tell you. I also wouldn't venture to guess *if* it will continue to survive. I take it one day at a time. I don't think of futures. We have a home in Beverly Hills, two gorgeous adopted children, Dinielle, now seven, and Jason, here. Past that, we're just a couple trying to survive the many pressures put upon a marriage.

"It's not easy for a man who is married to a starlike lady," she continues. "All the fuss is made about you. People knock your man aside to get to you. Yes, they even call him 'Mr. Uggams.' They don't mean to be hurtful but they are. That has an effect on a man. It's an ego breaker. One could say it's the man's problem but I don't think so. In a marriage it's *our* problem. I believe in marriage. I mean . . . I'd hate to see it abolished. I believe a marriage is worth having. Anything worth having therefore is worth fighting for. Besides, I'm not so certain I'd like to be single."

She remembers her "bachelor" days—"what there were of them"—and recalls she was never a "player"—that she always dated but one man at a time. "I'm relationship oriented. Even if I was suddenly a divorcee, I wouldn't swing. It's not my style. I need one-to-one comfort. I'm a homebody. It's an event when we put in a public appearance."

Her "public appearances" are confined to paid ones by and large. She loves to work. What's more, she must. "When I married, I decided to quit, although Grahame didn't ask me to. Actually, since I was working when we met, it was understood I would always work. But something within me—that fifties mentality, I guess—made me feel I should stay home—do the housewife number. After three months Grahame and everyone else around me was pushing me out the door. I had become impossible. I have too much energy not to work. It's not the applause or recognition I need as much as the outlet. I could quit the business as long as I had something else to do. At the moment I'm learning to play tennis. I can't give you much of a game but I sure can give you some stunning outfits."

When not doing summer stock, she tries to confine her on-the-road work. "Dinielle is now in school and thus can't travel with me. She resents my being gone and she resents my taking Jason and leaving her. Obviously the only way to solve this conflict is for me to become a great big mooovie star and never leave Hollywood. And I'm trying. *Roots* was without question the most exciting adventure of my life. It was a turning point in my career too. To have been part of that experience for its historical, political, and social significance was to have a dream come true in one's lifetime. And also for very selfish reasons, it's wonderful to know that long after I'm dead and gone, I will have left something behind that will be remembered."

She is being remembered now and she loves it. Perhaps because of the emotional outward display of "remembrances," she is speaking out about herself for the first time. She has been deeply moved this past summer and autumn by the "black folks" who have visited her backstage. It is no longer "Miss Uggams." Now it is the more comfortable: "Hiya, Leslie." They reach out and touch her, as though she were one of their own, which she most indeed is. She hugs herself and says: "Oh, God, how I love them touching me! How I love their thinking they now know me. I'm Kizzie and I'm me. But we've come together. The door has been opened and I've been welcomed back home, not as 'little Leslie Uggams' anymore, but as a grown-up woman, and a black woman at that."

CHAPTER TWENTY-TWO

LORETTA LYNN

"I was nervous . . . a lot. Too many responsibilities, too many conflicts, and too many guilts made me take too many pills," said Loretta Lynn. "It felt like everybody was pulling on me—my kids, my husband, my fans, my career—and there were those really bad migraine headaches. So . . . I began taking 'nerve pills.' City folk call them tranquilizers but either way they're drugs. Every time I felt nervous, I'd take me a pill. If it didn't work, I'd take another. Time came when I was taking them 'round the clock. And at bedtime I had me still other pills to get me to sleep. It was some kind of problem. I guess you can say I was addicted, 'cause that's the truth."

The truth is very important to country music's First Lady. "I don't want to pretend to nobody that I'm something I'm not. Lots of folks put me on a pedestal. Well, I don't want to be there anymore. It's hard enough entertaining people, putting on a show, without putting on that you're some kind of other person. I've nothing to hide. I had me some problems so I saw a psychiatrist . . . have for three years now. He helped me to a place where I now accept myself. What you see is all me and not some legend. And that's good!"

It is very good today for Loretta Lynn. She has been drug-free for a year now. "Ain't nearly so nervous no more. And I did it all myself. No hospitals or other drugs. I just faced up to me and my problems. Pills are a form of escape and I don't have me the need to run no more. Even the ole migraines are gone and they used to hurt so fierce that I would pass out sometimes right on stage. Through psychiatry, I changed. I don't try to be everything to everybody no more. I'm only one woman and I can't give all of me to every ole body that pulls on me. I've been a guilty wife and mother near all my life until I accepted I had to work—not just for me but for them. My career was putting bread on the table, a roof over their heads, and an education in their minds.

"That ole doctor in Nashville, he helped me learn to enjoy each part of my life instead of putting them at war with one another," she continues. "Okay, I hardly raised my kids and that hurts me to heart. But I didn't have me that much of a choice and best as I can see they turned out pretty good. And mama, here, now, she's doing pretty darn good too. I'm up from a scrawny ninety-three pounds to a hundred twenty-five. Fat and sassy," she says, slapping at her thigh and laughing. "Truth is, I'm feeling so good, I'm dangerous!"

There is a physical change in Loretta Lynn beyond the weight gain. She no longer looks fragile, as though a harsh word would cause her collapse. "I ain't fragile at all," she says. "Actually I've gotten mean. The doc said lots of my problems were caused by my not speaking my mind . . . by my holding things in. I was afraid of hurting people's feelings. I'd never get mad. Now I'm hot stuff. I just speak right on up, say whatever it is that's on the tip of my tongue. And sometimes it's some kind of mouthful. Because of that I'm finally enjoying my life and my work. I ain't poor little Loretta no more. I can say no. I work now—not 'cause I have to but 'cause I want to. So I might just as well have fun doing it. Ain't nobody twisting my arm so I might as well not pretend there is. When I go out on stage today, I try to entertain me first. Truth is. I gotta tickle me before I can tickle my audiences."

She was "tickling" them in SRO numbers at that
moment in her Las Vegas debut at the Aladdin Hotel. She is the first queen of country music to headline
on the Strip and she didn't think she'd enjoy it. "I
ain't used to settin' in one place for too long. And we
sat for a fourteen-day spell here. We're going to be
doing it four times a year. But you know, it was fun.
Mooney [Loretta's husband of twenty-nine years]
came up and we had us a good time. Actually,
anytime we can be together is a good time. It don't
happen too often."

Because it "don't happen too often," theirs has
been a marriage in conflict. It was Mooney Lynn who
took his Butcher Hollow, Kentucky-born bride into
show business after the birth of their fourth child
(they now have six). It was Mooney Lynn who gave
up his own work to drive Loretta throughout the
country's heartland to promote her and her records.
Mooney Lynn believed in his wife's talent. Some say
he *drove* her to the top. Still others insinuate that as
he drove her there, he nearly drove her out of her
mind with his ambition. But when she became an
American institution, he withdrew . . . by choice.
Explains David Brokaw, the Lynns's longtime friend
and business associate: "Loretta was Mooney's vision.
They married when she was fourteen (she is now
forty-two) and he was her husband, father, and mentor. He was a man who took great pride in being the
breadwinner. With Loretta's success he became a
househusband. You would have to know Mooney to
understand how difficult this kind of role reversal was
for him. It created enormous pressure on him and
Loretta."

Loretta Lynn agrees. "It creates some kind of strain
on a woman's brain when suddenly she's the one who
is making the money. Suddenly you are a very big
deal in people's minds and they fuss over you—puff
you all up and all while your husband, who made it
all possible, stands on the side watchin'-and-a-waitin'.

That was hard for Mooney. Hardest of all was when some folk at fairs or at the Opry would say, 'Hey, boy, you got some kind of good thing going. Your ole lady works and you don't have to do nothing.' Mooney would stand there smiling but with his fists all doubled up. Had he done what he wanted to, they'd still be picking up the pieces of some of those folk. He's a proud man. So . . . he decided it'd be best for both of us if he stayed home . . . became a farmer, worked the fields—which he does daily—and cared for the kids. The farm today is his pride and joy. That and a bottle of beer makes him happy."

She laughs but there is an edge to her laughter. "Mooney's drinking is the one thing that bothers me," she explains. "When he gets lonesome, he drinks. With me being away two thirds of the year, he gets lonesome lots. So do I, which is why I'm on the phone to him every day. If I still feel lonesome, I turn on the TV for company. Sure I could have me other kinds of 'company'—I get lots of offers—but when I ask myself if that's the kind of company I want, the answer is no.

"And I don't worry much about Mooney and his 'company.' Ain't no women out there who is going to take my Mooney from me. Not if she values her life. Yes, sir, I'd fight for my marriage. This part-Indian gal would go on the warpath for it. I've been fighting for my marriage for years now and I've just about won the battle and the war. We came close to divorce twice, but, you know, even if we had gotten unhitched, Mooney would still be the person I would go to for advice. He's smart. I trust him. He is head of our house and I wouldn't want it any other way. I have a deep love for that ole Mooney of mine."

Says David Brokaw: "In some ways the Lynns are like kids. Like the last time I drove them from the Opry to their home in Hurricane Mills. They sat in the backseat of the car necking, like teen-agers. And until you've seen Mooney's huge hulk of a hand caressing Loretta's face, you can't know what this woman means to him."

One of Loretta Lynn's changes, she says, is about not asking herself which means more . . . her career or her marriage. She accepts both have a place in her life. Yet when asked, she admits if she had to do it over again, "I would have my family—have that normal life I missed out on—but I don't know if I'd go into show business again. I don't think so. It's an unnatural life. Lots of pressures. And it's cutthroat. People are always doing-and-a-saying ugly things . . . making up stories. I didn't want any of my kids to follow in their mama's footsteps but Ernest [twenty-four], he's out there now, hootin'-and-a-hollerin' and he's pretty darn good. So, I guess I'll help him. Maybe it'll be different for him 'cause he's a man. With a woman . . . well, I missed out on my kids and all the psychiatry in the world can't ease that heartache. If I had me an education, I could have done something else—something close to home. But I didn't. There was nothing I could do but sing. And here I am still singing. But within two years I'm cutting back by half. That's right, by half! I've told Mooney I want to buy us an even bigger house, one with maybe forty or fifty rooms, and fill 'em with runaway kids. I mean, I wanna grab me an armful of kids who need a mama and love 'em up real good in my own home. And Mooney says: 'Just tell me when, woman, so I can get the hell out of here.' I guess he's had him his share of raising kids," she laughs.

Loretta Lynn laughs a lot these days. She even brushes aside the death threats that continue to arrive by mail. "It helped lots when Dinah Shore told me she used to get some too. I didn't feel so singled out. Dinah said you just have to go on living your life, so now I do. Time was when I would bounce all over that stage thinking it's harder to hit a moving target. But now I can take it easy, sit on a stool, relax, and sing." But she doesn't get too relaxed. "I still travel with three armed bodyguards, as there just ain't no accounting for some people."

She has the same attitude about the "some people" who would have you believe she and her baby sister, Crystal Gayle, are feuding. Loretta's brown eyes (if she had them) are *not* turning blue (they already are) over sister Gayle's success. "I'm tickled pink for that gal—tickled pink for her and for me. I helped start her. Crystal and I, we know this business. When asked, we tell folks right away we love each other. Feudin' is for other folk. Same with me and Dolly [Parton]. Folks want to make something where there is nothing. Nothing but liking and admiration. I admire Dolly. It took some kind of courage for her to step out from country into middle-of-the-road music. I couldn't do it. Like someone asked about me doing the disco sound. Well, I don't know what that is, so I guess I won't be doing it. Maybe my mind might want to try it, but I just know my mouth couldn't do it. It wouldn't fit for this coal miner's daughter."

Speaking of which, Loretta's biography, *Coal Miner's Daughter*, soon goes before the cameras at Universal. "I'd like Gregory Peck [her idol] to play Mooney. They're talking 'bout Sissy Spacek playing me. Ain't ever seen Sissy but I hear tell she's a fine actress. But I would like Faye Dunaway. With them cheekbones and that face, she'd look pretty good being kissed by Gregory Peck." And Loretta Lynn laughs. But as stated, Loretta Lynn laughs a lot these days.

CHAPTER TWENTY-THREE

DIANA ROSS

Pandemonium! Klieg lights, cameras, and limousines blocked the entrance to the show-business mecca. "Kid, until you've played the Palace, you haven't got it made," they used to tell the hopefuls. Now, in what was the summer's single social event, that "skinny kid" from Detroit, Diana Ross, had arrived. Along with her, if one was to judge from the interior of the theater, had come Noah's ark. There were two of everything, hand-in-hand, sashaying in silk and swishing in chiffon. They were not unlike the sideshow at the circus—an opening "act" for the star attraction.

Thirty minutes after the scheduled "blast-off," Diana Ross appears as if by magic on stage, emerging from behind two mimes. Wearing a white whatever, she and it unravel to film-screen proportions. We are treated not to *Birth of a Nation* but *Birth of a Star* as pictures of Diana Ross as Diana Ross and Diana Ross as Diana Ross flash quickly on and quickly off. It is a tacky and tasteless display of ego. The crowd practically capsizes the ark in its excitement. They love it! And they love the two acts and two hours in which Diana Ross is center stage, mainly lost in glitter, flash, a few wigs, and a variety of costumes that some might even call clothes. She is rock 'n' roll rotten rather than show-business chic.

But the crowd cheers, screaming as they stamp their feet in what is now the ritualistic standing ovation. History repeats. The claque killed Garland's greatness and perverted Liza's spontaneity. They almost made a fag-hag of Streisand and now they are robbing the single most exciting starlike presence in show business today of her chance at greatness. And it's a pity, for Diana Ross fills a stage with natural glamour. She is that wondrous and rare occurrence . . . a star. Many call themselves by that apellation but only a chosen few have that magic, that genius that radiates from within. Diana Ross nearly drowns in overblown arrangements, production, and frills. Hasn't anyone ever told her that the great don't need distractions?

And still the crowd screams. And the lady, touched, responds on this, her Palace debut. "I wanted to be all you wanted me to be and so much more." The crowd roars its approval. Too bad no one has advised Diana that "more" can often be "less."

Our meeting is to take place at the Carlyle Hotel, which is veddy, veddy chic. The Kennedy clan has called it home, as has Candice Bergen. It is a plush hotel, bigger, brassier but not better than any other in town. She is staying in a duplex the size of Dodger Stadium in Los Angeles. It is very expensively decorated—"hodgepodge lodge" at its worst. It is very much like her act—overdone. One wonders if she will be the same?

From the moment she casually enters the living room, wearing the simplest of pale blue dressing gowns, her hair pulled tautly back from her face, I am struck by a quality that no one—not Berry Gordy, her manager, mentor, or former premarriage lover—can create. To use an est (more of that later) term, the lady has got "it!" Without makeup (she refuses to wear so much as an eyelash off stage), she is beyond beautiful, tilting the sex machine at "spectacular." And she doesn't work at it. She just is! Everything about her is real, including the guarded look in her eyes. There is none of the I'm-so-happy-to-meet-you bullshit. She doesn't play that game. She'll wait and decide if she's happy to meet you, and if she is not, she'll let you know.

As she settles into a settee (at the Carlyle, they're settees, not couches), she is pounced upon by three little girls, her daughters, Rhonda, Tracee, and Chudney. Screaming, laughing, they smother her with hugs and kisses that are amply returned. They have just returned from a day at Coney Island and Diana, pretending not to know where her brood has been, asks the baby, "Where you been, girl?" To which the adorable little smart-ass responds, "Only the nose knows" and collapses in a fit of giggles, helped along by a mama who is tickling her unmercifully. Suddenly Mama remembers there is an interview in progress. "Listen, you guys," she says to her girls, "I'm having this here interview and I really would appreciate it if you would leave us for a while." No dice. "Okay, in that case, if the man asks *you* any questions, you'll have to respond." The girls screw up their faces and march out. One throws off, "I ain't talking to no innaviewa," as a parting shot. It delights her mama.

"Well, you can tell your readers that Diana Ross has children and that she *really* has children." That is very obvious and it is also very endearing.

"Obviously your girls don't like you very much," I say in jest. She looks rather stunned. "You know, that's exactly what Arthur Ashe said the other night." She is not name-dropping, but sorting out what seems to be a mystery to others but which is so natural to her.

Diana has lots of close friends but you know what? Her kids are her closest friends. Young as they are. She's had a lot of guts having that many with only a year or so apart. And they adore her. Diana needs her kids. They're her rock . . . her anchor. They are really what it is all about for her. Only her kids can cure that

special loneliness. And don't let all that noise
around her fool you, she's got the lonelies too.
You can't be *that* big and escape them.

CHER

Lonely . . . funny, the last thing Diana Ross
seems at that moment is lonely. The duplex is over-
run with children, their governess, and her parents,
whom she has flown in from Detroit for the occasion
of her Palace opening. Her father is a tall, regal man.
Her mother, also tall, nibbles at chocolate-chip cookies to keep her weight *up!* She is shy, but not about
her motherly pride. That is obvious. And the phone
rings constantly with sisters and brothers calling from
North and South. Lonely? Diana? Perhaps. The only
element missing is Robert Silberstein, the man to
whom she is married but whom she is reportedly di-
vorcing.

"My children do like me," she says almost to herself. "I guess it's 'cause I'm straight with them. I also
don't clutch. I hold them like sand . . . letting
them sift through my fingers when they must. Love
isn't about clutching. No . . . children . . . love
. . . you can't clutch any of it. It comes . . . and
it goes.

"I used to wonder if I'd ever be able to let go of
my kids, but I don't fret about that anymore. I can. I
will. I do. But I will be there to cup them—to be
there for them, as long as they need. When they are
ready to go, off they will go. In some ways they have
already gone. Young as they are, they are not connected to me. Yes, I am their mama but each is a very independent little person. Already. And that's good. I
don't want them to be an extension of me. Fly, little
ones, fly! That's what I want for my girls."

She has not yet turned her attention to me—to
dealing with that *person* before her. There is no
doubt she is aware I sit there pen-in-hand, but she
will deal with me when she is ready.

Sometimes, you feel an aloofness from Diana
. . . as if she is not available. Even on a film
set, Diana is always nice to people but again, not
often available. She keeps a distance. She doesn't
just open up. She is a secretive person . . .
self-protective.

BILLY DEE WILLIAMS

Suddenly she turns toward me, quite composed
and about as beautiful as any one woman can look
without being a fantasy.

"Do you know where you're going to and do you
like the things that life is showing you?" I ask,
feeding off her theme from *Mahogany*. She beams.
"Do I know where I'm going to?" she echoes. "No
. . . but I have intentions. And do I like the things
that life is showing me? Oh, yes. Oh, yes, indeed. In
fact I'm liking them more and more every day." The
question, "Why?" produces "because I have realized it
is *my* life. Mine! And each day I am finding what
works for me."

What currently "works for" her is being Diana
Ross. She loves to perform. "It was difficult for a
while. Very difficult. But I looked at that and saw no
one was making it difficult for me but me. But then,
isn't that the truth in all things. Isn't it always us who
makes things the most difficult. There I was, living
out of a suitcase, always on the run, and thinking it
hard. Well, it was hard but I was making it harder,
making it into some kind of tragedy when it wasn't.
How could it be? I was doing what I was born to do.
Listen, if I was not a professional singer, I'd be a
singer. I mean I'd stand on a street corner and sing.
That's what I was meant to do. And money—and oh,
goodie, how I do love it!—that's the bonus. So what
were the difficulties? Meaningless in comparison. I
just hadn't accepted them—accepted that they come
with the goodies. Do you know what I mean? Damn!

I must stop doing that. I must stop saying, 'Do you know what I mean?' It's a cop-out. I'm going to learn to communicate—to get across exactly what I mean to say. I am going to make my thoughts very clear."

I think Diana is at a very new place in her life. She now has a need to express herself—to be Diana Ross and not to let anyone else speak for her. She is out-front. She is working on her instincts and allowing them; seeing just how correct they might be. She is coming of age. Like the lady may not have had much formal education but she's got common sense and a cat's wisdom.

BILLY DEE WILLIAMS

The "cat" sits there, trying to make her thoughts very clear. "I grew up during my last pregnancy. Right here in New York, as a matter of fact [Beverly Hills is her home]. I remember sitting in the bathtub and being very pregnant and very miserable. Sitting-and-soaking. I was thinking if I pulled the plug, I could go down the drain along with the suds. So I asked myself, 'Diana, how come you're so miserable?' And I heard me respond: ' 'Cause I'm pregnant and bored.' And I was. Was I ever pregnant and ever bored! But a voice responded: 'Okay, girl, you are going to be pregnant and bored for a while and that's that! Why don't you just accept it instead of knocking yourself out with it.' And suddenly I saw that I did have that choice—that we all have that choice.

"So I accepted I was pregnant and bored and would be until I delivered and in the acceptance I became cool. I realized nothing is forever. In time I'd be out there, doing it, being that whole other Diana Ross.

"I learned something that week, learned I have this incredible ability to deal with the difficulties in life. If I just stay with them! In other words, if I feel my hurts, my angers, if I experience them, they pass on by. Like . . . 'Okay, Diana, this hurts now. Feel it. Know it. But also feel and know that all things pass.' Frankly, I'd rather deal with the pain here-and-now than let it creep up on you at some later time."

She is talking obliquely but the source of her pain is evident. The papers that particular week have blasted it in their gossip columns. Splitsville! Divorcetime. Mrs. Robert Silberstein is to become Miss, or Ms. Diana Ross again. Funnily enough, lots of people are happy about that—even those supposedly close to her. Theirs is a peculiar reasoning but it has to do with a kind of sick she-belongs-to-all-of-us-and-to-no-one-man-in-particular. Strangely, she does not look like a lady who sings the blues privately or publicly. She is radiant.

"To get to the next place in life, one must accept that life is about ups, downs, and in between, and that often what happens is beyond our control. But . . . how we react to it is not beyond our control."

It is obvious she is going to do her est training number. Like Valerie Harper, Cloris Leachman, and John Denver, she has attended the seventy-two-hour "kiss-the-boo-boo-and-make-it-go-away" fast-food type of therapy. Like her fellow followers, she is near ecstatic about its results. "Est did incredible things for me. Yet it didn't teach me one thing I didn't already know. It is all so basic. All of us know we have no 'choice' in the tragedies that befall us. We don't make fires or earthquakes or cause the death of a loved one. These events are beyond our control. But . . . how we react to these tragedies, *this* we can control. We can, or cannot make ourselves sick over them. I choose not to."

She is curled up, catlike now, excited, wanting to make her point. "Est made me aware that all of us can get to have things as we want them. If we want miserable, we get miserable. If we want happy, we get happy. It's true. It really is true! We get what we want. Each day we have a choice as to how we are going to feel. I make that choice. I refuse to fall apart."

There are many who claim, anonymously—not because they fear her but fear the power of Berry Gordy—that Diana Ross, even before est, was hardly the kind to "fall apart." Said one former Supreme groupie, "She's a street nigger and don't forget it. For all her glamour, this girl, skinny and scrawny as she seems, will kick your ass all over town if you mess with her."

Asked if the est experience has changed her from something quite other than the explosive bundle of energy that sits before me, she instantly responds: "No! I am not transformed. I am the same Diana Ross. When I was a kid, I was always fighting, always protecting my kid brothers and sisters. And when anyone knocked me down, I'd scream, 'I may be down, you SOB, but I ain't down.' They always knew what I meant. Well, that's still Diana Ross. Only, est helped me to accept her as well as those things about her and her life that she can change as well as those she cannot. I mean, like today, even if I'm down, I ain't down unless I choose to be down. And I don't choose, 'cause down ain't up. I now take the responsibility for my own life—my unhappiness and my happiness."

More specifically, please, I ask. "Well . . . a lot of what was bothering me prior to est was the 'Supposed-to-bes.' I was *supposed to be* home; I was *supposed to be* a dutiful wife; I was *supposed to be* an available mama. I'm not *supposed to be* traveling. I'm *not supposed to be* doing my thing. A wife *is supposed to be* all kinds of things that I wasn't and which I was killing myself for not being. But, thank the Lord, I learned I had to be me; that I had to obey my own inner 'shoulds' and not society's or anyone else's. As I said, est didn't transform me. It just helped me to be me. Today, I just *am* and as I am, I have come to realize, is okay. And I did doubt that. I most surely did."

But when those doubts started and what they were more specifically about is not learned. Not because Diana Ross is evasive—hardly—but Diana Ross is less concerned with her press image than with the steady stream of personal visitors and phone calls that rob us of our interview time. If the kids wander in, she's right there with them in their play. And so what if a best girl friend just pops on by without calling first? She is, after all, one of Diana's oldest and closest friends, and that too takes priority. I'm amused and not at all put off, although frustrated. This is not the standard interview, but then Diana Ross is not the standard "star." Somewhere, somehow, the lady has learned that her personhood comes first. Somewhere, somehow, she has learned that her private world, more so than her public, is where her real happiness lies.

I first met Diana in 1965 and couldn't stand the broad. No matter how many times we were introduced, she couldn't remember my name. But friends kept saying if we two ever sat down and rapped, we'd like each other. I doubted it. But the time came when we did sit down and let me tell you why I love Diana. Like me, she's a funky, get-down broad. Like me, she is a very complex person. Before est, she couldn't take any criticism. She'd go into herself . . . withdraw. Then she would punish herself with it. No more. Now, she listens, evaluates, takes what she feels is beneficial and dumps the rest where it belongs.

Then, too, Diana always feared people were trying to invade her armor. Not that you could. Before est, the chick wore a breastplate that was a foot-and-a-half thick. Now, a lot of Diana's defenses have come crumbling down. The armor, at best, is maybe an inch thick. She's a very out-front person. And she's okay with herself . . . freer. People can't hurt her like they used to.

CHER

And how did people hurt her? Few things rile Diana Ross more than being thought of as "plastic" or as Berry Gordy's invention. Yes, he discovered her, and yes, he was her mentor and yes, he was her pre-marital lover, but *no!* she is not a windup doll—a dimwit dummy from Detroit.

"It bothers the hell out of me when people think of me as Berry's bionic woman," she fusses. "Plastic? What is that? What do they mean? Why do they persist in it? When this all began—when I was a kid singing with the Supremes, it was pretty much all Berry making the decisions. And why not? What did I know? What did any of us know?"

It is explained to her that the "plasticity" leveled at her is often about her "costumes" and wigs—a veneer, a lacquer that although highly glossed has little substance beneath the sheen. She again fumes. "I love clothes—even those that fall into the category of costumes. Years ago I wore them for different reasons than I do now. Once, they were outer trappings to make me feel better about myself than I did. You know, sometimes when you don't feel so terrific inside, you hide that from yourself and others by looking terrific on the outside. But today I want to look and *feel* good from both places and I do.

"When I put together a show," she continues, gathering up momentum, "I give people what they want—what they think *is* Diana Ross. The glamour. But I also give them me. People want the glitter . . . the fantasy. And why not? What's wrong with dreams of splendor? But when I sit quietly on a stool and sing to them, from me, from deep within, I'm giving them the sum total of Diana Ross. I'm giving them the woman who cares about people—what they think and what they feel."

But are you the final word on Diana Ross? she is asked.

"Today I only record those songs I love. If I don't love it, I don't sing it. After all, that is me before the mike in the studio and not Berry. But I never want to be the final word on Diana Ross. No, change that! I never want to be the *only* word on Diana Ross but I do want the last word. Even today I'm not surrounded by the 'Aren't-you-wonderful!' people. I've got many who tell me honestly what they think of my work. And I listen. But only Berry can top my decision on *some* things. You know why? Because he knows more about Diana Ross in certain areas than the lady herself does. But . . . and listen to me good here . . . I would never at this point in my career do *anything* I personally did not believe in. I went that route once—with the Supremes. We had to in order to get where we eventually did. But no more. But I have no beef in listening. Like recently I was talking with Jack Nicholson and he said, when he acts, he lets the director direct. That's me too. Now, when I begin directing, then that's what I'll do. But till then I dig direction, and I take it very well. That doesn't mean I give up me or what's inside me. That's what makes Berry and I so good together. We have mutual trust. I'll try things his way and then he'll tell me to go inside my gut and do it my way. Then we choose the best."

She is very protective as she speaks of Berry Gordy. Respect and love shine through. "There is always something someone you love and trust can show you. But that final product on stage, on screen, on record . . . that's me. Berry gives me every chance to pull out the best of Diana Ross. I give everything I do my best shot. If it makes it, great! And if it doesn't, well . . . I don't kill myself. No more. I just say, 'Well, Diana, next time it'll be a killer.'"

Berry has been a great mentor for Diana . . . a papa to a little girl who started in this business at fourteen. But she has worked her ass off. And she's only touched on some of her greatness. Diana is going to be bigger, among the biggest of the big. And she's willing to work for it. That plastic shit thrown at her is just that . . . shit. Diana is far too inventive, too unique to be plastic. This is a highly creative artist. She'll jump out and do things you would never expect. Funny how she's grown. She was such a terrified little girl when we made *Lady Sings the Blues* but that terror was turned into constructive energy by the time we filmed *Mahogany*.

Stardom requires a single-mindedness and a devotion few people can give. Diana has it and gives it. She *is* a star. A real, honest-to-goodness, blazing, God-given star!

BILLY DEE WILLIAMS

Diana Ross knows it, loves it, and is totally honest about the knowing and the loving. "I love being Diana Ross, the star," she says. "This lady worked damn hard to get where she is and now that she's there, she is going to enjoy every single minute of it. And I am!" she explodes. "I am! I am! I am! I just love being Diana Ross, successful. And I love being Diana Ross, mother. It's all good."

All? How about Diana Ross, wife? What effect does her superstardom have on her marital relationship? "Although I can turn *that* Diana Ross, the public one, 'the Star,' on and off whenever I need to, there is a conflict with Diana Ross, wife. That's difficult . . . for the man, not me. He makes it difficult. But I understand. Being a successful woman, making a ton of money, making lots of decisions, is hard enough for the woman but it is murder for the man. In our society women are not supposed to be the successes. That's a man's province. Men fell small when their wives are big. We all grow up with this notion of what a husband and a wife should be and what roles each should play. Well . . . I'm a very good wife and my husband is a very good husband. It's just getting it together—*really* getting it together that's the problem. That part of the Diana Ross image is hard now . . . very hard." Her voice trails off and she does not hide the "very hard" from her face. She *feels* her difficulties.

Diana's complexity feeds her . . . makes her the enormous talent that she is. She will always be in search of greatness, and that has to make it hell for any man living with that kind of woman.

BILLY DEE WILLIAMS

Being Diana Ross's husband has to be some kind of bitch! I know, 'cause I've been told how being Cher's husband isn't exactly Terrific City. But Bob [Silberstein] seems to handle it . . . better now, anyway, that his groups, like Rufus, are beginning to make it. It's just so damn hard for a man being married to one of us gals. The bread we earn, the adoration we get . . . man, you gotta think of the guy. He's raised to be the provider and a chick like Diana doesn't need anyone to provide for her.

Then, too, women like Diana and I are selfish. When you dwell on yourself as much as we do— when you have people fawning all over twenty-four hours a day telling you how "divine" you are, it's hard to come off that pedestal to be some man's little woman when the whole world is screaming "Star!" at you. And that screws things up. It's easy for a Diana Ross or a Cher to forget as they stuff themselves on that glamour and glitter that another person exists; one who is little girl and part woman. Often she gets neglected . . . bruised. And Diana . . . she's one of the most little-girl type women I know. An imp. A delight. Yet she is also a sexpot and a star. Well, you try being married to that kind of schizo combination. It's just got to be some kind of hassle!

CHER

In July the "hassle," according to newspapers, resulted in the death of the Silberstein marriage. Diana, claimed reports, filed for divorce. "Except I didn't," she says spontaneously. "I started to, stopped, and stepped back. I was being ruled by emotions, forgetting the most important one: love. I love this man; this man loves me. We also *like* each other. So I canceled it out. We are sitting down and talking about where we are at and where we might be able to go together. We *have* to do this. You can't just throw the kind of love we share out through the window of a divorce court. Maybe we can make it; maybe not. But we gotta take another look before we pack it in."

Are the conflicts mainly that of career vs. wife? "Yes," she admits. "Like, recently I was on tour in Europe for seven weeks. What was Bob to do—follow me around? He has a life and a career too. Yet I *wanted* to make that tour. I *needed* to. And I refused to feel guilty for the want or the need. Remember that day in the bathtub when I felt I could easily go down the drain? It was then I realized I'm only a shell of me without my work. I can't give it up—can't just stay home and be bored or unhappy because somewhere, a long time ago, someone—probably a man—wrote that a good wife should be at home with her husband and family. I cannot, nor will I be, that kind of wife or mother. I love my work. I love my family. And I have learned what you give your husband and your children has less to do with quantity than it does with quality. I don't have to prove that with my girls. They *know* I love them. My girls and I . . . we *know* all about us and our love. But with my man . . . with his needs, it's different. But I love Bob and, frankly, I don't think there is that much love to be had in the world that you give it up without a fight. There is much hell on earth *and* much heaven. If it is heaven you prefer—and I do—then you gotta get yourself moving in that direction."

The roadblocks to "that direction" are numerous. The film work, the concert tours to Europe and the Orient, they carry their price.

No matter what Diana says, she feels the conflict of her priorities. You can't be that kind of superstar and not feel torn between your roles. And we're crazy ladies. We want it all. We want time for our kids, time for our husbands, time for our stardom, and time for ourselves. It's enough to get you crazy. Only Diana is not crazy. Est helped her put her parts together. I was with Diana and Bob the other night [the same Diana was reported to be candelight dining with Warren B.] and they are a great couple to be with. Lots of laughs. They dig on one another. And you don't have to ask me if she loves him, I *know* she does. And she's never "the star" when with him. I tell you, because they do love each other, it would really be a drag if they split.

CHER

Diana and Bob always seem to be in tune. He is a fun guy . . . a good guy. I like him. They really seem to have something going. I'd like to think they'll find each other but sometimes, sadly, even those who do love one another miss and have to move on.

BILLY DEE WILLIAMS

By the time you are reading this, Diana may have moved on, but then again she may not have. The decision, despite the numerous tugs, mainly destructive, will be her own.

A lot of people want from Diana without knowing what it is they really want. Some even think they love her—some do—just as many resent her and her success. That's true of all us alley cats who leave our alleys in the slums and make it to Beverly Hills. The jealousy can kill you and what you got.

CHER

Some people you worry about in this life, but not Diana. She is a survivor!

BILLY DEE WILLIAMS

The "survivor" is nobody's fool. She knows "there are a lot of people who get off on jealousy . . . who enjoy tearing others apart. I know some people want to split me. Well, that's life. And it hurts. But I deal with that. Also I'm lucky. I have some very good friends of longtime standing—people who don't 'yes' me to death but who listen and support me when I need both. They accept that I'm a person with feelings and one who is going through a lot of feelings right now at this point in my life. Of course I can handle them . . . alone. I'd rather not. But I could 'cause I'm a great handler. I never allow me the luxury of falling apart. I don't even allow me to have myself a good cry. That's just not me and I accept that. I was born to take care of things—to mother. I was born to take responsibility for myself and others. I can mother me if needs be. Meaning . . . if my marriage fails, I'll be hurt, but I'll scoop me up in my arms and tend to my hurts and my needs."

She seems so sure . . . so positive. But at no time does it come across as bravura or as a toughness born of anger. No doubt the lady has sung her own blues ... but very privately.

> I've seen Diana when she's been unhappy . . . uncertain. She may seem tough to some, but let me tell you, the lady's got more vulnerability than any ten women I know of put together. She can be hurt.
>
> CHER

"Tough?" echoes Diana Ross as though surprised someone would ascribe that quality to her. "Without fears . . . doubtless?" She laughs. A big throaty, oh-you-gotta-be-kidding kind of laugh. "Honey, I've got my doubts and fears like anyone else. I'm not always 'up' although I more often am than I'm not. But there is always some kind of negative voice nibbling away at you. I don't go through life denying the negatives. Like when I'm doing a new show, one I'm really excited about, a little voice in me says, 'Diana, you are going to be fucking great!' And almost instantly another little voice inside responds 'Oh, no, you're not, girl! You are going to fuck up!' Well, I hear both voices—thank the negative for letting me know she's there and then move right on to do what I must—which is be as 'fucking great!' as I know how to be. There is always the nagging fear. Always the 'no, I can't.' But there's a louder voice that says 'Yes, I can' and that's the one I choose to listen to. I intend to be happy."

And if she isn't happy at that very moment, then every signal she was flashing from the stage and is now flashing from the settee in the gaudy Carlyle Hotel is a lie.

"You know my parents were at my opening the other night," she says quite softly. "That meant a lot to me. But they've never been able to tell me—not in words—what they feel about me or my work. They're not expressive people. And once, oh, just once, I would love to hear my mama and my dad say, 'Oh, Diana, I am so proud.' I would just love to hear that. I know it's foolish of me, 'cause they show it without saying it. But just once . . ." And suddenly tears bunch in those expressive eyes of hers and fall very softly down her hollow cheeks. "Well . . . they really do tell me in their way. They always have. They were there when I began *Lady Sings the Blues* just as they were there when I was five and sang my first song for folks. It was my daddy who passed the hat so he could then buy me a pair of patent leather shoes. They were always there . . . in actions if not in words.

"I remember when I was such a little girl, I would walk a long, long way out of the neighborhood, away from Mama, just to see what the rest of the world looked like. Mama never scolded. She gave me that freedom. She always knew I would find my way back. I was trusted. And I never did get lost. I always did find my way home."

The "sun shower" has passed and Diana Ross is again *simply* and utterly beautiful. And very simply she muses, "I was just realizing how everything I just said has been true for my entire life. I have never been lost. Not really. I may have gone too far in one direction or another but I have always been able to find my way home. Always."

CHAPTER TWENTY-FOUR

JESSICA LANGE

"I was an inexperienced, naive child," says Jessica Lange. "I had to learn an actress is a piece of equipment. When the job is done, the plug is pulled and the equipment stops. So do the relationships that seem so caring. It's not that people mean to be cruel or cold, it's just ... business."

Jessica Lange was talking about the rise and fall of Jessica Lange. In 1976 she was our most publicized film personality—the girl for whom King Kong went ape. For the near eighteen months of its making, Jessica toiled as Kong's love interest. When the film was released, it bombed. And despite all her publicity Jessica Lange was a victim of the fallout.

There is nothing to quite equal the embarrassment an actress feels when she has been blitzed after multimedia exposure. In an industry that remembers its failures as vividly as it lauds its successes, Jessica Lange was strictly for laughs in Hollywood. She was washed up on the shores of Malibu, drowned in the sea of bad notices. Now, three years later, Jessica is once again working in the much spoken about and awaited *All That Jazz*.

Another actress would feel enormous pressure making a "comeback" film. Not Jessica. "I have nothing to come back from," she explains. "Like when people ask if *Kong* hurt my career, I reply: '*What* career?' I didn't have one prior and I haven't exactly had one since."

Jessica Lange is a stunning woman both visually

and verbally. Her soft blond beauty comes as a surprise. In *Kong* she looked rather plain. In person she is breathtaking. And . . . without trying. Her perfect five feet eight inches, 130 pounds are clothed unpretentiously in jeans and sweater. Her hair falls casually to her shoulders. Her makeup is in her dressing room and not on her face. Verbally Jessica is stunning because of her candor, despite her very real fear of interviews. She is a private person who would prefer not to reveal her feelings but who accepts that as "equipment," part of the business in which she is employed demands interviews.

"I don't feel any pressure in making *Jazz* because I don't feel I *have to* make it—have to be a star," explains Jessica. "I would like to be good in this film. I plan to be good in this film. I would like and I plan to have a career in films but . . ." The "but" is a big one. "I'm success oriented," explains Jessica, "but only to a degree. The minute success jeopardizes who I am, I don't want it. I was swallowed up once by this success thing and afterwards I vowed never again."

She is referring, of course, to her life in the aftermath of *Kong,* to the hoopla created about her by the film's producer and her discoverer-and-contract-holder, Dino De Laurentiis. She was a part-time model and bar maid in New York City—"doing neither particularly well—when her modeling agency sent her to the *Kong* show auditions. De Laurentiis took one look at the then gawky ("I was a hundred and five pounds") Lange and dismissed her from contention until a cameraman told Dino the screen test showed Lange dynamics that she, herself, in person, did not. Thus De Laurentiis signed Jessica to a seven-year contract and the star treatment began.

Kong took eleven months to film and Jessica at no time saw the rushes. Because of the furiously intense filming schedule, she also at no time saw herself. "I had no idea of what was happening to me or what I felt about *anything.*" When the film was completed, she was whisked off on a five-month, worldwide publicity tour. That too prevented her from "touching base" with herself. And then it was over. "All that love that was lavished on me was gone . . . vanished. With it had gone two years of my life. I suppose had another film been waiting, life would've been easier. But there wasn't any and so I drifted into this postpartumlike depression. I sort of languished in it and Hollywood for a year. Then my survival instincts took over. I began to readjust my sensibilities. I got used to being just another face again."

What she means is . . . she got used to being Jessica Lange again. Having been "swallowed up," she left the swallower and returned to New York, where she resumed acting and singing lessons. She became part of the city's life, frequenting its museums, the theater, and concert halls. "I got back to my real pleasures—a home [she has a small-but-elegant Park Avenue bedroom apartment], my family, my friends, and my dogs [Jake and Masha]. I resumed reading and just doing the quiet things that make me happy."

That, too, if one didn't know Jessica Lange, would read like a Sidney Skolsky Hollywood tintype—the-gorgeous-actress-who-is-really-just-a-simple-folk-at-heart. But that is really Jessica. As she says, "I didn't crack in Hollywood because I was lucky to be 'landlocked' in Minnesota."

She is referring to her roots. Born in Cloquet, Minnesota, twenty-eight years ago, Jessica recalls her Midwest environment as "provincial but solid. That part of the country, its values and ethics, grounds one. It also breeds strength. I recently bought a home there. Not that I think I'll ever use it, but knowing I have roots in Minnesota still comforts, still grounds me. As does my family. My two sisters are my two closest friends. My parents raised us all with a great sense of our own selves. They always encouraged me to get out there and live as I saw fit."

*   *   *

Which is exactly what Jessica has always done. At twenty she left the University of Minnesota and her art history scholarship for Paris. "It seemed like the right time to make that move." With her went one suitcase, one hundred dollars, and one man, Paco Grande, to whom she was married for several years. Paris grew her, she says. On her own [Grande came and went about his life as did she with no questions asked or recriminations received], she studied acting and mime. "I was happy in Paris," she says, "even though I was poor. I had walk-ons at the Opera Comique and 'walk-ups' to my fifth-floor apartment with the bathroom in the hall." She returned to America, and New York specifically, to further study acting. She lived in yet another fifth-floor walk-up, this time in Greenwich Village, and worked three nights a week in one of the village's more famous bars, the Lion Head, noted for its noisy and rather rowdy writer clientele. Although she hated the work, she needed the solvency that and the $500 a month she earned as model brought her. "I didn't much like modeling either. I thought it silly work," she explains. "I just couldn't get into taking terrific care of my fingernails or paying that much attention to my face. But it was a means to an end: paying for acting lessons."

With *Kong* in the past and *Jazz* in her present, Jessica is still taking acting classes. But she is paying for them on her own. To do the Bob Fosse film, she had to ask out of her De Laurentiis contract. That meant giving up minimally $1,000 per week (she will not reveal the exact figure). That she was "land-locked" in Minnesota helped. "As I said, I was taught to get out there and live as I saw fit. I wanted to do *Jazz*. I felt it was an important film and that it was important for me to work. I don't regret giving up all that financial security for a second. I don't worry about being down-and-out because I've been down-

and-out and it wasn't so bad. Being poor didn't make me unhappy. Money is nice to have. Freedom is even nicer."

Jessica's freedom includes a dissolution (but not legally) of her marriage to Paco Grande, now a cameraman who does quite well on his own. "Officially we're still Mr. and Mrs. but we've actually not been married for several years. When it becomes important to either of us to be legally divorced, we will. Right now we enjoy a friendship. I think Paco and I will always be friends. The men I have known best have always been my friends."

Which is why she is comfortable today working with Bob Fosse. Their "friendship" began shortly after Jessica firmly ended with Grande. Although she and Fosse split some time ago, they remain close. "But I had to audition for this film," says Jessica. "It was no gift. Bob is far too much the professional to give out 'gifts' to former girl friends." Nonetheless another of Fosse's former "ladies," Ann Reinking, is also in the film that stars Roy Scheider.

Jessica Lange hasn't thought past *Jazz,* although several scripts sit on her coffee table. "My priority now is to keep working but not necessarily in film. I'd like to do theater, regional or Broadway. Good work rather than stardom is my priority today, although both are quixotic. I guess I'm just not planning my future but letting it happen." Which is also what she is doing with her near three-year relationship with ballet dancer/superstar Mikhail Baryshnikov. The couple met when she was filming *Kong* and he, *Turning Point.*

Although Jessica admits she "is not seeing" anyone else, she does not claim the same is true for Mr. B. "I accept the man and the relationship as it is. I don't try to control or program it or him. What matters to me is . . . Misha [Baryshnikov]. He is quite the kindest man I've ever known. And giving [Masha is a gift from Misha]. There is such a feeling of life, of excitement, with Misha. For him every day is new. He thrives on the challenge."

Many who know Baryshnikov think Jessica, too, must thrive on "the challenge" if she thinks their relationship will result in marriage. When asked if she hopes to marry one day, Jessica Lange avoids the question at first. Her very blue eyes look down and when they finally look up, she says in a very small and soft voice "I would love to have children someday so . . . yes, I hope to be married." But the one time "inexperienced, naive child" is older and wiser. She doesn't say to whom.

CHAPTER TWENTY-FIVE

ROBERTA FLACK

FIRST TAKE (SD 8230)

Only the voice reveals it is Roberta Flack. It is musical, interesting to the ear, and seductive. Without her trademarks, an Afro as wide as her hips and a body that is overstuffed and overfed, she could be any young, attractive woman casually dressed for an afternoon in New York City. She is without jewels and without makeup. She is also without bra and what-you-see-is-what-you-get and it ain't bad.

She is the unexpected. The intensity one associates with her and her work is somewhere else. She is, in its stead, friendly and chatty. An hour after the *session* begins she is still friendly and chatty but she has revealed nothing while she has said a lot. Hers has been afternoon teatime talk. Of diets and music, of dishing and dirt.

It is learned she "loves" Lena Horne and Muhammad Ali. It is also learned she has had "enough beef and pork to last me a lifetime" and has shed her forty pounds with a diet consisting of fruits, vegetables, and fish. No vitamins and "no pills," she adds meaningfully. Herb teas have made the difference in her diet and that fascinating shared information leads to the revelation that "my skin is so much better because of eating properly." She is also experiencing no difficulties, as she used to, falling asleep at night or waking up each morning.

New Track: "Everything is beautiful, just beautiful," she beams. Not that she ever had difficulty attracting men, she insists. "The most attractive thing people see in me is not my physical appearance but my musicianship." But being thinner, she admits, does have its advantages. She practically exposes two of them as she leans over to pick up a cigarette. And that little trick has nothing to do with her musicianship.

Overdub: Soul. "People are all wrong about this soul thing. Who is to tell me that Lena or Leontyne or Ella don't have it? I'll beat 'em with their bottom lip if they do. Soul is what you feel and *everyone* feels. Some just express it differently than others." Expression, verbal and nonverbal, brings her to *He Be Done Did,* a book she is writing for would-be teachers who label a child stupid because they do not understand his ghettoese. She has taught inner-city children and speaks wistfully of someday opening a school which will use her still developing methods of education. She has just been awarded an honorary doctoral degree in humanities from Hood College in Frederick, Maryland. Concurrently she is working toward a Ph.D. in language and logistics at the University of Massachusetts. Obviously she is not just "talking-that-talk" but is sincere about the possibility of a future involvement in the education of the young.

Music Intro: "Take the A Train." She just "loves" New York. "It's so honest. You can see anything on the streets of New York and, honey, you do!" But azaleas, "rainbows of them," have won her heart and she launches into a rhapsody about pastoral living in Alexandria, Virginia. She and John Denver—our sunshine freaks. "Everything is beautiful," she beams, "just beautiful!"

PLAYBACK

Never mind "Where Is the Love?" Where is the Flack? The woman's wit is as lively as her intelligence. All the words are right. She talks *good* but she remains at arm's length. She comes from a distance outside of herself . . . uninvolved, unemotional, and invulnerable.

Could the same be said of her music? Yes, it is pure. Yes, it is perfect. But it is not "out-front." Somewhere between technique and perfection, the singer emerges. But does the woman? She states: "Music comes first from my heart and then goes upstairs to my head where I check it out before letting it out." One can never criticize Roberta Flack's musicianship. It is faultless. One may not like what one hears but that has nothing to do with her professional expertise. She is an *artiste*, one who says, "I cannot function without my music. Before I am a mother, lover, teacher, I am a musician. Take away my music and I wouldn't be anything."

Which of course is not true. Take away the music and she is still Roberta Flack, *person*. Her words are her defense, the invisible shield that protects. She, the *person*, cannot be hurt, if it is safely hidden behind she, the musician. "Music comes before anything," she says and that is understandable as one examines her early life when there was precious little other than her music to make Roberta Flack feel good about Roberta Flack.

CHAPTER TWO (SD 1569)

Initially she is hesitant about brushing away the cobwebs that shroud her memory. She sugar-coats her childhood, preferring not to meet again the lonely and alienated child she once was. One of four born to Laron and Irene Flack (February 10, 1940) in Black Mountain, a small Piedmont town near Asheville, North Carolina, she was five when the family moved to Arlington, Virginia, where her father worked as a draftsman and her mother as a domestic and cook for Wakefield High School. Undoubtedly the single most important event in her childhood was the rescue and resurrection of a piano her father found in a junkyard. She learned to play it by "ear," but by age nine she was started on formal lessons. She owes that to her mother, "who wanted it for me because she had wanted it for herself."

She is more than just vague when she initially speaks of her mother. "She taught me to be a woman" and "a wonderful cook" is the best, or the most, she will recollect. Of her father she is somewhat more revealing. "Our relationship was kind of strained. I was like him in temperament and that caused the problem." What problem? "We got mad about the same things," she explains while explaining nothing. "But we loved one another. He loved me but in a strange way," she adds while adding nothing. "Well, that was the way it was and it didn't seem to do me any harm," she says matter-of-factly. "My parents gave me everything they could—although I was never spoiled. Why I never even knew we were poor until I had the means with which to compare. Sure there were hard times, but they didn't seem that way. Once, eleven of us lived in one room in a cellar. I still have the scar from the time when my brother pushed me into a potbellied stove. But I never felt underprivileged. Not in that sense."

Hers was a different kind of deprivation. She returns to her mother and speaks of her dos-and-don'ts for little girls and just because they are little girls. She says they gave her a sense of womanhood. "Women's libbers would find my mother's preaching on what was and what wasn't in a girl's domain very deteriorating in terms of a young girl's growth, but I found it gave me a sense of security to know what was and what wasn't expected of me." She recalls the first coat her mother bought for her from a second-hand store—"the first *woman's* coat." It was a tweedy sort of thing with a great big fox collar. She paid it little mind, preferring her older and shabbier and unisexless coat until her mother "straightened my head." She said, "You are thirteen, young woman, and it is time you appreciated that fact."

"My mother was a very sensuous woman. She passed that on to me. She made me feel good about being born female."

Later she is to say of her mother, "She is truly a great, noble black woman. Strong. Very strong and yet . . . soft." The words are spoken with reverence and an emotion never explained. Still later, when asked if she was close to her mother, she first replies "relatively" and then, devoid of self-pity, responds, "I was never close to anybody. Not close, close. Not my mother or to any member of my family. I had one friend throughout my childhood, a little white girl who, like me, was president of her Junior Red Cross Chapter."

A further examination of her relationship with her father journeys her back to graduate school and its seminar program, for which she was working on a concerto that she would play with the National Symphony Orchestra. She recalls the day she was at home, practicing the piano in the family room. She was there "fingering," when her father came in to watch baseball on television. He requested she stop her practice so he could enjoy his game. She refused. The verbal yet nonverbal tennis game of his asking and her refusing ended when he arose to slam shut the piano on her fingers. "He might just as well have used an ax blade and hacked off my hands. I thought what he did was the worst thing anyone could do." She left home because of it and took up residence with her piano teacher and her family.

She does not immediately respond when asked if she felt loved as a child but in characteristic fashion hedges. "I think probably at one time in my life before I knew the complete and total satisfaction that comes from accomplishing so much [she means her music] before that . . ." She stalls, out of alibis. Then suddenly, "Yes, I did feel I had lived a very neglected life. I used to make that statement quite often to myself. Not only wasn't I close to anyone in the family, but I felt they couldn't have cared less about me, particularly when I went out on my own. No one ever called. There was just no communication between them and me. Later, when I recognized my love for them, I was able to move toward them. I couldn't wait around for them to tell me how much they loved me. I *knew* they did! And don't ask me how I knew. I just knew. They *had* to love me. We needed each other. So I started acting towards them like I wanted them to act towards me and we've gotten closer and closer over the years."

She refuses, however, to look squarely at the child whose name was Roberta Flack. She insists music was not that child's salvation but just "her thing."

"I didn't play hopscotch or jump rope because I preferred to play the piano." Music, she insists, was not an escape. "I was a fulfilled child because of music." Why then was she a near two hundred pounds by her teen-age years? "Because I loved to eat," she snaps, refusing to invest any deep psychological meaning to her eating. But the truth remains she had a pitifully few friends when she was a child and found acceptance and admiration only through her musical performances. Music gave her a sense of personhood and the acclaim she earned felt like love.

She was not popular with boys, and she does not claim to have preferred piano practice to dating. "Nobody ever asked me," she admits simply. There was one boyfriend and he arrived on the scene when she was fifteen, and there he stayed until she finished college. "But we seldom saw one another. I was still a kid and very, very fat. He was a kid too, and we were never alone together. We never got to *do* anything, if you get my meaning. And we went for six years like that. By the time I graduated, he had done his thing with the Navy and we were worlds apart—spiritually, emotionally, and intellectually."

Her childhood was not made easier by her blackness. "Black people hated being black then and feeling bad about one's blackness was the code of the day," she says. "I was more brown than black and that was enviable. I was never much good at street fights and used to get beaten up something bad, but I always won with my last words. I'd scream 'You black———' at them and run like hell. You just might say I grew up with a negative black identity. Most blacks my age did. Why, it has only been in the last decade or so that black people have begun to learn and appreciate their true identity. But I was a product of my times and when I was fifteen, to be black was to be ugly. A few years later it was beautiful. Well, my head doesn't turn that fast and it took me some time to adjust to that change. It was hard for me and for a lot of other black folks to relate to Black Pride or Black Consciousness. They weren't born the day I was. Yes, indeed, it took some time but I've happily come full circle today."

She remembers the scars—like the music competition held in Richmond where she and her mother had to stay at the rat-run "hotel" for blacks while the white contestants stayed at Richmond's version of the Ritz. And she remembers her first day as a student teacher—the first black woman to hold such a job and how she received a pelting of crab apples from whites as she walked tall to her classes. The present has contributed its own wounds. When performing throughout the country, she jets minus the Afro and other Flackisms. Thus she is afforded the same treatment other "casually dressed" black women receive when they seat themselves in the first-class cabin of a plane. The stewardess invariably demands, ever so sweetly, of course, to see her ticket, assuming that the black woman has made a mistake and belongs in coach class. "Only rich whites are rich enough to travel casually" is the thinking. "Someone like me, we've got to be tricking the airline if we seat ourselves in first class."

She has made known her displeasure at this subtle discriminatory practice. She receives letters of apology but the beat goes on. About this she is not bitter. "I have plenty of that so-called black rage but I don't believe in dumping it indiscriminately. I don't think it belongs to every white person. Anyone who is white is not necessarily a bigot. Times have changed and are changing. In another twenty or thirty years things will be very different. I foresee a coming-together of people regardless of race or religious differences. I think it is people's basic need and nature to love one another."

Her own "basic need and nature" emerged when she was twenty-two. He seemingly did not have a special significance in her life other than he was her first. No man had special significance until Steven Novosel, a jazz bassist. Their interracial marriage was opposed by both families—his disowned him ("His father told him from a hospital bed as he recovered from a throat cancer operation that if Steven ever came home again, he would kill him") and her own, in the person of her brother, refused to give her away at the ceremony ("This, despite our paternal great-grandfather having been white"). The marriage ended in divorce in 1972. Of it she says, "It was great. All marriages are great until they cease being marriages. Ours failed because *we* failed to communicate. It seemed we just couldn't speak about those things that really hurt." Of her ex-husband she says, "He is today a friend, one of those fantastic good-as-gold people. He was a wonderful man to be married to. Where other men might bring their wives tulips, Steven brought me roses. And he threw them at my feet."

Theirs was never a great love affair, she admits, but "it was a good, good thing. Maybe without family hassles we might have made it. Then again, maybe not. Actually, the interference brought us even closer together and that is what we had in our marriage . . . closeness. I liked him and he liked me. Above all, that man treated me like a queen. Like a queen! No one ever did that before."

PLAYBACK

Many would treat her like a queen today. As a multi-Grammy award winner, she is at the apex of her industry and is treated like the royalty she is. Few artists would be indulged as she is by her record company, Atlantic. Most often, she takes *minimally* six months to produce one album. "My muse doesn't rush," she explains, "and then, I'd rather be a musician than a *mad*sician."

The "queen" is not impressed with the homage paid to her. In fact, she mistrusts it. She has come to her position, "the throne," with considerable struggle and late in life when one realizes that most of our rock/pop stars are barely voting and/or drinking age. Her rise to "eminence" began at fifteen, when she won a scholarship to Howard University, where she was first a piano major before switching to music education. She studied both voice and instrumental music. Work on her master's degree was suspended when her father died and she accepted a position teaching English at $2,800 per year at a black school in Farmville, North Carolina. She was hired to teach English literature but the "facts-of-life" dictated she teach basic grammar to twelfth-graders. She also taught music. A year later she passed the examinations to teach in the District of Columbia and did so for seven years in three different junior high schools. In her spare time she played the organ at church as well as directed its choir. She also coached the voice students of her own voice teacher. Additionally, she worked as an accompanist for opera singers at the Old Tivoli Gardens in the fashionable Georgetown section of Washington. Slowly she gravitated to accompanying herself, and by 1967 she was singing five nights a week at a small but popular club in Washington. That led to Sunday brunch performances at Mr. Henry's. Although the afternoon's work only produced twenty dollars, it gave her something beyond money—a reputation. Eventually she was hired to sing at Mr. Henry's in a room built solely to show-case her talents, and although it was primarily a gay club, her singing drew fashionable elite who were not of that sexual persuasion. Such music luminaries as Burt Bacharach, Al Hibbler, and Carmen McRae became part of her audience but it was jazz pianist Les McCann who arranged for an audition tape of her voice, which he sent to Atlantic Records. Her first album for that company, "First Take" sold 150,000 copies and from it came the Grammy award–winning, "The First Time Ever I Saw Your Face." Her second album, "Chapter Two," was a certified million-record seller, as was her third, "Quiet Fire," even before it was released.

QUIET FIRE (SD 1594)

Legend would make her an overnight success but actually she is a Johnny-come-lately, and as such the product of experiences both positive and negative which have made her strong, determined, and even fierce, to some. She will not be bossed or bullied, co-erced or coddled, into being what and who she is not.

"I am not going to sound like Judy Garland before she died," she says. "Nobody is going to use me up. I am going to be who and what I am and not what agents, record companies, promoters, or producers would have me be. Sure, there is this public Roberta Flack. But there is also the private and she isn't to be denied. No one is going to make me think I've got to have two Brink's trucks escorting me to my grave when I go. I'm not killing the *me* for money or fame."

Her reputation in her business has quickly become that of "difficult." She allows no one to "mess with" her. She sees her industry as a potential "head-wrecker" and tries to let none of its ugliness interfere with her music—"which is what really has me out there." She finds it is not always that simple, not al-ways possible to just "make music" and walk away from the *personality* to be the *person*. She has found she cannot leave the managing, booking, and accounting to others. "If I do, I get ripped off. And even when I'm standing there, I can be ripped off." Like it or not, she sits with her lawyer and accountant to study the books. "I just don't sign checks but examine each and every one of them. If there is one little thing I don't understand, I don't sign." She hates being *that* Roberta Flack but finds she is without choice unless she chooses to lock her doors and make music for herself. "There is no way in this business you can surround yourself with people who you believe will not rip you off. Eventually the very people you trust the most become the people you most mistrust. The temptation to steal, and the opportunities, are always there."

She finds it twice as difficult for the black woman in the entertainment industry. "Through the ages—whether it was Billie or Bessie—she has been totally unable to defend herself against that ruthless kind of person who takes her money but is not married to her; who tells her how she should live and beats up on her if she doesn't comply. The attitude, therefore, of most people, including blacks, about black female singers is that they are promiscuous and that they will align themselves with men to whom they are not married and who feed them such negative things as dope or booze. These women are seen as people who cannot hold on to anything—least of all themselves. Well, that ain't this lady. Most people in my business approach me with that stereotype in mind and they find it difficult to believe I'm not into that, that I've made it without resorting to any of those things. They keep searching for my weakness. They feel if they can find it, and then feed it, they'll own me. They'll supply anything, feed any vice you have, to keep you recording or performing. They'll hook you to hook you.

"Unfortunately many black men come on the same way with a gal who sings and who is black," she continues. "They, too, think they know what you need to survive—that if it were true for so-and-so, it has to be true for you. So the *you* becomes an object, one that must fight being that object constantly."

KILLING ME SOFTLY WITH HER SONG (SD 7271)

She is "out-front" now. Pure Flack. Real. Vibrant. There is no "technique"—just the woman.

"I've been hurt by men and I've been saddened by death and I've been abused. Name me a black person who hasn't," she says. "All black women in show business are potential victims. Let me tell you, it's damn tough for a black woman hanging out there on her own. It takes enormous strength and insane courage. Insane!

"And they have the nerve to call me *difficult*," she says with dripping irony. "You know why they do? Because this black woman will not let anyone do her in. And it's a struggle, an everyday fight. There is no one out there to protect you. No one. It's you, baby, and you alone."

And she hates it. Alone is not the state she truly desires. She has built a "shelter" in Alexandria, Virginia, where she lives with fifteen cats and seven dogs, all refugees from the pound where she has done volunteer work. She also lives with a husband-and-wife "couple" who are employed as caretakers and companions. When hiring them, she said, "I don't care who you've worked for in the past but I do care that we are able to talk to one another. 'Cause that's what I need in my home, someone to talk with."

She needs that outside her home, too, but experiences difficulties in finding it. She would prefer being with friends to being alone but has very few close companions. It gnaws at her. "You have to have somebody. You just have to. Somebody who is there. It means something. And I don't just mean a man. I've been so tempted at times to call a girl friend and say, 'Hey, c'mon and hang out with me.' But it doesn't work. It does something to their heads. All of a sudden they see me as someone other than me. They see the performer, the so-called 'star' and they say, 'Oh no!' "

She is alternately angered and saddened by her observation that people do not wish to be close, are even afraid of drawing near in a relationship. "No one really knows Roberta Flack but me. Some have gotten a few close looks but they have not been able to deal with the person, as she is too far removed from the personality. I'm not about minks and diamonds and limousines. That is not me. Most people would have me be that."

She truly believes that ever since the Roberta Flack, personality, emerged, people ceased being interested in the Roberta Flack, person. "People have this idea of how show folks should be. Well, I'm not show folk or show biz. Take away the gold records and the pretty, long dresses and I'm me. And *me* is seemingly not what's wanted."

She places the onus on others, on *their* not wanting closeness. The reverse, except in one brief, unguarded moment when she admits, "I don't give people the opportunity to get close," is not seen. She has no ready-made answer as to why people are denied the opportunity for closeness, but it would seem that any woman who has stated that it is "you and you alone out there" and who believes "you can be ripped off just standing there," is not long on trust of others. Yet this very same woman also says "I believe in mankind, believe in the goodness that is in all men." Perhaps the contradiction can best be explained by calling Roberta Flack a realist who is also an idealist.

"To live is to suffer," she says. "To survive in life is to have found a meaning to that suffering. Long ago I came to realize this is not paradise or the Garden of Eden we live in. To try to find some meaning in one's existence . . . that is the only way to survive."

She is searching for meaning, a *new* meaning, one

other than her music, by searching for relationships, particularly with males. She has had "affairs" since Novosel; one most notably was with a notable black man prominent in national affairs. That is not open for discussion. Nor is the relationship she enjoyed with a younger man. Embarrassment prevents that. Only till recently she felt "I was too old for such nonsense." But now that Victorian viewpoint is vanishing.

FEEL LIKE MAKING LOVE

She is first realizing one is never too old for romance, be it based in love or sex, she says. Poignantly she explains how for the fiirst time in her life, she *feels* young, feels what most young women of twenty feel—her desirability as a woman. She is the newly liberated woman, having recently freed herself of forty unneeded pounds but, more important, having freed herself of the negativism forty unneeded pounds add to one's personality. Although she will never have the body of Pam Grier or the sensual grace of Lena Horne, she has her own "thing" and it is surprisingly sexual. It is an attitude more than a physical presence, a womanliness, a "smell" that says "I enjoy being a female." She is currently dating many men and "digging" every minute of it.

"I can never go back to my teens or my twenties to relive what I didn't have then, but I can sure have the fun of what I missed now. I am free, fancy free! And available. Ready for crushes and if any gentleman cares, even looking forward to them with great exuberance.

"I love men," she continues, still "warming" to her subject. "I truly love men. Happily, my so-called *position* in life doesn't prevent me from meeting a man. That's not my problem. But meeting a man I would want to spend any time with, *that's* the problem. I also love love," she admits with sighs to prove her point. "I'm basically an old-fashioned girl who likes to be wooed and would love to be courted. I like flowers and phone calls. Romance. Sure I love getting down to the nitty-gritty but nowadays, it seems folks just get right down to the grit and forget the nit."

She is laughing, and is almost schoolgirlishly gay. When asked what qualities appeal to her in a man, she giggles, "His sex. He has to be a man. That's basic! A man who likes women, but most important, who likes *this* woman. I like real tall men but don't let that discourage the shorties. My only absolute must is that a man be intelligent and not afraid to show it. He must also not be afraid for his woman to be equally smart."

The relationship she searches for is based on additions rather than subtractions. She does not wish to be minus one career to be plus one man, but would prefer to share what and who she is with a man who can appreciate both. Despite the problems she experiences in the workday of Roberta Flack, she feels much joy in what she has accomplished. There are the riches, of course, but the joy is something more. It is the joy of achievement. She needs to share that.

"I would love to live with someone I love, just move in and be with him, be together. Marriage? I don't need legalities. I need a man who could really love me and who would let me love him. Oh, Lord, how I would love to do that! I have such a need to be loved and to love back." She thinks of children and admits to wanting to know the experience of having one. "But there are already too many children and perhaps the world is not yet right to bring in more. I think I shall adopt and I will love her as my own."

She stares at the question, "Are you happy?" and one sees the answer begin in her heart and then rush "upstairs" to be checked out by her award-winning mind. What emerges, this time, is pure heart.

"No, I am not," she says simply. "In truth, I am happy-sad or just plain sad. Happy? How could I be? I am lonely. I have no one to lay with."

CHAPTER TWENTY-SIX

BROOKE SHIELDS

The question arises: who and what is Brooke Shields? Is she a beautiful princess held captive by a wicked witch, a puppet who dances to the tune of a master manipulator? Is Brooke an unwilling child star forced into hard labor by an overambitious mother's fantasies? Or is Brooke, as it has been suggested, a tough-beyond-her-fourteen-years "pro," a nymphet who uses her incredible beauty to arouse dollars-and-cents interest?

Brooke Shields is certainly a phenomenon. In the next few months, she will be seen in three movies, *Tilt, Wanda Nevada,* and *Just You and Me, Kid,* as she films *Morning, Winter and Night.* She already has to her credit—or discredit—depending on your point of view, the controversial *Pretty Baby* in which she played (at age eleven) a prepubescent prostitute in a whorehouse. Then, too, there is the recently publishd *Brooke Book,* which sells for $3.95, and a commercial, made in Japan, which is reported to have paid her $250,000 for one minute of film. And Brooke's manager, mother Teri Shields, portrayed by the press as a booze-soaked "broad," the "wicked witch" in other words, now asks for and gets a staggering half million for her daughter's film appearances. It could be said that Brooke is a very rich girl indeed. It could also be said—and has been—that she is poor in the essentials.

Discovering truths about Brooke Shields takes time and patience. Teri Shields makes repeated dates and repeatedly cancels them. Seemingly, she thumbs her nose at what has been mainly a hostile press. Perhaps she feels with the monies Brooke Shields Industries is raking in, she can play the fame game by her rules. They are rude rules and they breed antagonism.

Yet when Teri Shields, with daughter in hand, is finally at your front door, preconceived notions are jarred. Although there is a guarded look in her eyes, her general manner is friendly. There is an earthy, "lived-in" quality to Teri. Her total lack of pretension in dress and attitude is surprising. She would be instantly likable if she didn't instantly announce upon her very late arrival that she must leave earlier than anticipated. No apologies are made.

And what of the "captive princess"? She says "hi" and when asked if she would like coffee says, "I would love some" and proceeds to rattle around in an unfamiliar kitchen making her own. She is assisted by her friend, Judy, an unexpected "guest" at the interview, as is Lila Wisdom, Brooke's godmother and Teri's close friend. That it is unprofessional, and rude, for them to be there either does not occur or does not matter to Teri Shields.

Brooke, after ordering out for Big Macs and serving coffee to all, settles down on the living-room floor to a wrestling match with a huge German Shepherd who is almost her size. And her size is now five feet eight inches, what with her having grown two inches in the past two months alone. She is staggeringly beautiful, this child/girl/woman, and her beauty is unembossed by cosmetics. Happily, Brooke's personality is also unembossed. This kid is strictly *au naturel*.

"We're moving," she announces suddenly, "to a big house in Jersey and we're going to reconvert the barn into a stable so I can bring my horse, Magic—Peter Fonda gave him to me after we finished filming *Wanda Nevada*—home. It's going to be a terrific house. I'm going to fill it with animals and friends."

"I hope for their sake and mine not at the same time," thrusts Teri Shields.

Brooke giggles. "Ignore her," she says, meaning her mother. "If you encourage her, she'll continue with the jokes." This time, Teri laughs. "Anyway, we never lived in a house before," says Brooke. "It'll be fun. And I'm going to have lots of dogs. I think someday maybe I'll be a veterinarian."

Only a Big Mac silences the babbling Brooke. With french fries in one hand, a hamburger in the other, and a dog's head and front paws in her lap, Brooke looks like any other teen-ager. "Well, I am like any other teen-ager," she says. "Almost, anyway. I know my life isn't typical—never has been since I started modeling at eleven months—but Mom tries to keep it usual. No matter where we go on business, Mom sees to it that a friend my age comes along so I'm not bored or just surrounded by grown-ups. And at private school I try to be just one of the kids. I know and they know I'm *that* Brooke Shields but not at school. I don't dress up for classes. Some days I look like a slob."

"Brooke!" says friend Judy exasperatedly. "You always look perfect. At your most gross you're gorgeous. You just can't help it, poor child."

The "poor child" is laughing, as is Judy, who continues, "A lot of the kids have seen *Pretty Baby* but no one talks about Brooke actually being the girl she plays."

"Boys don't approach me one way or the other," adds Brooke. "Some are cool and others are kind of shy. Mainly I have a pretty good rapport with boys, but still sometimes I have to be the one to ask them out, like to the movies. And why not? What's the big deal in a bunch of us going to see a film. It's not like we go out alone 'cause I'm not allowed to date yet. Someday, when I'm a B-i-g G-i-r-l . . ." And again Brooke is laughing, naturally, easily, and her laughter and overall demeanor dispel much of the fear about her emotional well-being. This young girl is delightful.

"Most interviewers come to find out how 'disturbed' I am," says Brooke. "They dig for dirt about me and my mom. And when they can't find any, they make it up. People think because I played a prostitute that I have to be weird. But it's people who are weird. Do you know one interviewer actually asked if I thought I'd grow up to be prostitute now that I have played one! And the things people have written about my mother. Awful things. And they don't even know her. My mom doesn't push me or make me do anything I don't want to do. In fact my mother has always told and taught me about all the other avenues open to me in life besides acting and modeling. She keeps saying I'm young and that I have many options. She's always encouraging me, making me feel good about me. And when I'm working, she's always around. People say she makes a pain of herself and maybe she does but for a reason: me! My mother sees to it, first in the contract and then on the set, that three hours of school, one for recreation, and one for lunch are provided for me. She also ensures there is a social worker who doubles as a tutor in attendance. Finally she oversees that I work only four hours a day and never before seven A.M. or after six-thirty P.M. She becomes a pain only when someone tries to break those rules."

"I'm like a hovering hawk, ready to swoop down on any infraction that affects Brooke," says Teri. "Yes, I know the social worker could do that but I don't trust my daughter to anyone's care but my own. I was thrown off the set of *Pretty Baby* for this and it's possible I'll be thrown off others, but Brooke will be protected whenever, wherever, and for whomever she works."

Brooke has been working since infancy. Obviously not by choice. Brooke doesn't argue that fact but says: "I like modeling, like posing. But what I like best," she adds, fighting back more giggles, "is the attention. Who wouldn't like a whole bunch of adults fussing over you?" And Brooke on acting: "That I *really* like 'cause you get to dress up and pretend to be what you're not."

Would it bother her if suddenly she were no longer in demand as an actress or model?

"I'd be unhappy but I'd hardly have a breakdown."

"But people would like to think *I* would!" quips Teri, which causes both mother and daughter to fall apart. The fun between them is real. It's the easy banter of friendship. Mother and daughter so obviously like *and* enjoy one another as people.

"Not always," corrects Teri. "I wouldn't say I 'enjoyed' Brooke while she was making *Tilt*. She became this addict, this monster who would wake up at the crack of dawn to play the pinball machine that the producers so kindly put in our apartment. Not one but two."

"It was wonderful!" interrupts Brooke. "In *Tilt* I'm supposed to be a pinball wizard and that's what I became. I was real good at hitting targets and jiggling the machine. When we move to Jersey, I want us to get four or five pinball machines for our playroom."

"I just decided we don't need a playroom," jabs Teri. Again the girls laugh.

"I hear John Travolta likes pinball," says Brooke. "Oh, I'd like to meet him! Almost did. Three times. But . . . well, one day, I'll meet him."

Shades of every teen-age girl's fantasy. Would Brooke like to meet a "special" boy—a Travolta of her own? "If you remove the Travolta I can answer the question. No!" she says emphatically. "All the other kids think going steady is neat, but I'd hate it. I wouldn't want to be tied down. Maybe I'll change my mind with I'm a B-i-g Girl. But now I'm having too much fun and that to me is what acting is. If it felt like work, I wouldn't do it. And when it does feel like work, I'll stop doing it.

"Actually, I'll stop when I have a baby," she continues. "Of course, I'll get married first but I think the best part of being married is having a baby. One would be just fine. I'm an only child and it's been terrific. But then I'm not really an only. My father [Frank Shields, from whom Teri has been divorced ten years after ten months of marriage] has provided me with a stepbrother and -sister and two half-sisters. They're a neat family. I see them every Sunday after church."

The radio in another room captures Brooke's attention. "Listen, that's Blondie!" she squeals. "My favorite group."

"This week!" interjects Teri.

"No really. They're super!" insists Brooke. "I may sing with them. Blondie, herself, said I could. It's a real possibility. What's really real is my singing with Leif Garrett on his TV special. I'm going to dance too."

"Well I hope you do both better than you cook," sighs Judy. "But then you would almost have to."

"That pizza was *not* that bad," snaps back Brooke. "As a matter of fact, with all that cheese and sweet sausage, it was delicious. So what if it was floating around in a foot of sauce. I'm not expected to be Julia Child."

Teri Shields is laughing. Later, when Brooke is not present, she laughs again, recalling the moment. "She's very special," says Teri, who again has made no effort to look "beautiful." Mother is obviously *not*, as some writers have suggested, living out her own fantasies of what a successful model should look like through Brooke. "That's because, contrary to what has been reported, I was never a model. I worked in the garment center as a receptionist and bookkeeper. Every now and then my boss would yell out from the showroom, 'Hey, Teri. Come put on a coat so Mr. Rosenbloom can see how it looks.' That was the extent of my modeling career. People invent stories about me . . . about Brooke and me. For the record, I have my personal problems; who doesn't. I am not, however, an alcoholic. I do not drink every day. Nor is Brooke my entire life, my *reason for being*. Till recently there was a man but . . . well, I'm only forty-six and hopefully there will be another. Meanwhile there are my friends who share my interests and my life. I'm attached to Brooke as she is to me but I don't think unhealthily or abnormally so."

Teri Shields understands why many people feel Brooke should not have been allowed to appear in *Pretty Baby* but she does not agree. "Brooke has known the facts of life for many years. I like to think I gave her a healthy view of sex. I continue to educate her on the subject. And I will always try to guide her so that she will not be hurt. Ultimately she will make her own decisions. Each person is entitled to that. But while she is my baby, I will watch her. And Brooke particularly needs watching now that she has reached puberty. That's such a difficult time for a girl. It's ironic, and regrettable, that while she is going through her most important 'changes,' I am going through mine. I tell her because of where we both are at, we have to be extra understanding of one another."

When challenged about Brooke's future—about the long-range effects of so-much-so-soon—Teri says: "Maybe I'm stupid or oblivious or both but I don't worry about Brooke. This child is firmly grounded. She has something terrific: self-respect. She'll never be used or abused."

There are many who think Brooke has been and *is* used and by Teri herself. Should a child, one who is partially dressed, pose for *Penthouse*? A pop poster of Brooke is forthcoming. Is Brooke's sexy-for-fourteen "look" being exploited? "Brooke has yet to discover she has 'wiles' to win men's hearts," says Teri. [It's true. There is nothing seductive in Brooke's attitude or manner.] "When she does, I hope she will use those 'wiles' carefully. I would not like her to be the misuser anymore than I would the misused."

As Teri Shields prepares to depart for a previous engagement, she agrees to another meeting to further discuss her management and possible exploitation of Brooke Shields Industries. "Why not? I have nothing to hide." she says. "I'll phone tomorrow to arrange a date." But true to past form, Teri Shields doesn't phone. Several days later a friend does to explain . . .

"Teri had to leave town unexpectedly . . . personal problems."

That goes without saying.

CHAPTER TWENTY-SEVEN

ANN LANDERS

"Eppie" Lederer blew into her living room with a force to rival the galelike winds that were stirring up Chicago's Lake Michigan sixteen stories below, and apologized. "Only one man in the world could make me late and it was him on the phone . . . Hubert Humphrey. What courage that man has! He's going to beat this thing, you know. It'll take more than cancer to knock Hubie out of the race.

"See this?" she asks as she waves a bejeweled pendant. "It's the vice-presidential medal. A token of his affection. Yet I never could budge him on Vietnam. 'Hubie,' I'd say. 'The war is an obscenity—one we cannot win. Talk to LBJ. Get us out!' Instead he got me to Vietnam, thinking a first-hand look and a conversation with Westmoreland would change my mind. But it didn't. 'General,' I said, 'our involvement in this war will have a corrosive effect upon our country and its youth for years to come.' And Westmoreland—what a handsome and genteel man—just looked at me askance and said: 'Madam, where do you get your information?' and then proceeded to explain how all he needed was another 100,000 men to win the war once and for always. To which I replied: 'General, where do you get *your* information?'

"Terrible war. Terrible aftereffects," says Eppie, shaking that famous head with its wingspread hairdo that instantly identifies her to sixty million readers in 940 newspapers as Ann Landers. "The war and the Nixon administration have undermined morality in this country. Disgusting how those Watergate people are cleaning up with their books. What a deplorable example. No wonder people are angry. . . . Here, have some chocolate cake! No? What about some cheese and crackers. Got some *wonderful* cheese.

"All this anti-Semitic and black sentiment. All from the war and the Nixon years. You never saw that kind of thing in the fifties when we were peaceful. But negative times bring out negative thoughts and actions in people. When people are insecure as they are now, they look for scapegoats. Jews and blacks have always been vulnerable targets. All minorities are. I tell you," says Eppie Lederer, the eye of her storm passing directly through the beige and bronze of her living room, "the Vietnam War did more damage to the national psyche than we know.

"Look at what happened in New York City during the blackout. Some blacks saw a chance to get something for nothing and they took it. And they reasoned . . . why not? The system isn't working for these people. They see the pie and they want a piece of it. When they can't buy it, they take it. They don't see it as stealing, which is another sad commentary on the times.

"And these are times to try men's souls. Like that Anita Bryant dame. Why I would sooner leave *any* grandchild [she has three] of mine with a homosexual than I would with her! Where does she come off saying homosexuals recruit our young when any psychiatrist will tell you that's not their bag. Such lies . . . such distortions. Boy, if there is one thing I distrust it's someone who thinks God talks directly to him. Listen, have a piece of fruit!"

She is a marvel, this Esther Pauline, "Eppie" Lederer, a truly bionic and wonder woman. Soon to be sixty, her energy is that of ten and at half her age. As Ann Landers she writes her own daily column and radio show, her speeches, and such pamphlets as "Teen-Age Sex and Ten Ways to Cool It." She is currently compiling *The Ann Landers Encyclopedia of Problems—From A to Z*, which Doubleday will publish next spring. All this proves there is a lot of money to be made in chicken soup. And make no mistake, it *is* chicken soup Eppie Lederer dispenses to the masses. She is a former Jewish princess from Sioux City, Iowa, who now as Queen shares (some say reluctantly) her throne with her twin sister, Pauline Esther ("Po-Po"), better known to millions as Abigail Van Buren or Dear Abby.

"Dear Eppie" employs eight secretaries to assist in answering the one thousand letters that arrive daily. "I couldn't call myself a counselor if I didn't make help available to all who ask for it. That's time-consuming work. Since I do not consider myself an authority on anything, I go to the authorities to get my information. I'll leave no source untapped—to the Pope if necessary!—to get answers for my readers. That's why I never feel guilty playing God. I give each reader the best counsel I can provide, and at *no* cost, through the very best experts in the field. And then I let go. I try to be right for my people but if I'm wrong, I don't torture myself."

Eppie Lederer so obviously enjoys being Ann Landers. "Honey, if I didn't love this work, I'd be bananas in a week. Speaking of which, how about a banana . . . nice, ripe one. Maybe some melon? . . . For twenty-two years I've been performing a service, being a friend to some people who have no one. I take these people's problems very seriously but never personally. If I allowed myself to feel all the world's emotional pain, I'd be a basket case even *before* I'd be bananas. Being Ann Landers is no phony baloney with me. And my readers know this. After twenty-two years they've come to know me pretty well.

"And the rewards are more than money," says Eppie, gathering up strength for another Big Blow.

"Like at the airport café in Fort Worth last week the waitress just put her arms around me and hugged. I like that. Boy, is it good to feel that kind of love from people! I've never had anyone say anything but the nicest words to my face. Behind my back? That's something else again. The anti–gun control and the anti-abortion people hate me. But I believe guns kill people and that a woman's body belongs solely to her. And nothing, bubs, is going to change my mind.

"Not that I'm always that irretractable," powers on Eppie. "Why, if someone had ever told me years ago that I'd reverse my position on interfaith and inter-racial marriages, I'd have sent them to the Menninger Clinic to have their heads examined! But today statistics prove interfaith marriages work as well, or as badly, as any. Even I, Eppie Lederer, a nice Jewish girl, would now date and perhaps marry a man of another religion. I guess I've come a long way, baby.

"But the name of the game is staying-in-step. Never look back, I say, because there is never anything there to see. Not really. In my day any girl who 'fooled around' before marriage was considered a tramp. But times change. Many women today enjoy a sex life without the legal bindings of marriage. Are they tramps? Hardly. They are adults living their lives as they see fit. I make no judgments *except* where teen-agers are concerned. Their bodies may be willing—all *too* willing—but their emotions are weak. They are simply not mature enough, other than physically, to handle an adult relationship.

"The role of woman in today's society has changed and I've changed with it. Which is a darn good thing, 'cause the day this kid stops growing and changing is the day she should get out of the business. Listen! Are you sure you wouldn't like a piece of chocolate cake? You can afford it. You're in great shape."

As is she. Her face is either miraculously or surgically unlined and her body, as her clinging brown jersey pants suit displays, is firm and trim. "I watch what I eat," she explains, "watch it go from my plate to my mouth. Cake, cookies, ice cream, I eat them all. But I exercise thirty minutes and walk three miles each day. That and a twelve- to fourteen-hour work-day keeps me lean. Then, too, I've always been blessed with terrific amounts of energy. And good health too. I haven't had so much as a cold in a year. Knock wood! Which is why I'd never retire. I feel too good. Besides, what would I do? Play cards with the girls? Shop at Saks? Neither is my bag. No! So long as I'm vital, so long as I have something to give and people let me give it, I'm giving it. No retirement for this girl. Not while I'm in the one slot I was meant to occupy . . . living the exact life I wish to live. Besides, I'm an active rather than a passive person. I have great strength . . . a handle on things. I'm in control."

Such statements have made Landers/Lederer seem unreal, without emotions or needs, to many people. Some believe Lederer hides herself to protect the Landers's image. "Not so," says Eppie earnestly. "I know many think of me as steel-plated but . . . I'm not a leaner, or a complainer. I'm a very secure woman who was a very secure child. I felt loved by my parents. And then there was Po-Po. There still *is* Po-Po. We were always so close, the other sides of one another. I am a very lucky person in that I have never known pain or failure. Nor have I ever been lonely. Some speak of an inner loneliness or an inner pain that is indefinable but there. I've never felt ei-ther. Nor have I ever felt frightened by life. I'm just basically strong . . . fulfilled and happy. And you know what? I'm sick of apologizing for being who I am. I'm not protecting any image. And I'm not steel-plated. I do have needs.

"Like right now, I feel the need to be married. I hate the thought of spending the rest of my life with-out a husband. It's been more than two years since the divorce from Jules and I'm ready to meet *the* man. And Lord knows I'm trying! Why not? I had thirty-six years in a wonderful marriage. It was such a shock when *he* ended it. But the shock and the pain and anger is gone. Actually it went within a day of counseling. I searched my heart and I truly felt I had done everything I could to be a good wife. I was faithful . . . supportive, and he was very good to me. I simply couldn't believe it at first when I heard there was someone else."

A look that passes over her face says she still has difficulty believing it. She does not deny this, nor does she choose to pursue it. "What difference why there was another? Once I knew she existed, I knew my marriage could not: that there was no way I would want to keep it together. No . . . I simply wished him well. I still do. I hear she's a lovely girl. I hope they are happy. Me? I'm looking for my own happiness. But it's not that easy for someone like me to meet a man. Times have changed, but in some respects I haven't. I'm still a 'Shirley,' a nice Jewish girl who believes in saving 'it' for the wedding night. I couldn't be comfortable having sex without marriage. Some men respect this; others . . . well, they're not for me."

She is finding that many men are not for her. Those who see her as "Ann" instead of "Eppie" are ruled out, as are those who view her as a celebrity. She admits many potentials are initially threatened by her image. "They think I'm going to be hard-boiled. They're wrong. I'm not a ball-breaker. I'm Eppie.

"It will probably take one helluva man to marry me and for me to marry," says Eppie, "but I had me one and I'll have me another. Right now I don't know who or where he is. But . . . he's out there for me and I intend to find him. I must. I have been so darn lucky. I have so much to share. And not being married is like trying to clap with one hand.

"How about you," the "storm" says as it shifts

course. "Are you married? No? How come a nice Jewish boy like you isn't. Listen . . ."

Eppie, you wouldn't. Eppie, you couldn't. She did.

"The next time you're in Chicago, I know this nice girl . . . very refined, pretty . . ."

CHAPTER TWENTY-EIGHT

CAROL BURNETT

"I want to marry again," said Carol Burnett, "but not to an actor. Two performers in one household makes for ego problems. I need a man in show business who is successful in his own right, a guy who won't feel threatened by my success and who will be dominant in our home."

Carol Burnett made another significant statement that summer day in 1962 as we lunched shortly after her divorce from actor Don Soroyan. "I want children, a houseful, and if my career goes as planned, I'll only be gone three or four hours a day [Broadway was then her goal] and thus won't be an absentee mother or wife."

Fourteen years later Carol Burnett is in her thirteenth year of marriage to Joe Hamilton, a successful producer and a man who is secure both in his work and in his home. Together they have "produced" *The Carol Burnett Show*, now entering its tenth year on television and three sun-bleached and beautiful children—Carrie, twelve; Jody, nine; and Erin, seven. There are also eight Burnett stepchildren from Hamilton's former marriage who frequently visit the Hamilton homes in Beverly Hills and Malibu Beach. A houseful of kids is what Carol wished for and it is what she got. And guess what? She works as little as three to five hours, four days per week, which makes her more an absentee star than mother.

By what miracle Carol Burnett has achieved a healthy relationship with both her husband and her children, as she has maintained her starlike and award-laden status, is the question. Few other Hollywood couples share the successes the Hamiltons seem to have.

Carol Burnett gags when she hears herself grouped as part of a "Hollywood couple." Then she giggles. "Oh, that's a hoot! Joe and I . . . Hollywood?" She hoots some more. "Wait and I'll change into a sequined gown so I can look more the type." Actually she looks terrific in a sleeveless, orange, scoop-necked sweater and white slacks that hug a body more associated with a girl of twenty than a woman of forty-three. Her husband, Joe, at that moment out of earshot, persuing the newspapers as he sips his morning coffee, is also attractive. Miraculously, he seems impervious to the bedlam his daughters are creating as they engage in a bloodthirsty game of bumper pool—their roars all but drowning those of the ocean which spills onto the sands just outside the Hamilton's summer home in Malibu. Carol, nibbling canteloupe, is also impervious to the noise of her girls but not to the "Hollywood couple" tag. That continues to tickle her.

She has changed greatly in fourteen years. It is more than a weight loss and an attractiveness that bloomed late and which television does not capture. It is about serenity. Is it possible this is the same woman who wept as a recent divorcee those years, "I get so lonely I could cry?" I think not. This Carol Burnett is, to use a worn cliché, "together" and it is doubtful both that she would feel loneliness today *or* admit to it. She has become a very private person, who despite her accessibility to the press, hides behind such lines as "I'm really very dull—not a Marisa Berenson or anyone of the jet set. Just an ole married lady who happens to have her own television show and thus a modicum of fame. Mine is really a very average life."

Contrary to her poses—and they are that—Carol

Burnett is not dull. When she appears "itsy-poo" (her words) in articles written about her, it is of her own doing. Everything is always j-u-s-t w-o-n-d-e-r-f-u-l with Carol, her husband, the marriage, and kids. She resists the pokings of the press into privacies she shares with a very few. She has been wisened sadly but well by prior press experiences that ripped at her. Today Carol Burnett is like a successful, high-class stripper: she reveals just so much and no more. Furthermore she admits to this and makes absolutely no apologies for her refusal to bare all. Most definitely this Carol Burnett is different from that of fourteen years ago!

Much of the change is recent and is credited to her studies in yoga and meditation. Both have been well chronicled by the press. This morning, in Malibu, she is explaining that "nothing bothers me anymore. I live as much as possible in the now. No more the regrets for what was yesterday or for what tomorrow might bring."

If you are curious as to what "regrets" Carol Burnett might have, perhaps when she writes her autobiography—"at age seventy-five"—your curiosity will be satisfied. Till then . . . Happy Conjecture! The most you are going to get of Carol Burnett today is at 10:00 P.M. each Saturday on CBS. She feels she owes you—the public—nothing. To her credit, unlike other stars, she doesn't gush-and-goo about how she owes it all to this-and-that-one. Her only debt that she feels is to herself. "A public doesn't own a performer and *no* performer owns a public. For either to think otherwise is dangerous. I own me and no one else. My worth doesn't change with or without an Emmy award or a renewal or cancelation notice. I love my work—I love the people for whom I perform—but I need neither to survive. I no longer look without for answers, but within. I haven't reached my goal—that of fully knowing who and what I am, but I have upon occasion reached the God that lives within us all. Meditation has helped me *know* God, which is far different than believing in Him."

And this, seemingly, has made her serene. It is remarkable to watch her over the course of the week. She is so comfortable within her clothes, herself, her marriage, and her home that one is tempted to take her pulse to see if she is alive. How can this be the same woman who entered yoga because of "terrible tension" and "incessant headaches"? She explains *how*. "I have learned to please me first. If I do that, then it follows I can be pleasing to Joe and the children. And all else lines up after that."

It results that hers are more than just words. Home-hearth-and-Hamilton, as everyone connected with Carol attests to, means far more than a hefty Nielsen rating. But she has it all and the trick that gorgeous morning is to get Carol Burnett to reveal how she has attained the "impossible dream"—how she has so successfully combined the various Carol Burnetts.

Again she reacts to a phrase. "There are no *various* Carol Burnetts," she states. "Wife, mother, person, performer, are not separate entities to be managed. We're but one. The kids come first, period. That's instinctual. Since the kids also come first with Joe, I'm not at odds with anything. My *basic* life is about my family."

She has managed that by arranging bankers' hours, only no banker ever had it so good. Other than for Friday, which is a dawn-to-dusk taping day, she works an average of four hours a day. She has insisted on one week off each month and her summers are totally free. Thus she sees as much of her children as any mother. Dinner in the Hamilton house is served promptly at 6:30 and *all* members of the family are present and accounted for. Unless Carol and Joe are invited out to a friend's home—which is their usual way of socializing as opposed to nightclubs or "openings,"—Carol is home to bed down the youngest at

8:00 P.M. and the eldest at 9:00. Says Joe Hamilton: "Few other mothers give the quantity and quality of time to their children that Carol does. She tends to all their needs—except, unfortunately, the discipline. That she leaves to me."

According to their friends there is much Carol Burnett "leaves" to her husband. Mitzie Welch, a Burnett buddy of near twenty years and who with her husband Ken is one of the TV show's special music coordinators, says, "It would be very easy for a woman in Carol's position to castrate her husband. Carol never does. She is very protective of Joe and never wants anyone to think she runs the show—which she doesn't—or that Joe merely hangs on. Carol goes out of her way to let us know who is boss, which, incidentally, is unnecessary. By nature Joe is a very strong person who commands respect. He *is* the boss. He never was and never will be a Mr. Burnett, while Carol most definitely is Mrs. Hamilton."

Mrs. Hamilton insists she does not feel the least bit protective of her husband. "Joe takes care of himself. I'm not on guard in public. I don't play the shrinking violet so that Joe can appear to be the blooming rose. I don't have to make Joe feel important because he *is* important. What's more, he knows it. Joe has a very strong sense of who he is. We don't have to play at that."

And indeed they do not. Hamilton, when questioned privately, was charmingly candid. "I don't feel a Mr. Burnett because I have been a successful producer long before Carol exploded onto this business. Remember, I'm the guy who *hired her* for *The Garry Moore Show* [which elevated Carol to stardom]. Also I produce film features and TV specials which have nothing to do with Carol. I am not, nor have I ever been, threatened by Carol's success. Hell! I've been producing for seventeen years and have only been out of work six months in all that time."

There is no doubt when speaking repeatedly with

Hamilton that this is a strong man, one with his own sense of self and serenity. Mitzie Welch's capsule comment is eminently believable. "From the beginning Carol respected Joe's talent. She also saw his strength. I think she married him for that. She needed it. She also needed his compassion and his humanity. Joe, the person, commands Carol's respect."

In assessing the Burnett/Hamilton working relationship, Tim Conway, one of the show's costars, says, "No one on the staff doubts the buck stops with Joe. His decisions are final but he will never make Carol do anything she feels is wrong for her." Artie Malvin, another ten-year man and another of the show's special music coordinators, adds: "One learns quickly not to go to Carol for special favors, as she instantly defers to Joe. And I think her deferring is spontaneous rather than a calculation to make Joe feel important. He doesn't need that."

Hamilton reveals that Carol defers in many areas of their married life. Their new home, built at her insistence, was nonetheless overseen solely by Hamilton. "All Carol asked for was a yoga room and a closet the size of Minneapolis, and she got both," says Hamilton. The family finances are also largely left in Hamilton's hands. "Carol has no idea how much money she earns per week or per year. She doesn't want to know," says Hamilton. "Carol would rather put her energies where she feels they are most needed, which is herself, our marriage, and the children. Believe me, she is no slave to her stardom. If the show was canceled, she'd be depressed for a week, maybe two, and then she'd gather up the girls and go surfing or hiking or just browsing about."

"Carol and Joe are the only people in television who schedule rehearsals around PTA meetings," laughs Mitzie Welch. "They hang their kids' drawings all over the office and there is always a new anecdote about the girls we must listen to." As Harvey Korman, a friend and a costar, says: "With Carol and Joe you are dealing with old-fashioned, old-world parents. They are very united in raising the kids together. They are intent on teaching the girls to respect themselves and the rights of others. Although one doesn't get *that* close to what goes on within the Hamilton house, I would venture the girls have received a very solid foundation. There are values and ethics at work here."

The Hamiltons shield their children from the press. Although I was introduced to the girls—who were totally disinterested in the fact I was there to do a story on their mother—they were not available for interview. Only twice have they been photographed and both times it wrecked the Burnett serenity. "It is hard enough for an adult to handle success and publicity without foisting it on a child. Adults whose names and faces frequent the front pages of newspapers usually veer very left or very right by the adoration or its reverse, so think what that can do to a child! I don't want the girls thinking they are special—lording it over their classmates because their picture is in the paper—when they are not. They are special as people but not as celebrities. When they go out and earn their own TV shows, they become fair game. Right now I want them to live as normal a life as possible. Believe me, that *Carol Burnett thing* never steps past our front door. Even out, I'm not bugged a lot. Lots of people find this hard to believe, but I don't get mobbed. I don't have that Elizabeth Taylor type of fame. Thank God! Yes, there are autograph seekers and that's kind of nice, except maybe when you're trying to be *très* elegant stuffing fettuccine in your face at your local pizzeria. But as I have told the girls, fame is nothing to be distressed or impressed by because it comes and it goes. The only thing that remains is *you* and that's important."

That last statement is very important in understanding Carol Burnett. Fame came very rapidly to her and in the form of enormous love. Then it was followed by some really bum years in which she was much more "out" than "in." Her career was struggling—in peril actually, when *The Carol Burnett Show* debuted ten years ago. In polls among would-be advertising/television experts, it was one of two shows given the least likely chance of making it. In other words Carol Burnett has experienced that "fickle finter of fate" and as she explains, "I'm not about to put all my eggs into that lady's [meaning the public Carol Burnett] basket. Had I done that, both the eggs and I would have been pretty well scrambled by now." Thus when she tells her girls "the only thing that remains is you," she knows of what she speaks.

Both the Hamiltons worry about becoming "impossible parents." Says Carol, "Joe is even more prudish than I. He would prefer none of the girls yet see a film rated Parental Guidance. He is also selective about what they read and more importantly what they wear. Now I'm a nut of a different kind. I just know when the girls begin to date, I'm going to want to chaperone. I'm also going to want to wait up for them . . . at the door . . . with a list of questions. Joe promises to lock me in the closet if I do. I think maybe I better take all the locks off the closet doors very soon."

Asked how she will then deal with youth's new sexual morality, considering her own puritanism, she says, "I haven't the vaguest idea. I'll probably go to my yoga room and breathe a lot." She laughs, but then suddenly she adds: "Our kids are very sound physically and emotionally. They know Joe and I treasure them. We also trust them. Each will make the right decision for herself." Only one potential problem with her girls gnaws at Carol. Both she and Joe "have an open dialogue with the girls. I worry about losing that one day. You know how kids are: they grow up and suddenly think their parents don't know anything anymore—aren't hip."

"That's a needless worry," says Hamilton. "The girls really dig Carol. She is their mother, *first,* but she is also a friend."

"We don't pry into our kids' lives," says Carol, "but as I've told Carrie, who is soon to be a teen-ager, 'If ever you want to talk with your ole lady about anything, I'm here.' You can't do much more than that. Funny, when I was a girl growing up, I so much wanted feedback from my mother, but she was an alcoholic and couldn't give it."

Her answer is an instantaneous "No!" when asked if she worries about ever losing an "open dialogue" with Joe. "We're adults. We're also let's-sit-down-and-talk people where there is something that needs discussing. No, I never worry about the future for Joe and me as husband and wife. Besides, I never think in terms of *forever,* although I hope our marriage will be just that."

Their friends and associates believe the Hamiltons have a shot at lifetime marital longevity. "These are firmly rooted people," explains Tim Conway, "rooted in themselves and in one another. There's a oneness here based on mutuality of interests and goals."

There is also sex. Harvey Korman recalls that in April, at his golf tournament in Palm Springs, "The Hamiltons were like teen-agers—holding hands and smooching. It was really rather touching." Artie Malvin finds the affection between Carol and Joe "minimal in the work situation but there. It's a quiet thing . . . a look that passes between the two or a touch. And every lunchtime Carol takes her tray into Joe's office."

"It's the only place where she can watch *All My Children* in peace," says Hamilton. "My being there is incidental."

"It is also where Carol can be totally Carol," says Mitzie Welch. "Not that Carol is ever false or phony—hardly, but there is that part of her no one sees or touches but Joe. That part of her is very deep and takes full responsibility for her own life. Carol doesn't ask Joe to make her happy. She works at that herself. He is the same. In other words they don't place demands upon one another that neither can fulfill."

Artie Malvin adds a final point. "There is a give and take in their relationship I've seldom seen in any marriage. In ten years I've seen them disagree and argue, but healthily. Carol has never walked off her set in a rage—Joe has never put his foot down arbitrarily—because they can talk things out. In working with them, because they are so totally above board, there is no guesswork involved. I would suspect there is as little guesswork involved in their at-home relationship."

Joe Hamilton nods his head in agreement. "We're not likely to hold things back from one another. From the day we met, we kind of had this sixth sense with one another. It's called being tuned in. Like at work, although we've never discussed this, intuitively we knew not to bring our husband-and-wife relationship to the set. That would have been a terrible trap. At CBS Carol is the star of the show and treated as such and I am the producer. Although we can, and do, bring our work home, the roles remain at the studio."

If one is to believe all those closest to the Hamiltons, theirs is that miracle . . . a problemless marriage.

"The hell it is!" snaps Hamilton. "No marriage is problemless and all take work. Even ours. Happily, Carol and I have always had the ability to look at our problems and knock them down to size. And while we're at it, let's clear up another misconception about Carol. She is not problemless—just very private. She is still hesitant about standing on a stage, as Carol Burnett, and singing a straight song. She still cannot take a compliment—particularly one about her appearance—with any great ease. She still has her depressions, as we all do, periodically. She still spreads herself too thin. If someone needs her emotionally, she runs. Having dealt with her own pain, she can understand and feel another's."

And what is Carol Burnett's pain? Hamilton shrugs and is purposely vague. ". . . her childhood, the lack of parental attention and love . . . the trust she put in others which was sometimes misused. Carol remains, despite her years in this business, a lady with thin skin. She is hypersensitive and easily hurt. She cannot understand why some have a need to lie or distort the truth. This makes her appear 'simple' to some but I find it rather beautiful. I never interfere in her press or personal relations but I do react when she's hurt. I feel bad for her but I do not try to protect—at least no more than any man tries to protect the woman he loves."

And does Carol Burnett Hamilton need protection? "Yes, sometimes," says Hamilton slowly. "She still reacts inwardly when she is angry or hurting. Like if a guest star comes on too strong or is rude and obnoxious, Carol, instead of speaking out, goes inward. I can always spot it. She becomes quiet, much *too* quiet. A shield rises between her and the world. You cannot be gruff with Carol. Nor can you attack her. Both make her withdraw and when that happens, no one and nothing can reach her until she decides to be reached. My wife is a gentle lady and she is beautiful and yes . . . there are times because she is gentle, because she is beautiful, that she needs protection."

The very next day is one of those times when Carol Burnett needs, it would appear from the chagrined look on her face, protection. She is being asked directly why her marriage works and the question is producing mass discomfort. The shield rises. "Well, Joe has this terrific sense of humor," she begins. "We giggle a lot. And we never get bored with one another. Do you know that in thirteen years I've only twice taken a separate vacation?" She is straining. "We're so

. . . compatible. That's it, compatible!" But suddenly she finds safe turf and the shield rises. "You know what's particularly terrific about Joe? His working relationships. His head is screwed on straight and he is totally without BS. And he doesn't need to be loud to get his way. In fact, at meetings, the louder people get, the quieter Joe becomes until his quiet becomes so loud that people stop to listen. But he is never dictatorial. He'll never make me, or any employee, do anything that goes against the grain." She laughs. "Joe often says I don't always know what's right for me but I intuitively know what's wrong. I'm not exactly sure what he means but it sounds terrific, doesn't it?" Again she laughs, comfortable now that she has shifted from what has been the personal to the professional. By doing so, she has managed to avoid speaking of the emotional content of her marriage and the feelings she has for the man with whom she has shared the last thirteen years. Nailed for having done so, she says with characteristic candor: "Look, if I ran around talking about the meaning of my marriage, then it would no longer be mine. To share what is solely Joe's and mine . . . well, then it would belong to others and not just to us. Something vanishes when you share it indiscriminately. Our marriage is *our* marriage. People know we get along—that we like each other . . . *love* each other, and that's really all they need to know. What they see is what they get."

I try one more time. "Carol, what does marriage fulfill within you?"

She looks anxious again and I expect her to begin Yoga breathing exercises and meditate me out of her life. "What does marriage fulfill within me?" she echoes dimly. "My need to have a date Saturday nights," she hoots, and before I can interrupt, she's off and running. "Wouldn't it be awful to have to go through all that dating stuff again—wondering who

would call and would he have a car and would he try
to get fresh. Ugh! The thought is awful."

A silence grows within the room. Only the ocean
can compete with it. And then suddenly the silence is
gone, broken by a very soft voice that says, "We allow
one another to be. Just to be. That's a gift, you know.
There are many such gifts in marriage. Before, when
we talked about 'forever,' I wasn't totally honest. I
don't think in terms of 'forever' but . . . there has
never been a doubt in my mind that Joe and I could
make it forever. I can't imagine a problem arising in
our lives that would be insurmountable. You asked
what marriage fulfills in me. How does anyone really
answer that? It's an anchor . . . a comfort. It's companionship of the kind I wish for everybody. God!
Knowing someone cares for you . . . *loves you,*
that you feel good with, safe with . . . who you
love and care for . . . what else is there?

"I know," says Mrs. Joe Hamilton, "that this will
sound horribly 'itsy-poo' but there is nothing lacking
in my life . . . nothing further I could wish for.
We have everything. *I* have everything and I'm not
talking about possessions or fame but about *here* and
now, with Joe, my children, and me."

CHAPTER TWENTY-NINE

CLEO LAINE

Cleo Laine stood ankledeep in roses, violets, and marigolds, the gifts of an adoring audience who had strewn the stage of Carnegie Hall in flowering tribute to her artistry. It was an audience of all sizes, shapes, and colors, a mixed bag of sexes and sexualities. Hand in hand in their musical appreciation, they harmonized well with one another, erasing for the evening the line between "straights" and "heads."

The mingling of such masses could only have taken place for Cleo Laine, who is, at her very best, "a mixed bag" herself. Musically she is somewhere between Ella and Sarah with a little Leontyne thrown in for spice. Artistically she is closer to Streisand. The total effect, however, is unequivocably Cleo Laine, whom *The New York Times* called "a national treasure" and whom Leonard Feather, America's most recognized musicologist, termed "the greatest all-around singer in the world."

Cleo Laine is British born and bred and only recently exported to this country. She is a black woman who is also white and a white woman who is also black. She is neither more one than the other. Among musicians, both here and in England, she is the current most revered name in music. In her native land she has disproven that a Jack-of-all-trades is a master-of-none by moving with vocal ease from Jazz and pop singing to center stage with several opera companies. As an actress she has appeared in such musical comedies as *Showboat* but also in such "heavies" as Shakespeare's *A Midsummer Night's Dream* and in the title role of Ibsen's *Hedda Gabler*.

Her reputation in America is first blossoming. She was initially heard here in 1971 when her husband, John Dankworth, suddenly realized that those strange sounds Americans made were really that of the English language, and since his wife sang in English, the two should be wedded. He rented Alice Tully Hall at Lincoln Center, where his wife proceeded to convince those that attended, a handful at best, that all was not lost in the British Empire. The "man" from *The New York Times* was near orgasmic in his following-day review and he, as much as her RCA recordings, is credited with beginning the Cleo cult.

Since then there has not been a Cleo Laine concert that has not sold out in the major cities where she appears. Mike Douglas and Merv Griffin appearances have been helpful, as has been a show-stealing segment on a recent "Cotton Club" special. Within her industry Cleo Laine sits at the stairway to superstardom; roses, violets, and marigolds, and the consistently used "the greatest" strewn upon each step awaiting her ascent. She sat there twenty years ago, to be exact. Then in England she scaled the heights effortlessly and enthusiastically. Today she hesitates. Once you have climbed Everest, to climb it again is anticlimactic. She has "done her thing" in England and has been handsomely rewarded for it. A "rerun" in the United States, although flattering and tempting, is not her *raison d'être*. The promise of prize plums means as little (or as much) to the lady as the rotten tomato thrown by one reviewer who after lauding her professionalism damned his praise by adding, "She is however a bit of a cold fish."

Upon first meeting, Cleo Laine seems to fit that description. She is not bright, bubbly, or bombastic as she sits, almost wearily, in her suite at the St. Regis Hotel in New York where she, her husband, and hotplate are entrenched for a three-week run at the hotel's nightclub. She is pleasant but pooped, her bubbles and brightness stranded somewhere between Pittsburgh and Peoria. This is the last leg of her three-month tour of the States and she is feeling its effects. A younger woman might have been bombastic, as a crash through the doors to fame usually erases fatigue. But Cleo Laine is no young chick, no hit-record *pheenom*, about to enter the Big Time. She is "forty-something-or-other" and without the urgency to be a superstar in this country. If she were not pushed, prodded, and poked, she would undoubtedly sit at the bottom of that staircase to superstardom, ponder its heights, and then go home unless an elevator miraculously appeared to trip her to the top.

She is making instant coffee, oblivious to the three phones that continuously ring. She looks amused, as though enjoying a private joke. She is. Instant coffee and hotplates in the St. Regis as consumed by "the greatest" does have its irony. She laughs, a deep throaty chortle, and then dumps herself into an oversized and overstuffed chair. She sits and looks directly at the questions coming toward her. Without makeup and without trying, she is a remarkably handsome woman, distractingly so. She is as instant as her coffee. There is no prepared-by-press agent "junk," just Cleo Laine. The "cold fish" proves to be "English reserve." Yes she lacks the *burning* intensity that halos most stars, but in her own evaluation she is not a star but is, in the following order, a woman/person; wife; and mother to Alec, fourteen; Jacqueline, eleven; and Stuart, twenty-six; the last born of a marriage that preceded the one currently entering its eighteenth year to John Dankworth.

It is he who has the ambition for Cleo Laine, he who pushes, prods, and pokes at his wife to climb Everest once again. But he is not the stereotyped "greedy" male pimping for his talented woman. Dankworth is a master in his own right, a musician, composer, arranger, who has during the last twenty-

five years frequently earned his Musician of the Year
award. He is no Mr. Cleo Laine. He *was* before she
was and he *is* as she is becoming. Upon meeting Cleo
twenty-five years ago when she auditioned to be his
band's singer, he instantly felt "she had the stuff of
greatness." It is a matter of pride—his, not hers, that
insists she be recognized throughout the world and
not just in England.

The Dankworths like one another and if that reads
like an unexciting statement that is how their relationship at surface seems. Neither is given to
describing the other or their relationship with any
great excess of emotion. Passion? Forget it. They are
both too English for that. But they do giggle at one
another a lot, do disagree, contradict, and com-
promise. They work as well and as naturally together
in a hotel suite as they do on a stage. He credits the
success of their marriage to "total incompatibility."
As she chokes on her coffee, he elucidates that they
have "just about nothing in common. She loathes
blues and reds, which are my favorite colors, while I
dislike the browns and greens she favors. She is terribly working class, poor girl, while I, coming as I do
from a middle-class background, am rather snobby.
Frankly I'm a bit of a social climber."

"Impossible is what he is," she states soberly. "Positively disgusting the way he awakes, bright-eyed and
ready to push off into work. Ugh! Everything about
me is half of John. I wake up slowly and can, at best,
do two things at a time to his ten. He thrives on
America's double time, loves the pace here. Not me.
I'm falling apart. After this tour I'll come apart at
home, become a virtual slob, while he'll rest an hour,
maybe two, and then rush about working like stink."

"It is the price a man pays for marrying a *much
older woman*," stabs Dankworth, who is in reality a
few years older than his wife.

"He *is* impossible," she says, scowling but obviously

enjoying every moment of Dankworth's explanation of their "total incompatibility."

"You know our differences often work to our advantage, however," he says quietly, suddenly serious. "I can be so damned intellectual. Cleo often helps me to see the heart and soul of matters. She is the emotional one of us two, the *feeler,* so to speak. She, more than I, gets involved in life and in particular with people. She cannot look at social injustice or brutality without bleeding all over the place."

The inference is that he can but he fools no one. Dankworth is no heart-on-sleeve man. But in England, with his wife, he helped organize the charity gala for Bangladesh and the Wavedon Allmusic Plan, a nonprofit charity that presents concerts and music education courses for children. The latter takes place within their 115-year-old home set on seventeen acres in the English countryside. They have converted what were stables into a mini concert hall where both teach as well as perform. But Dankworth's emotional involvement in life is deeper than that of "do-gooder." He is emotionally involved with his woman and the involvement is color blind. He is almost annoyed when it is intimated that it takes courage for a person to marry outside his own color. "I married a woman, not a skin tone," he snaps. "That she was black was beautiful. That she was white was beautiful. That she *was*—that's the miracle." Musicians, he claims, are all basically color blind. "You hear a person's soul in the music he or she makes. It is that which you come to love or dislike." Their marriage has never encountered any difficulty in England. "I think the kind of racial interference most interracial couples experience is more indigenous to America than to England, where we have never known the racial strife you Americans have."

A partial truth. Racial interference, as Dankworth calls it, exists on a much more subtle level in England, but exist it does, as witnessed by Cleo Laine's

father and by the lady herself. Born and raised in
Southall, Middlesex, England, Dinah Clemintina
(Cleo) Campbell, was often called "nigger" and
"fuzzy-wuzzy" as a child. Her father, Alexander
Campbell, was the "town black," and one of but
twenty-five West Indians living in all of England in
the 1920's. The townfolk were more likely to close
than open doors for him, but since he was a proud
and fiercely motivated man, he circumvented man-
made obstacles by making work for himself when it
was denied him.

Minnie Campbell was a farmer's daughter who left
home, hearth, husband, and middle-class respectabil-
ity to marry Cleo's father, an act which found her instantly disowned by her vehemently white parents.

"My mum didn't give much of a damn about public opinion," says Cleo. "She was a strong woman
with a mind of her own and a fierceness to survive
that was as strong as my father's. They were a bloody
good match. Nothing and nobody could break them.
When Dad couldn't get work because of his color,
they went into the boardinghouse business, renting
rooms to foreigners. Hard times? Plenty. But we
kids—and there were three of us—never felt it. We
had a rip-roaring childhood. Real hellers we were.
Our parents raised us with equal amounts of love and
clouts. We got what we deserved. Pride was instilled
in us at a very early age. We were the Campbells and
best not to forget that! I remember once visiting my
mum's sister, my aunt, in her elegant home in London
and hearing her say 'Oh, Minnie, how could you have
made such a mess of your life!' M'mum didn't say a
word but marched me by the hand out of that house
and my aunt's life. The last thing Minnie Campbell thought was that she had made a mess of her life.
M'mum knew real love and a sense of accomplish-
ment. All of us kids adored her as we did our dad.
Thanks to them we grew up with a sophistication
most people lack—even later in their lives. In that

free-wheeling boardinghouse atmosphere in which I was raised, I grew up without prejudices. Exposed as I was to all kinds of life-styles, I became very accepting of people. I never learned to fear other nationalities because I *lived* with them, lunched with them, sat on their knees. People were people, and among them some were good, others bad, but the goodness or badness had nothing to do with race, creed, or color."

Because of her eclectic upbringing, she finds the attention given to her mixed heritage and marriage in this country unnecessary and annoying. When she states, "I do not feel black any more than I feel white but only feel human," it is not an Oreo-cookie cop-out but the words of one raised in special circumstances by special parents. She dislikes being classified by color and thinks of the practice as "an American social disease. . . . It is labels that keep us apart from one another. The black-is-beautiful movement is currently at its peak in England but I am somewhat at odds with it. Not the thought—black *is* beautiful—but with the brother/sister aspect of it. *Nobody* becomes my brother or my sister through a shared skin tone. I will not like, let alone love, someone because they are also black. For me loving someone and being together with him or her has nothing to do with color but is about who that person *is*. I see that it is different here; how the terrible injustices blacks have had to face in this country have necessitated a banding together, a creation of a family feeling in order to survive. But that has not been true in England even with its undercurrent of racial hostility. There have always been laws to protect minorities—laws that demand racial equality and make it mandatory for blacks to have the same freedom, advantages, and opportunities as whites."

Although sincere, she is naïve. Earlier she has admitted her father was denied work because of his blackness. She has also stated that her mother was disowned because she married a black man. Obviously then, laws cannot be enforced on the mind. Nor can they always be put into practice. Had her parents' financial difficulties not been predicated on color, she would not have been forced to leave school at fourteen to learn a trade. But because her family struggled and because they had the foresight to realize she too might struggle someday, she was gently maneuvered from her dreams of singing to the more practical reality of hairdressing.

Music began for her at age three when at a talent school recital she was pushed on stage. Liking the results of her singing, she also had to be pushed off. As a child when schoolteachers asked "And what do you want to be when you grow up?" she would answer, "A singer" and to their arched eyebrows which bespoke of a skeptical "Oh, yeah?" she would say, "Yeah! Oh, yeah!" Her mother, until apprenticing her daughter to the local hairdresser, reinforced her daughter's desire by taking her from one audition to another. Even when Cleo shoved her musical dreams under a hairnet to pincurl-and-wave, she was "auditioning" at parties at which her brother would arrange for her to sing. Throughout her other *professional* life—from hairdresser to milliner and on to cobbler and pawnbroker—she "starred" at local sweet sixteen parties and their like.

And suddenly she was married. She no longer remembers exactly when, only that it was "a silly marriage although George was a nice enough man, a really good bloke with whom I should have lived but not married. But in those days a good girl—and I was a *good* girl—didn't live with a man unless she was a tart. M'mum would have had m'head. As it was, if I lingered past a respectable hour Saturday nights, she'd have the police out looking for me. George was my passion but it was mainly physical. He never agreed. He thought we weren't all that bad together—that if we just hung in, the marriage could work. I didn't think we had enough together as people to make it worth fighting for. Sex is lovely when with the right man but there is more to a lifetime relationship than just sex."

She does not deny that John Dankworth was a contributing factor to her marriage's collapse. "When I realized I fancied John, I knew my marriage was over. I'm strictly a one-man woman and when I find I'm fancying some bloke I'm not married to, the relationship I am part of is in trouble."

Theirs was hardly a classic case of love at first sight. The first two years of their association, "we barely said hello to one another, although now that I think of it, I always fancied John," says Cleo.

"Damned if I knew," he responds. "She always looked and acted very married." As Cleo's marriage floundered, they began "seeing one another." Marriage, however, was not proposed by Dankworth. "Cold feet, mainly," he explains. "I didn't see me as the marrying sort."

Until she decided to divorce George regardless of what decision Dankworth made, it was a difficult time for Cleo. "But I knew I had to leave." Simultaneously she also knew she had to leave Dankworth's band. Although it was not a calculated move to force Dankworth's hand, it did that nonetheless. "I called Cleo ostensibly to wish her luck, fully confident that marriage was not for me, and ended the conversation by asking her to marry me. Of course she had the damn good sense to accept my proposal to become Mrs. Dankworth but she would not accept the other role, that of my group's singer. Instead she went on to become the toast of London."

"The toast of what? You must be kidding," she interjects. "I wasn't the toast of anything. I made a modest splash . . ."

"It was a deafening roar," he insists.

"A *splash*," she continues, "in *Flesh to a Tiger*, a play that had a modest run in London theater. It was a good bit of luck. I had never acted before and I'm sure the only reason I was hired was because the producers tired of interviewing. I was the first of a hundred and one girls they had seen who actually had what the part called for—a West Indian background."

"She was brilliant," says Dankworth. "I always say of Cleo she started at the top and worked her way sideways." He is not putting her on. The "stuff of greatness" that he first saw in her twenty-five years ago he is still in awe of. She, however, takes "this supposed great talent of mine for granted. I just don't see me or it as John does. Not that I'm humble about what I do. I sing well. I know that. And I am always professional but . . ." She leaves the sentence in midair. "Actually John is the one with the major talent—the musical genius. People in England think they are being snide when they whisper he is really my Svengali. But that's true. He is. His taste in music, his creativity—they are the forces that combine with my voice to make my work fun and successful. John is the one with the drive. Fame is his dream—for me, not for him. I don't have that dream—that driving need today. Music is my love. It has been a major part of my life *all* my life. Music unifies our marriage. It also solidifies it. Music is the language we speak in harmony. In other words, music, not money or fame, is my joy. I love to sing. I *need* to sing and I'm sure I must have ego needs that keep me in this blooming business but since I have never been analyzed, I don't know what those needs are. I have never felt nor do I feel neurotic, though I may be. I don't feel a desire to be loved by masses. I am content and know I have been very fortunate in life. I knew love as a child and I feel loved as an adult. The only conflict I ever suffered through other than the divorce from George was that involving me—my role as wife and mother. When the kids were but tots, I would torture myself thinking as I worked on stage or in television studios that I ought to be home acting like a proper mother.

But when I did that, it was an utter disaster. Within the week my children got to hate me; my husband got to hate me; and I got to hate me. I'm just not very good at housewifery. I'm best at singing and at being married to a man who understands that his lady would not be at all happy if he expected her to stay home and iron his shirts."

"As you can see from this ragged rag I'm wearing," says Dankworth, offering his shirt as evidence.

The properly disdainful look she casts in Dankworth's direction barely covers the smile she is trying to hide. "Actually I'm a lady who needs to be married and who needs to have family. In truth, I see more of my kids than many nine-to-five working mothers do. When I am home, I am *really* home and so happy to be with my children that they glow from it—as do I. I guess it is not about quantity of time spent with children but the quality of that time. It would not have been good for them had I been forced into full-time motherhood. It is better for children to have a part-time mother who is happy than a full-time one who is disgruntled."

She thinks, mixes some instant coffee, and smiles. "You know, there is nothing missing in my life. I feel quite complete, thank you, although I wouldn't mind being a millionaire."

"A most noble ambition," interrupts Dankworth. "It runs in the family. Her father, at eighty-five, is still rushing about Edinburgh trying to prove he is the proper heir to the royal Stuart family's fortunes."

"And if he does, you don't get a penny for being such a Doubting Thomas," she cautions as he laughs. "Oh, wouldn't it be loverly to be that rich," she says, "to be really stinking rich!"

When reminded that if she climbs that staircase to superstardom, she will undoubtedly be rich beyond the Stuart treasure, she says, "Oh, but it wouldn't be the same. I'd have to work for it and that's no fun. No, let John work for it. He enjoys that. Me? I'll sit back and watch, be encouraging from the background. Isn't that what a proper wife should do, dear?" she asks Dankworth.

He throws his hands up as if in defeat and as he mutters "totally incompatible, totally," she giggles.

CHAPTER THIRTY

JOYCE BRYANT

PART I - THE BEAUTY IS BLACK!

Her nightmares began in Brazil. As did her depressions. They followed her to New York, where the woman hailed in the 1950's as "the black Marilyn Monroe" would inexplicably become hysterical at premieres and parties and be led, near incoherent, to her sky-high Manhattan-chic apartment. There, the nights held hidden terrors . . . voices that urged her to the windows. "Press-and-push," they crooned. "Press, push, and peace will come," they promised. One night she was found, huddled on the floor of her bedroom near an open window, one hand stretched toward the promised peace.

Her voice—that miracle of a four-octave ranged instrument—began to falter. A tonsillectomy was performed. Complications arose. Do not sing, advised the doctors. But a manager insisted she "honor" her commitments. "Honor" is often a five-letter word spelled m-o-n-e-y. Within weeks, while appearing at the Apollo Theatre, she collapsed. Her throat felt as if jagged glass were being scraped against it. "Make her *honor* the engagement," commanded her manager of a doctor. "It is only possible if I spray her throat daily with cocaine," advised the doctor, "and that might make her an addict."

"I don't give a damn what you have to do; just make her sing!"

She was lying on a bed, behind closed bedroom doors, when she heard her manager speak those words. "No, that isn't him," was her first thought. "It cannot be" was her second. "Oh, God, don't let it be!" was her last. And she wanted to die. But she didn't. The Joyce Bryants of this world do not die easily.

Joyce Bryant did not take cocaine but she did "honor" her Apollo engagement. She gave the patrons "a fashion show"—wearing those famous skin-tight, clinging dresses that had made her "a black sex symbol" and whispered words of love to her audiences. The day after she closed, Joyce Bryant packed a single bag and closed the door on a life she could no longer live. Although she had earned upward of a million dollars from '49 to '54—maybe more, maybe less, she never knew exactly—she left with but $2,000 to her name. A day after her departure her former "friends" descended like so many vultures on her lavish apartment and stripped it. But Joyce Bryant didn't care. She wanted to leave behind everything that reminded her of who and what she had been. She discovered, of course, that she couldn't—not then, not now. But in 1954 Joyce Bryant—or what was *left* of Joyce Bryant—flew "home to Mama." Today, at fifty, after a long, arduous odyssey that has taken her on well-worn rocky roads down which too many have traveled, Joyce Bryant has come home to . . . Joyce Bryant. No longer does she wish to "leave behind" the girl who once was. The woman who now *is*, Joyce Bryant, reclaims all she has been and makes no excuses for mistakes made.

Today's Joyce Bryant lives once again in a sky-high Manhattan apartment but it is neither chic nor her own. It is a borrowed sublet. There are no ermine and pearls to garnish what was once the most heralded "black body" in show business. Thus there are no vultures hovering about. Gone, too, is the $5,000 per week she once earned. But the beauty is still there. Earthy and yet elegent, like the mythical phoenix, this beauty is rising from her *own* ashes.

For reasons she cannot explain, her blackness was always a source of pride to her. Yet in Oakland in 1927, when she was born, and later in San Francisco, where she was raised, the phrase "If you're black, stay back" was the slogan of the day and oddly enough mainly with her black peers. She rejected their prejudice just as she would later reject those of whites who could not fathom black-as-beautiful and thus would label her as "Eurasian."

She was one of eight children; her father was a chef for the Southern Pacific Railroad and she remembers that "he was seldom ever home. We were poor when we should not have been. He earned good money but . . . he gambled and he womanized. During his absences my ma would rail against him but she would always take him back. He would stay a day, a week, a month, and then . . . gone, leaving her pregnant. I never understood. She was miserable . . . always miserable, hating this man—or so she said—and yet always having his babies—babies she'd be too miserable to care for. I was a mama at eight. Not my own—hers. I was always a mama. I never had time to play after school—when I went to school, which wasn't often, as Mama was sickly and just hung around. I never had any friends. I was too busy being mama. And she . . . she could never muster up enough strength to do much of anything except pray. There was always that. She was, and thus we were, Seventh-Day Adventists. We were God-*fearing* folk."

She was an isolated child who loved to listen to opera, "moody music," her family called it. She also painted and sculpted but no one—not her mother or her teachers—took her talents seriously. "I was a girl and a black girl at that. We weren't supposed to have talent. We weren't supposed to have dreams. We weren't supposed to have *anything* or *be* anything. We were *colored* girls and we had no expectations for our lives. I was raised to be nothing, but a 'good' nothing or God would punish me." At this early age she began to dream "of getting away!"

At nine she was hired out as a family helper. This of course was in addition to her own household chores. At ten she was enrolled in the Seventh-Day Adventist school. Had she attended regularly and had not the "urgings to escape" already rooted within her, she might have achieved *their* goal for her. She might have become a nurse, then a teacher, and finally a minister's wife, where she could do both His and his work.

Religion was the dominant and dominating factor in the Bryant household. "Although we had precious little of anything else, we had an abundance of Adventist rules—no pork, no shellfish. No skating or dancing or any kind of socializing where you might meet corruptors . . . spoilers. Of course drinking was taboo, and sex . . . sex was the greatest of all evils, a 'thing' reserved for procreation. I grew up believing in evil and in the two things with which I was threatened: reform school and hell."

She never speaks of love in her childhood, or of warmth or acceptance. And never is there a hint of childhood fun . . . of being a child. At nine she reached puberty and her sex education consisted of her mother's bark: "Never let a boy kiss you or you might become pregnant." At ten, on a church hayride, a boy kissed her. Terrified but unable to voice her fears, she became anxious. She stopped eating and sleeping. Weeks later she fainted in class. Under interrogation at the nurse's office she wailed: "I'm pregnant!" Horrified, the authorities summoned her mother. Outraged, the woman stormed, "How did it happen?" Joyce, through sobs, told her of the hayride kiss. "And then?" raged the woman. The child was confused. "And then nothing." It was then the child was given fuller facts of life, but with the admonition not to let "it" happen, not unless she wanted damnation and hell.

At fourteen Joyce Bryant eloped. She married a young merchant seaman from whom she fled on their wedding night when he asked for his "rights" as her husband. Upon her return home she was forced by her father to "honor" the marriage contract. But she couldn't no matter how hard her husband tried. "I couldn't yield to this sinful thing he was trying to do to me. And then that is how I saw it . . . as something *he* was trying to do to me against my will. It was wrong, wasn't it? It would be awful, wouldn't it? Wouldn't it? Wouldn't it? Stop! Stop!"

The marriage was annulled.

That same year, with an older cousin, Joyce was permitted to visit an aunt in Los Angeles. There, experiencing a new permissiveness, Joyce went to the movies for the first time. And to a roller rink. And with her cousin, to the Cobra Club, one of those then typical piano bars in L.A. where people sat around and sang along with the trio. When Joyce "sang along," the others stopped. Unaware, she continued. Upon conclusion there was applause. Lots of applause. The manager instantly asked her to sing for the night. She refused. Show business is the devil in disguise. He offered her twenty-five dollars—more money than she had even seen. Get thee behind me, Satan! An hour later after "breaking it up," the manager offered her a hundred dollars a week to be the star singer. "A hundred dollars a week!" she echoed in disbelief. "Okay, one hundred twenty-five but not a penny more," he countered, thinking she had found his offer unacceptable.

Joyce Bryant's mother would have found his first *and* his last offer unacceptable, which is why it was decided not to tell her the truth. Although Joyce loved performing, a part of her that had been programmed, "felt sinful." Her mother helped the feeling grow when she said upon learning of Joyce's true whereabouts: "I'll pray for you." According to Joyce, "she was afraid I was harboring evil within me and that evil would now cohabit with the evil that was all about me."

In truth Joyce was well protected from "the evil" by the Sepianaires, the trio that performed at the club. They sheltered her. One of its members, an older man, became her first lover. "I lost my virginity but not the feeling that sex was repugnant. I was sixteen and unable to give that man anything other than my body. There was no pleasure in sex. Just disgust . . . guilt. I was turned off. Although he was good to me, I eventually had to leave him, and thus the club. The relationship had grown too complicated for me to handle. What did I know of being a woman?"

She had no difficulty in obtaining work. She had a local reputation and thus worked steadily in a series of small clubs that grew progressively bigger as her following grew. She lived alone and pretended she liked it. She did not drink. She did not date. "I was living the clean life. I thought that was *my* choice. Actually I was living *their* choices. I was doing what a good, *colored* girl from an Adventist family should do. And I was so lonely and alone, it is a miracle that I did not fall victim to the pimps and pushers that hung out at every club I played. And they hit on me . . . tried to recruit me into the ranks. How I hated them even then!"

No one understood better than Billie Holiday. The late singer had entered Joyce's life unobtrusively. She came to hear Joyce sing and stayed to become her friend. There was an enormous mutual need that Joyce now recognizes. "Billie would big-sister me. It was as if she saw in me all she had been. She also saw in me all that could be her. She wanted to save me that. I was so young . . . so vulnerable and so confused. Billie wanted to spare me from what could be . . . from what *was* for her. She knew guys were hitting on me—*wrong* guys, and she was afraid I'd get messed up.

"Funny, Billie would come to see me wasted . . . strung out on Lord-only-knows-what but she would always talk straight. It would break my heart to watch her struggle. She'd fight to kick the habit and to break free but . . . there was always someone there to hook her again. Crazy ole Billie couldn't save her own life but she was like a tiger with mine. She wanted to keep me straight. It was because of Billie— what she said and . . . what she became—that made me resist every kind of drug for years." For years but . . . not forever. Later, like the woman Joyce Bryant admired and loved, she too would become . . . "strung out on Lord-only-knows-what."

She was nineteen when the "big break" came. Pearl Bailey, upon taking ill during her engagement at Ciro's, then *the* place in Hollywood, recommended Joyce as a fill-in. The Ritz Brothers, a comedic institution, upon seeing her, brought her east to the Riviera, then the poshest of nightclubs built onto the side of a cliff along the Hudson River and overlooking Manhattan. She arrived for the engagement as an up-and-coming singer. She concluded it as . . . a rising star and yet . . . by her religious values, a fallen one.

In one of those twists of fate for which there is no explanation, a designer named Zelda took it into *her* head to design for Joyce *sight unseen*. She arrived at the Riviera, carrying two of her creations. "They were skin-tight, fish-tailed, backless, and cut to the nipples in front. They fit perfectly. I remember looking in the mirror and thinking 'Who is that woman with the body? And with such a body.'" There was no more thought on Joyce Bryant's part. She wore those dresses and others like them and thus began the black Marilyn Monroe label. Thus also began the war within her . . . the fight for the control of Joyce Bryant. "Sometimes, not often, I would hear my mother saying: 'To this you have come!' It was the voice of judgment. I had become what she had feared: a purveyor of sex. I often wonder . . . did I want to hurt her? Was I rebelling against her and the rules of my childhood? Those answers are still hidden. And in those years I didn't . . . seek-and-ye-shall-find. I was Joyce Bryant, rising black phenomenon . . . the toast of the town."

And she was. Walter Winchell, then one of the most powerful of syndicated columnists, rhapsodized about her daily. Lee Mortimer, also a columnist of national note, wrote of her in '52: "In time, or in no time, Joyce Bryant will rank with Ethel Waters, Sarah Vaughan, and Lena Horne." A year later Mortimer wrote: "We can now say Miss Bryant is on a par with that illustrious trio." She was *that* talented. Her salary soared to $5,000 plus per week. In addition to her nationwide nightclub appearances, there was national television. Prominence and propositions. Nonstop lights . . . cameras . . . action. Always action. Too much action. She began having trouble sleeping.

The "sexy" and "catlike" Joyce Bryant is how she was described. Without knowing exactly when or why it began, she used more sex than song in her act. Which was strange. She could sing but "The bombshell couldn't detonate in bed," she admits. "I was all promise and no fulfillment. In retrospect it seems ironic. It *was* ironic. Worse, it was schizophrenic. On one hand I was being heralded . . . rewarded for being this 'sex thing' while on the other I was rebuked . . . chastened . . . reviled by my upbringing."

But she continued on what seemed a merry way. To compete with Josephine Baker, with whom she was appearing at a benefit, she painted her hair with silver radiator paint. It became yet another Joyce Bryant trademark. Although Ms. Baker took Ms. Bryant's little "trick" quite well—"she sort of smiled and tilted her head as if to say 'touche' "—her hair did not. Within a year of its painting, it fell out.

She laughs, a full from-the-gut chortle, recalling "the incredible things the young will do." But the laugh dies quickly as she remembers other "incredible things." In the early fifties many of the major nightclubs throughout the country were controlled by the syndicate—as were many of the more popular singers of the day. Joyce was an independent but "If you wanted to work, you had a drink with the boys when they asked." They asked . . . frequently. She was often seen about in the company of gangsters. "You didn't say no if you valued your life—professional and otherwise." But she insists she was never "one of the girls"—but a companion. "There was never a time that I was not treated with respect. But then I was a lady. That 'hot number' on stage cooled it off. Julie Podell would tell the 'boys' who hung out at his Copacabana: 'Hands off the Duchess'—that's what they called me—' 'cause she's just a kid.' I was never bothered—not physically."

But she was emotionally. Although she tried not to think about her "command performances," sometimes events forced her to. Like the evening she was to be mobster Mickey Cohen's dinner date. As he went for the car, she went for her wrap in the dressing room. Seconds later, in the club's parking lot, Mickey Cohen's body was polka-dotted with bullets. "That could've been me," she thought then. It almost was, a short time later. Appearing at the Copa, she noticed the same "gentleman" sat ringside each night. One evening "I made a grave mistake: I said thank you to him as I left the stage. He took it as an invitation." He sent flowers, champagne, a TV set—which in those days was tantamount to a diamond. Then one early morning shortly after her late show, her phone rang as she had raised the sheets and lowered the light. "It's Ralph," announced a voice. Not knowing any Ralph, she said something curt and hung up. Within five minutes she knew a Ralph. Her admirer kicked open her front door and then proceeded to beat up on her. Only when he felt she had gotten his message did he cease. He threw a handful of bills on her dresser and said: "Get your door fixed and be ready for me tomorrow."

Hysterical, she called her manager, who called Julie Podell. While she was hidden away for a few days, Podell used his "influence" to call off Ralph's ardor. Actually it was "Little Augie" who did the cooling off. In a little heart-to-heart, he advised Ralph that both his legs would be broken off if he didn't leave the Duchess alone. Joyce was not bothered—not physically—again. Unfortunately "Little Augie" was. His body, or what was known as his "remains," was recovered at Kennedy airport. Simultaneously Joyce returned to her apartment to find *everything* missing. A week later all was returned with a note that read "Love, Ralph."

She was now not sleeping regularly. "But I'm a nice girl," a voice within her would plead as she would lie in bed. "I truly am," it would insist. But another would be equally insistent that "nice girls and gangsters do not mix." Still other voices chastised her "vulgar display" of sex. And other voices called her a liar "and some less charitable told it like it was," she says. "They screamed . . . 'cockteaser!' "

To quiet her voices, she began taking sleeping pills. Although she had resisted for years the pushers who promised nirvana on heroin, cocaine, and other exotica, she hooked herself . . . with of course a little help from her friends. When she told her manager about her sleeplessness, he recommended a doctor who would "help" her. All her manager's doctors "helped" her, she says—to a dozen different varieties of sleeping pills. And when she slept too soundly, her associates—her "friends and family," which is how she then thought of them—found her other doctors who prescribed other pills. Within months she was like her late friend, like Billie, strung out and in constant need of fixing. Only today does she say bitterly: "Isn't it strange how none of those 'friends and family' ever said: 'Hey, Joyce. Maybe you're doing yourself some

kind of bad trouble?' Well, why should they have?"
she snarls bitterly. "I never missed a show, did I? I
worked regularly!

"No one ever knew I was a pill junkie. No one.
Not even me. I didn't face it. I didn't have to. I was
too busy being *that* Joyce Bryant. And she was something. A star! And . . . a lady. I was always a positive image. Black women were proud of me. I was
making it in a white world . . . moving in spaces
and places maybe only Lena had moved in. And I
was proud of me. In some sort of daze . . . some sort
of cloud, I moved through my life a black woman
who knew nothing of the black experience. I wasn't
born or raised in the ghetto. My upbringing was
more Adventist than black. From the time I entered
show business I was called 'beautiful' as though 'beautiful' was not something a black woman could be. I
was treated like exotica . . . a black rose. And once
famous, I, as a black Marilyn Monroe, moved in
white, not black circles. I lived in apartments *I*
couldn't rent as a black woman but which whites
could rent for me. I never played 'black clubs'—the
dives where some of our greatest black entertainers
performed—because I was never considered a 'blues
shouter' or a jazz singer. I was a black singer of white
songs. Prejudice was something that brushed against
me and which I flicked away like some bothersome
fly. Vegas didn't permit blacks to live in the hotels
where they performed or to socialize with the patrons.
I would be angry—for *me*—but not for my people.
Even in 1950, when I was first—when I opened Miami
Beach to black entertainers—I did so as a goddess
. . . a black goddess who was above their cross burn-
ings and *above* a black experience of which I knew
nothing. Yes, I was black, and proudly so, but it
wasn't the kind of pride I would someday develop."

Then she dated mainly white men—not out of malice toward blacks or an identity confusion—but
through social necessity. In the upper echelons in

which she traveled in the fifties there were stop signs
for black men. The system made them nearly invisible.
And the black men she had known in L.A. and did
see in New York were "mainly rounders . . . pimps
and pushers. I hated them—hated what they did to
their black women. And awful as the truth is, most
black female singers then were married to such
men—'tough guys' who would deliver the Saturday
Night Special to their working women—beat up on
them as they messed with their money and their
minds. Then I hated the black man. I was too
young—we *all were* then—to see how he was a victim
of white society and his own inner rages. Yet—and
isn't this the damnedest thing!—I always wanted to
marry a black man."

All of her men invariably proposed. "I was never
just a 'plaything.' How could I be when my 'play' was
all on stage? None of my relationships—and they were
always that—was ever about sex. One-night stands
were impossible for me. I had to care for . . . love
a man before I could entertain the idea of a physical
relationship. I was such a fake. A damn good actress
too, I guess, because people *bought* the idea of my
sexiness. Why, some members of my church went so
far as to label me 'a lewd performer.' And others
wrote that I 'seethed' sex. That's the word *seethe* as in
seething with anger. Which is what the psychiatrist I
eventually saw suggested was what I was doing on
stage. He said I might just as well have used a
machine gun as wear the gowns I did. He said I was
killing men with 'the promise.' And when I thought
about it—*really* thought about it—stripped away my
own blinders, I remember a part of me thinking as I
appeared 'catlike' on stage . . . sexy . . . revealing: 'Your eyes may shine and your teeth may grit
but none of this woman's body, boy, is you gonna git.'
Only now do I realize how angry I must have been at
men—and in particular . . . my father. Only now
do I understand why it was impossible to react to a

man sexually—to *allow* him any kind of control over me. I hated men. I blamed them for the babies of this world—babies *I* had to take care of. My father came and went as he pleased. I hated him for that, not thinking . . . not then, that it takes two to make a child. Between what I learned from my mother and the church and what I felt about my father and his relationship with my mother, no wonder I was frigid. And that's what I was . . . frigid, like in ice. And what an irony that my biggest hit record was 'Love for Sale.' Banned in Boston it was, and later . . . just about everywhere else."

She laughs but without amusement. "I never enjoyed my career," she says abruptly. "I was a pound of flesh and an object of lust in my last years and I've no one but myself to blame. I created the masturbatory fantasy that I had become. But why? That question still plagues me. It was not that I had lacked talent. My voice . . . my singing . . . moved people. Even through the image, *I* was felt. And yet," she says bittersweetly, "they always thought I was what I sang—the lady who had been around when in truth I had been less around than most women in this or any life. Folks didn't know that, though. My own kept writing . . . 'We're praying for you, Joyce. We're praying you will find your way back.' Today, my mama is *still* praying for me to find my way back to do *her* will.

"But then when she would write that she was praying for me, I felt as if a knife had been drawn through me. She made me feel my 'mortal soul' was in danger. I would feel so sinful . . . so guilty that I would run . . . anywhere, to avoid feeling my feelings. I had no peace. Pills brought sleep or pills brought energy but they never brought peace. I felt so alone. There was no one to talk to. Why was that? Why is it none of us gals who were big then were close? What is it we feared from one another? I was such a Big Star but I was such a little girl. Such a frightened little girl. Billie was a lonely soul but Joyce topped her."

It was carnival in Rio and one night, while attending a party in the Brazilian resort city, she heard a voice say: "I don't give a damn where I go from here or what I do next. Nothing matters . . . least of all me!" She was horrified. Who would say such a thing? Her horror turned to terror as she realized the voice she had heard speaking was her own. And thus began the nightmares . . . the depressions . . . the suicidal tendencies. Back in New York, through the haze of drugs, she sought counseling from her church. The Adventist minister listened and then intoned "My child, you are in conflict." She laughed. "Tell me something I do not know. Tell me whether or not I'm going insane."

Joyce Bryant believes hearing her manager say give-her-anything-but-make-her-sing prevented her from truly going crazy. She distinctly remembers hearing his words. Through the pain of realization that these "friends-who-were-family" were nothing other than business associates who did *not* care about her personally ("and that was the bitterest pill to swallow") came the decision to quit . . . to walk away from her fame and its fortune. Because "they" had her doubting her sanity, she saw a psychiatrist. After a month of reliving her nightmares, of speaking about her terrors . . . her conflicts . . . guilts, she discovered she was not crazy—that if anything she was finally taking a giant step toward facing reality.

Reality faced her instantly. There was to be a price paid for leaving one's *own* career. " 'But you're taking food from my baby's mouth,' said my manager. 'You are causing us undue hardship,' he added. So I gave him everything. I accepted a check for $2,000 and left, never thinking to examine the books—to demand an accounting . . . to see exactly what I had earned and what I was worth. He pleaded poverty—*my* poverty, insisting we had spent heavily in order to make more in the future. He was right about one thing. About one thing he didn't lie. I didn't have any money. He and other 'friends' who called me 'baby' and 'sweetheart' saw to that. Money-money-who's-got-the-money? They had it but I had nothing. A fortune had been made and a fortune was gone. With it the illusion of 'friends' and 'friendships.' "

> The vultures in this business—the agents, press agents, lawyers—are in it to make a buck and they make it by using you. Okay, that's cool. That's how business is. But when they're not straight with you, when they pretend to competencies they don't have, when they hang out with you 'cause you're a *meal ticket* and not a friend like they say, that sucks!
> MELBA MOORE, *Essence*, JULY 1973

Hers was an old story. Only today does she see a new wrinkle to the plot: her responsibility. "I shirked it. I was young and wanted only to be concerned with the creative end of the business—my music. Which is why I gave others power of attorney. *They* signed the checks—sent money to my family, who accepted the checks while they continued not to accept *me* and the way I earned my money. *They* had it all. I retained nothing. I trusted them because I *had* to trust them. I could not think for a second they were using . . . or misusing me. Don't you see? I couldn't be *that* alone. Someone had to be there for me. Someone had to care."

> Leave the managing or the accounting to others? If I do, I get ripped off. Even if I'm standing there, I can be ripped off.
> ROBERTA FLACK, *Essence*, NOVEMBER 1974

Shortly after she left the business, she was to discover not just the price but the *hidden* costs for not being "that alone." The Internal Revenue Service hit her with a bill for back taxes totaling $60,000. When she pleaded poverty, they issued a warrant for her arrest. At the ensuing investigation she was to learn "my earnings had been invested wisely—for others, not me. I was left holding a very empty bag." She would have received a jail sentence had not the arresting officer testified in *her* defense. "He saw my shock . . . my horror. He knew I was a victim . . . a truly unaware, trusting, and stupid victim. But that victimization was *nothing* in comparison to what I suffered at the hands of the IRS. They treated me like black cunt," she says with open hatred. "They wanted to know if I were a junkie. They implied that I had been . . . and probably still was . . . a hooker. They wanted to know to which pimps had I given my money . . . which male prostitutes had I paid for my pleasures. They made the most disgusting, vile accusations and insinuations. They tried to make me feel like slime in the gutter. I hated them for it. I hated them long after they became convinced I hadn't a dime and got off my case. But that took years and in those years they made me pay in ways far more costly than money."

She remembers it all well. Too well. Her body is contorted with anger that she does not express. It sits on her face and eats its way into her skin, making her grimace, causing her to look old and ugly. And then she relaxes. She remembers back to early 1954, the one suitcase clutched in her hand and the going home to her mother.

"I was so needy and so hoping she would accept me . . . tell me I was worthwhile. I even hoped she would love me. 'Ma,' I said. 'I'm never going back to that life. Not ever. Ma, I can never be *that* Joyce Bryant again. The price for her fame had been too high and I just can't pay it anymore.' "

Her mother's response was to whisk her off within *a day* to a church who "thought of me as a coup for the cause. Much had been made of my show-business defection by the nation's press. The church administrators descended . . . swooped down on me instantly. They hit on me right away. Sign on the dotted line for salvation. And I did. But then I would have signed *anything* that would ease my shame and guilt for what I had appeared to be—for the life I had seemingly lived and for the image that had been mine. It seemed I was so heavy . . . so weary of carrying so much guilt for so long a time. In thinking back, I cannot remember a day in my life until recently when I didn't feel guilty just for being *me*.

"So . . . within two weeks of my return I turned my back on one life and entered another, only to later learn I was leaving one exploitation for another. I answered 'the call' because I wanted to be embraced . . . protected . . . loved. I wanted God's forgiveness . . . His love. I wanted Him to clutch me to His heart. I wanted . . . I wanted . . . I wanted . . . from every pore that breathed I wanted. I needed peace and I hoped . . . prayed . . . I would find it as a missionary for Adventism."

Thus in the autumn of 1954, as she approached her twenty-seventh birthday, Joyce Bryant joined the Adventist school in Huntsville, Alabama, where she believed she would one day earn His love, a degree that would name her "minister" and the peace she so desperately needed.

ON THE ROAD TO SALVATION

> Being black means being beautiful . . . yes. But it also means struggle and pain. Every black woman knows of that struggle, of the pain . . . of the search to find herself and her place among others. . . . Eventually you learn self-love must come first in life.
>
> ARETHA FRANKLIN,
> *Essence,* DECEMBER 1973

Joyce Bryant "nestled in the bosom" of a large extended family in Huntsville. No longer was she the black sheep. The sinner had seen the light and repented. And repented. And . . . repented.

She repented at "meetings" throughout the South, "witnessing" before thousands who came to see this new Joyce Bryant. It was another kind of show business. This time she was center stage and starring for Christ. Her studies were secondary to "the cause." Not by choice but by *their* command. She was needed, she was told . . . needed to bring others to salvation. As a wandering minstrel, a singing evangelist, spreading "the word" on the conversion circuit—"a recruiter who believed in my Lord and my church"—she saw hunger, the empty-belly type, for the first time. She saw blacks in rags—although they thought them to be clothes—who were cold . . . sickly. She would look at these people disbelievingly. Later she would say to church administrators: "But how can we offer spiritual guidance to people who need creature comforts?" And her "teachers" would respond: "But you speak of earthly matters which are of no spiritual importance."

And when she did speak of matters that were of "spiritual importance," it seemed to her they were of no *earthly matter* to her teachers. In impotence she witnessed racial injustices within her church. "Our white ministers would refuse to baptize a black child. They would turn them away . . . send them to their 'own' church. I was outraged. Prejudice in the guise of Christianity? It's unthinkable, I protested. I argued with the church administrators. 'Why cannot blacks "join in Christ" with whites? God does not see color and we, his emissaries, should be preaching His love and not man's hate!' They didn't hear me. They *couldn't* hear me. They made me feel I was not worthy—sinner that I had been—of being heard. And something within me began to fester."

Yet she continued evangelizing. As she did, she

traveled the South and "experienced blackness—my own and those who lived with dignity but little else." Her mind wanted to disbelieve the poverty, the sickness, and the fact that many hospitals would refuse care for the critical because they were black. A new "seething" began to take place. This time she put her anger to work. She organized fund-raisers for blacks to buy food, clothing, and medicine wherever she was appearing for her church. She met Martin Luther King and whenever possible joined in his efforts to bring "creature comforts"—among other things—to . . . "my people." The struggle for civil rights was her struggle, just as she believed it to be the struggle of *all* people who believe in God and country. Her church disagreed. When she confronted them, asking that they take a public stand against discrimination and segregation, they refused. Again their reasoning was: "But these are of earthly matters and thus of no spiritual importance."

She experienced just how "earthly" it was and simultaneously just how spiritually important on a train ride from Washington to Huntsville. A roomette had been purchased for her, as blacks then could not buy such "luxurious" accommodations on public transportation in the South. Since roomettes are small, their occupants, other than at bedtime, usually leave their doors open to prevent claustrophobic feelings. Across the aisle from Joyce was a southern "gentleman" imbiding generously from a bottle of Southern Comfort. At first his advances, although obvious and unwelcome, were not threatening. But the drunker he became, the more obscene and demanding were his "requests." He did not like the fact that she did not feel compelled to obey his wishes. "Bitch!" he muttered. She closed the door. Thus began a pounding that lasted halfway through the night. And as he pounded, he screamed: "Open this goddamn door, nigger gal. I want to fuck you."

At 6:00 A.M. Joyce opened her door to permit the

porter to take her and her luggage into the Chattanooga station where she was to change trains for Huntsville. There stood her admirer . . . naked. He tried to force his way into the roomette *and* her and was prevented only by the porter, who grabbed her in one hand, her luggage in the other, said " 'scuse me, sah," and fled. Her "friend" followed. With frightening calm he advised, "You're soon gonna find out what we do to uppity niggers down here, gal." And she might have had not the porter called a local black family who arrived en masse to drive her first to their home and then . . . all the way to Huntsville.

She weeps as she tells the story . . . weeps for the kindnesses of strangers who risked their own lives to save hers. This was a new kind of "extended family" experience. The tears stop abruptly. She is again "seething." In her own home she cannot find a place for herself. She is that agitated. "Everyone in that car of the train heard that pig assault me. Everyone! But not one person intervened and not one person would have even had he raped me. And I knew as I stood on that train platform in Chattanooga that he could make good his boast—that I could 'soon find out what we do to uppity niggers down here.' I *knew* not one person, white or black, would come to my assistance. He could murder me and there would be no interference. The law in those years was not there for black people. The law then was to protect whites from us blacks. I suddenly realized on that rotten morning in Chattanooga what it meant to be black. I had no status. Worse, I had no protection. At that second I recognized how vulnerable *all* black women are. We are *all* potential victims to be raped by the system. Never have I felt as naked . . . as *unprotected,* as I did at that moment. And you cannot know what that feels like unless you have been a black woman living in the South *prior to* the law-enforced . . . liberty and *justice* for all. And I thought then . . . how dare my church say that racial injustice is of no spiritual importance? How is one's spirit to survive when it is so hideously attacked?"

> The air we breathe as blacks is poisonous, polluted by hatred. We choke on it. It defeats us sometimes. But being called "nigger" doesn't bother me as much as knowing there is that evil sitting up there like a cloud over this country. It is the cumulative unseen pressure that destroys blacks' confidence and their lives. It is the subtle crippler.
>
> RUBY DEE, *Essence*, JUNE 1976

Joyce Bryant, then, had many questions, few answers, and even less resolve. Although she would continue to voice her objections to church dogma, she would also continue to remain "nestled" but not comfortably nor quite within her church's bosom.

"Where would I have gone had I left?" she asks herself today. "To whom . . . to what? Then it seemed I had so few options. And then . . . too, I needed to belong *somewhere*. I was happy belonging to God—doing for Him. I hadn't yet learned that one must someday learn to belong to oneself. Then it was still . . . what-would-Mama-say."

So she continued her work, giving spiritual solace to others but "receiving precious little myself. The original aim was for me to become a minister. That meant classes . . . studies . . . formal education. But that never happened. I was 'needed' elsewhere, they said. So it was never about *me*—my needs—but about what I could do for them. Which is why I had said previously that I had left one exploitation for another.

"Still there were benefits," she says, "wonderful benefits . . . miraculous ones, actually. As I began truly giving of myself to others I'd meet as an evangelist or . . . as a black woman, I began changing. I found within me qualities I never knew I had . . . like kindness . . . compassion . . . love. And I had these things to give! Slowly I began to like myself. In the 'liking' came a self-respect. And it showed. I was happy. I no longer needed pills of *any* kind to make my life work. I could face up to life and . . . to me. In fact, I wanted to . . . needed to. Suddenly I had this desperate need to talk about all I had been through. Not as a 'witness' but as a woman. I needed to *be with* another person—to pour out my grief and my anger about who I had been and *why*. I wanted to make sense of the past.

"But there was no one within my church who was available to me," she says wearily. "My teachers had all led such 'circumspect' lives and didn't want to hear of mine. And I was told not to 'taint'—that was the word *they* used!—my fellow students. My story might be a corrupting influence, I was told.

" 'Take your burden to the Lord and leave it with Him,' I was advised," she says bitterly. "They couldn't understand how one sometimes needs a human hand to touch . . . to hold—that there are moments in a person's life when *human* compassion and understanding is needed. A woman often needs another woman to share what has been a woman's experience. And a woman often needs a man's comfort to see her through.

"But there was no such comfort. Not physically. Not emotionally. Not sexually. Certainly not sexually. There is only abstinence among Adventists. Including the two years prior to my joining my church, I was celibate for thirteen years! Can you imagine, for thirteen years I denied . . . closed off what had already been a denied and closed off part of me? Today I regret that. Oh, Lord, do I regret that! And how I regret that I wasn't stronger to deal with the men I met within my faith. I kept company with two: both of whom ultimately, upon 'looking into their spiritual hearts,' found me unworthy—*sinner that I had been*—of their love. Although God could forgive, it seems many members of his flock could not."

She speaks with a bitterness and an anger that she recognizes today but that she could not feel then. Nonetheless, even then she began to "drift" from her church. As the years passed, she moved from evangelizing to teaching Bible classes in Washington. She continued to organize fund-raisers. At such an event she was again "discovered" as she sang church music. An audition was arranged with a local vocal coach of reknown who advised she had potential as a classical artist. She became his scholarship student and within three months was singing with the Washington Symphony, often performing the "moody music" she had so loved as a child.

Joyce Bryant never considered "breaking" with her church. It is a word she still does not use. Yet, break she did. The event that caused the schism is still painful. She became aware that she was the subject of ugly gossip within her church. Worse, she became aware the officiators of her church believed the gossip that was started by an Adventist minister who accused Joyce of being a lesbian and of having stolen his wife.

Joyce Bryant was horrified. Once, in her past, because of her inability to totally relate sexually to men, she asked herself if she might be a lesbian but "because I never felt attracted to women, I knew I was not." But the rumor was accepted by her church as fact. This "scandalized" her. She called a conference of administrators and ministers, including the one who had accused her. She confronted him and under her cross-examination, he broke down and admitted his lie. Yes, his wife had run away, the man wept, but with another man. And he, so ashamed, found it easier to say it was with a woman than admit another man was fulfilling something in *his* woman that he could not.

To her amazement, as the man sobbed, his brothers

in the church went to his side with comfort and forgiveness. "Not one came to me," she says. "They elevated him in his grief . . . in *his* repentence. They
praised God. To me . . . they gave nothing. To me
they said: 'Joyce, you are strong. You can bear this as
you have borne so many other things in your life.
Forgive this man. He needs your love.' I heard but I
could not believe what I was hearing. Where had
been *my* forgiveness all these years? Why was I still
deemed so 'unworthy' if forgiveness is the key to the
kingdom. And I looked around at all those men and I
realized . . . I am a woman and in their eyes that
counts for very little."

A black woman's fight is both racial and sexual.
Both are painful and enraging.
DIAHANN CARROLL, *Essence,* JULY 1974

As she sits rigidly erect, Joyce Bryant resembles an
architect's paste-up of a building—held together with
spit and Scotch tape. "No one cared . . . gave a
damn about the damage done to me," she says quietly. "Why should they have? Hadn't I been a 'lewd'
woman in the past? Once lewd, always lewd, no?
. . . *No!*" she screams. "I was not that person anymore. Only they couldn't see that. And it took me
eleven years to realize they never would see that.
There was no forgiveness or human understanding
within my church. So I cut my cord . . . left them
but I never cut my ties with God. Not ever. It is man
who makes religion a 'God awful' thing. Not God. He
is about love . . . forgiveness. But I saw precious
little of that among his emissaries. I could not believe
how unforgiving they were—how prejudicial, un-
feeling. It is so horrible what man does in the name
of God!"

Abruptly the spit and Scotch tape give way and the
"building" collapses. Joyce Bryant is sobbing. She
tries to speak. ". . . last year . . . my brother . . . he

was so terribly ill. . . . A letter arrived . . . from an
Adventist . . . a friend of his . . . and that man . . .
that man *wrote* . . . 'If your sister would mend her
ways . . . maybe God will spare your life.' . . . And,"
she screams, ". . . and . . . my brother died. He died!
He died! He died!"

The "building" is reduced to rubble. She clutches
herself and alternately cries and chokes. And then
. . . abruptly, the "building" resurrects. Piece by
piece, it reassembles. "How dare that man," she rages.
"How dare he or anybody speak for God? How dare
he or anybody judge me? God and God alone is my
judge. What horror religious zealots make. If they be
what God and religion be about, then I am going to
hell. And sooner I be there than with people like
them!"

MOODY MUSIC

> With all my heart, I believe to live life is to
> dream it first. One is never too old to make that
> dream come true.
> MAYA ANGELOU, *Essence*, AUGUST 1975

At thirty-eight, Joyce Bryant allowed herself to
dream. At an age when many are established or entrenched or . . . settled in lives that are fulfilling
or not, she began anew. Where this courage . . .
this *tenacity* to hang in and hang on stems from can
only be a subject of conjecture. In 1965 Joyce Bryant
is *in*formally educated . . . a student of life who
has flunked several courses. Yet she refuses to be a
dropout. She refuses to be part of a passing parade.
An eternal optimist? . . . A believer? . . . Whatever, Joyce Bryant decides to pursue a childhood fantasy. She will be a concert/opera star.

Washington encourages her. Notices and word-of-
mouth for her performances with the symphony and
other local concert groups bring her to the attention

of Rosa Ponselle, formerly one of opera's more revered prima donnas turned vocal coach. She too takes Joyce as a scholarship student. Joyce studies and sings at the Tivoli Restaurant, where her accompanist is sometimes Roberta Flack. Heard by a New York impresario, she is asked to audition for the New York City Opera Company, and upon doing so is awarded a three-year contract. She is *near* ecstatic. But only *near*. Her family is again praying for her. True, they are not as upset as they would be had she returned to nightclubs—"opera had class . . . stature in their eyes. It was less sinful"—but they are still disapproving. Joyce Bryant is too honest to pretend that their disapproval, even at the age of thirty-eight, did not bother her. But she pushed *their* doubts aside and pursued her dream, "filled with hope." The one thing that filled her with fear was not professional.

"I was unsure of me as a woman," she says. "I was fearful of resuming a social life. I did not know if I could be a woman to a man." She found she could and . . . she could not be. There was a man "a wonderful man . . . a wonderful black man, and I had fun and comfort with a man for the first time in many, many years. He was kind and he was good. I think I loved this man and if he did not love me, he nonetheless gave me feelings of love. I felt he liked me . . . me, the person as well as me the woman. I never felt used for his pleasure. He made me feel good about us. But . . . I still could not feel good in bed. Not that I felt bad—which is an improvement—but, I couldn't feel what women were beginning to talk about publicly in the sixties . . . the joy of sex. I found it was easier to . . . leave 'the life,' leave the church, leave Washington, than it was to leave guilt. So I was to continue without sexual gratification. Although this was painful, I was not unhappy with this man. Quite the contrary. Had he been available, I would have married him. He gave me something precious and I thank him for that."

During their affair she needed "something precious." Her professional life was not what she had hoped. In her three years with the opera company, she performed but one major role—that of Bess in *Porgy and Bess*. Her reviews bordered on brilliant and initially that was pleasing. Eventually, as it became apparent she was not to be given the opportunity to play Mimi in *La Bohème* or the title role of *Aida*, reviews that spoke of her "seething passion" as Bess became bothersome. Not only did history seem to be repeating itself but why, she wondered, was she only being allowed to portray a "seething" black woman. The possible answer was unsettling to her.

Also unsettling was the attitude of her coworkers in the company. Mainly they were steeped in the traditions of opera. "To them I was an outsider—a saloon singer turned legit . . . and an *old* saloon singer at that. And an old, *black* saloon singer to boot. They were elitists. They felt I had not paid my proper dues. Whether I had the needed capabilities or not didn't seem to matter. They were terribly polite to me and always their prejudices came across as professional. After all," she says with mock sincerity, "they were arty liberals, so how could their prejudice be anything but professional."

> When you are black, always the proof is needed—always the credentials to show you belong. When you are black, yesterday's high C is just that—yesterday's. Always the need to prove that black is good; black is capable.
> LEONTYNE PRICE, *Essence*, FEBRUARY 1975

By mutual agreement her contract was not renewed at the New York City Opera. In an interim period she "starred" at cosmetics counters at Lord & Taylor, a New York department store, demonstrating beauty products for blacks. "What we don't do to survive!" she says jokingly. But it is no joke. Yet she fails to see that. Despairing but not desperate, Joyce Bryant "starred" at Lord & Taylor until she *could* star at the Los Angeles Civic Opera, which then led to nine months of concertizing in Israel followed by tours with the Italian, French, and Viennese opera companies.

"They were glorious times," she says in glorious tones. "I was allowed to sing a wide variety of roles. Europe treats its black women so differently than America. Had I stayed . . ." Her voice fades. But she could not, or would not, stay. It is more than her saying, "But I could never be an expatriate—I am an American." It is about wanting to make it in her homeland and believing she could. She was forty-three and arrived back in the States with a portfolio filled with triumphant European reviews. They were her proof that she was indeed a classical artist and not an old, black saloon singer.

Not one of the major companies in America would employ her. She was considered "too old" to first be establishing herself as an American name in opera. "This is a business," she was told, "and we only invest time and money in the young because *they* pay off . . . in time." She was without "time"—so they said. "And yet my voice was stronger . . . better than it had ever been. 'Listen to me!' " she would beseech. They would not. "I came home believing I had a future in opera. I could not find one person to share that sentiment. I found myself at a dead end . . . yet another. 'What next?' I thought. 'Where to to and what to do?' "

Perhaps because she was forty-three and at yet another "dead end," Joyce Bryant didn't look before she leaped. When she met a "reputable businessman" at a New York party who had been a former fan of that *other* Joyce Bryant and was willing to put his money where his fandom once was, she agreed. And why not, she reasoned. There were no strings—sexual or otherwise—attached. And wasn't he a wealthy merchant, written of frequently in society columns? Didn't he fly about in privately owned jets to such "privately owned" climes as Palm Springs and Palm Beach? He would manage her; she would sing. Between their efforts, he promised, she would regain stardom. His sureness of manner impressed her. Even more impressive was the sprawling apartment on Central Park West in which he established her at $1,000 per month—three of which he paid in advance. "Get the best arrangers and musicians," he told her. "Get together the best act possible!" he enthused.

There was no way her act was to top his. She picked up *The New York Times* one morning to see her "manager's" face on page one. He had been arrested for fraud . . . among other things. Later he would be tried, convicted, and jailed. She worried from her penthouse perch—worried about the name— her own!—on the three year lease. Since she hadn't a dollar, let alone a thousand of them, her worries were not unfounded. Yet the management company was "understanding," she says. "They let me stay on" and on, and on. "But they believed in me!" she persists. To the tune of $14,000 in back rent.

In retrospect Joyce Bryant knows rental agencies are not known for their "understanding." But she also knows she could not make a move. Although unaware of it then, she was in shock. She had commissioned arrangements, bought gowns, and found she could pay for neither. Again it seemed "there was no place to go. And there wasn't!" she says vehemently. "I couldn't get work in the States—and I was trying! Just to keep body and soul together, I took work in Puerto Rico, Bermuda, and Jamaica."

It is sometimes said "God writes straight but with crooked lines." Were it not a matter of *basic* survival, Joyce Bryant would not have been in Jamaica. And had she not been in Jamaica, trying to "keep body and soul together," *her* body and soul might never have come together.

"I saw this man and for the first time in my life knew lust," she says, not claiming he was the "love" of her life. "No, he was my passion," she says simply. "It wasn't just that he was a handsome man—I've known handsome men all my life—but the *first* to make love to *me*. He cared about my pleasure before his own. Actually his pleasure seemed to be in pleasing me . . . in all ways. He was the consummate lover . . . giving . . . warm, sensuous. I felt alive in his bed. And never used. Never that. We were together. For the first time I felt how lovemaking can be a sharing yet an erotic thing . . . an expression of caring yet passion . . . even with love. At forty-seven I experienced my first orgasm. I *came* alive! I cried. I laughed. I cried-and-laughed. Oh, the joy! The joy of knowing *at last* that I was a woman—a whole woman, and a desirable one at that. And I was near guiltless. How could sex be wrong when it made me feel beautiful—when it helped me to achieve unity—with myself and with another. And in Jamaica, in addition to the joy, I knew anger . . . rage. To have been denied such a feeling to such an age seemed criminal to me. It still does. But the miracle remains . . . at last the bird was set free."

The "bird," however, was faced with "feathering her nest." Her lover belonged to her Jamaica experience. In New York she was faced with the day-to-day job of . . . survival. Again, at a party, she was seemingly rescued when a group of businessmen, also professing to be former fans, offered to showcase her talents in their soon-to-be-opening West Side cabaret. In January 1975 their party-promise became a New York event. Joyce Bryant opened at Cleo's to rave reviews. She closed—"was fired"—five days later because she was losing money for the house. Patrons didn't eat or drink during her set. The owners wanted an artist but they didn't want an "artiste"—someone who would be in competition with their true motives for being in business—money. That very same week

Joyce's "understanding" landlord put her things on the street. She was evicted.

She fled to a friend's house in New Jersey where "I hung on by my fingernails. A part of me wanted to let go . . . to collapse . . . break down. A stronger part screamed: 'Girl, you haven't come this far in life to drown-and-die in New Jersey!' So I got up . . . again, and got a job selling 'sundries' in a notions store. I let the word get around that I would take any kind of singing job that would get me away . . . anyplace . . . but someplace where I can sing."

She was booked on one of those cruise ships that go nowhere for seven days and then spend seven more returning from where they haven't been. She didn't care. She sang for her supper . . . literally, and used her time alone to close the wounds that seemed to never have the time to heal. Although originally committed for just a two-week sail, Joyce Bryant, with "nothing else to go toward" sailed on to nowhere for three months "until the day came when I knew if I didn't get off that boat, I'd die at sea."

It was April 1975, when Joyce Bryant "landed" in Los Angeles. She was broke. Although food and shelter were but five hundred miles away at her mother's, "I could not face the . . . I-told-you-sos . . . the recriminations." Thus began a hand-to-mouth existence. She stayed at a friend's for a week—another friend's for a month; still another's for a day . . . an hour. Her last "residence" was with a friend whose occupation turned out to be . . . male prostitute. When he turned his tricks, he would turn her out . . . by necessity. With no place to go, she would haunt hotel lobbies, keeping warm and one step ahead of the Los Angeles police who hustled hustlers and bums out of lobbies and into cells. She walked the Sunset Strip, often through the night, particularly when the rent was due and her friend was working overtime to meet it. In her heart she felt as if "I had

finally come to the place I had always feared—hell.
And it was here on earth. It was a day-to-day living
hell and I cannot tell you why I kept on walking
through it . . . why I would not die. But I
wouldn't. I just kept going. I just did."

I guess I had more strength than I knew. To
have survived! A miracle. To have survived the
last years of my life . . . *just to have survived*
. . . a miracle . . . a miracle.
CICELY TYSON, *Essence*, FEBRUARY 1973

SEETHING WITH PASSIONS

Sure things were tough for us black ladies but we
made it, didn't we? We're still here, aren't we?
SARAH VAUGHAN, *Essence*, OCTOBER 1974

Joyce Bryant is still here; "here" being the winter
of 1978 in New York City. "Here" is also Joyce Bryant considering bankruptcy now that the "understanding" rental agency is suing her for monies owed.
And with interest. "Here" is a place in time where if
viewed on the motion-picture screen, one would
sneer, "Only in Hollywood." Her life often resembles
contrived melodrama. But . . . hers is real and not
reel life. This all happened to one woman and the
whys-and-wherefores are best analyzed by psychologists, sociologists, and . . . Joyce Bryant.

And Joyce Bryant is still here! With hope . . .
and with a growing insight that she finds disturbing.
Much of her past she had "laid to rest" . . . or so
she had thought. But speaking of her life has rattled
skeletons in her own closet. It has also shaken free
her anger. She is once again unemployed and resentful of that fact. "I'm a good singer. I should be working!" she says emphatically. Sharing that opinion is
someone firmly in her corner. More than a "second,"
he is, at times, punching it out for her—being what a

manager should be—competent and concerned. He is the by-product of one of her late-night Sunset Boulevard strolls.

She remembers the evening. Her friend was tricking and as she was aimlessly walking the Strip, she ran into her onetime accompanist, George Rhodes, who was now employed in the Sammy Davis hierarchy. Rhodes recommended Joyce as a guest for *Sammy & Company*, then a syndicated TV series. Davis gave her a shot in August of '75. In November, the day after the show aired, she received a message that a Jerry Purcell wanted to meet with her. She recognized his name, knew he was a respected manager of talent. It resulted he respected her talent and offered to manage her. Numbly, she agreed. When he asked: "Where do I reach you once [not if] I get you work?" she started to lie—to say something oblique like "I'm between apartments" but the words stopped and the tears started. In seconds the truth of her existence poured out in dam-bursting proportions. Purcell listened. When she was through, he took keys from his pocket and placed them in her hand. "For however long it takes to get yourself together, use my home," he said.

She is moved, even today, in the telling of the story. "For years I would comfort myself with the rage I felt toward men—how they had victimized me. There is a safety in that kind of anger as it prevents you from looking at yourself . . . from what truly happened. Yes, some men had used me. But I had *used* myself. *Mis*used myself. For years I laid blame and responsibility on others. No more. There were choices . . . I made them. Many were bad but I didn't know that. I didn't want to know that or . . . a great many other things about myself. But in the safety of Jerry's home—and when there is finally safety one can look deeply into oneself—I knew I had to look to myself for answers before I looked to others. I'm still looking. And when I can afford it, I'll look deeper . . .

with an analyst. And that will be soon. 'It' will happen for me again. It's all out there. It always has been."

Purcell has been "out there" finding it. In January of '76 he negotiated for Joyce to reopen at the under-new-management Cleo's. The press and public reaction prompted a summer opening at the posh Rainbow Grill "high atop the world at Rockefeller Center. And that's how I felt . . . high, atop the world," she recalls. "Earl Wilson was there. And *The New York Times*. Celebrities . . . friends . . . fans. It was a joyous occasion. There was a standing ovation and I cried. I remember thinking 'I'm home and I'm so very glad to be home.' "

The reviews promised "she is going to have a sensational second career." They stated she "has added maturity and luster to her considerable attributes of former years." They said . . . and they said. Yet today, other than for numerous auditions for Broadway shows and an album that she plans to produce with Lloyd Price, Joyce Bryant sits and waits with her added maturity and luster.

She is not waiting complacently. "Why hasn't it happened for me? Why?" she demands agitatedly. "There were such brilliant reviews at the Rainbow Grill. I really thought . . . this is it. But it hasn't happened. Sometimes I wonder, because I once rejected this business am I now supposed to crawl on my belly before I'm once again accepted? Well, I refuse. I'll never crawl."

She rattles off the names of superstars who "knew her when" and asks "Where are they now? Why won't they answer our phone calls? 'Cause I'm fifty, that's why!" she spits out. "Too old to come back. Too old for *any* woman in this business to get work on national television. And that's not sour grapes. In the fifties, when I was a legend, Patti Page was 'the Singing Rage'—the biggest thing to hit the recording industry. Rosie Clooney was also turning out one hit after another. They're both my age. Do you see them on *Donny and Marie*? And Ella . . . Sarah . . . institutions. The greatest of the greats. How many 'specials' do you see them on? We *older* ladies are put out to pasture. Well I'm not ready to graze. I want back in. My life is not over . . . it's *fiirst* beginning."

There is more truth than bravado in Joyce Bryant's words. *Her* life may indeed be just beginning as she finally frees herself. It is not a completed process. "I never learned—not till 'a moment' ago—to think for myself . . . to believe in me. I trusted blindly because I didn't trust myself. I needed to believe others loved me because I didn't. I was not raised to either trust or love myself. I don't think any of us little 'colored' girls were then. My mother meant me no harm. She didn't know women had options. And most women didn't. We were slaves even though slavery had been abolished. I think now we enslaved ourselves and passed that enslavement on to our daughters. We didn't dream. Why bother? Dreams don't come true. But prayers do . . . or so it was thought.

"I didn't dream as a child—not in the sense of *dreaming* to be 'something.' No, I dreamed about getting away . . . breaking free—but away from rather than toward anything. I was never comfortable with all the rules and restrictions of my childhood. But I never had any real ego strength to support my rebellion. I accepted I was evil because I wasn't strong enough to realize that maybe I was just different and that there is no one way that works for all people. But I've mended my bridges. Today my family still prays for me and I . . . well, now I pray for them as well. My mother is a good person, a product of her times and her environment. You can give no more than what you have received. She loved me as best she could. My father too. Yes . . . him too. All men make mistakes. I sided years ago with my mother because she was there . . . and I could *see* how she felt. I never knew, until I asked, what prompted his behavior. But whatever their mistakes, the fact remains they must have given me something good because . . . I'm still here!"

She is "here" alone, however, and for the first time in her life she is aware of being discomfited by her aloneness. She has found "late in life" that "I do not need a man's money—I'll always get by; history has proven that—but I now need the physical and emotional presence of a man. Oh, I could mouth all those 'liberated words'—how I've always taken care of myself and how I could live alone and like it—but . . . the truth remains I live alone and I *don't* like it. I would like someone else to help Joyce Bryant take care of Joyce Bryant. And Joyce Bryant admits, emotionally, she needs to be taken care of."

She is having difficulty meeting men. "What woman my age isn't?" she asks. "It's just like show business, past a certain age and a woman is thought to be washed up. Men my age prefer younger women. And the younger men I date want things from me they should have received years ago from their mothers. And I'm not interested in being a man's mother. I've waited too long to be a man's woman. And I can be that now. I am first full-blown . . . ripe . . . more woman today than I have ever been. And maybe that scares some men. Which is ironic. Why were men less threatened by the 'sexy mama' I portrayed than they are now a real woman with real needs? Is it being *too needy* to want companionship, honesty, tenderness . . . love?"

> Everything I ever wanted I have now. I'm fifty years old . . . a beautiful woman with her beautiful husband and her beautiful family in their beautiful home. That's what most of us women have always wanted.
>
> SARAH VAUGHAN, *Essence*, OCTOBER 1974

* * *

"I need to work but I *must* love . . . be loved," says Joyce Bryant tremulously. "I want to marry. Ready at last. And I would still like to marry a black man but . . . I will not wait for him any longer. I can't. I can't wait for him to realize that this black woman does not wish to deball him. I only want his touch . . . his tenderness. Why is it black men seem to have such difficulty in showing their soft sides? What prevents them from being their true selves? I want a man, a man of *any* color, who will not be afraid to let me lean. And I want that man to be able to lean on me when he needs to.

"Sometimes I'm so afraid I'll dry up from age and the waiting," she says. And then shuddering, she adds: "I don't want to spend the remaining years of my life without someone. I know of no woman my age who wants to grow old alone. This woman, *me!* needs, once again, *human* comfort, as spiritually I am never alone. Not ever. There is always Him. That has never changed. Only I have changed in my relationship to Him."

She nods her head in agreement with her thoughts. "I once felt I was letting down the thousands of people—and there were that many that I brought to Christ—when I returned to show business. But I don't feel that way anymore. They must find their own way just as I have had to find mine. I recognize, at last, that I have a *God-given* talent. When I sing for people today, I feel more like a missionary than I ever did. Now . . . I am truly selling love. My singing today is about what I feel for Him, for you, and . . . miracle of miracles, for me. Singing is sharing me in my most meaningful way. It is giving the sum total of Joyce Bryant to others. It is about my "seething passions'—be they anger, pain, or joy. It is about my womanness. It is about the *fact* that I may not have a dime but I'm a very rich woman. I have me and I have Him. I am about His business just as I am finally about my own."

Joyce Bryant rises from where she has been sitting and moves toward a window laced with ice. She looks out and beyond and searches the Jersey coastline silently for several minutes. Her eyes are aligned with the exact spot where once rose the Riviera and a child/girl emerged as a "black Marilyn Monroe." But not quite. Marilyn is dead; by her own hand, some say, and she is not. Slowly Joyce Bryant turns away from that window and moves toward others facing downtown Manhattan and Rockefeller Center where the Rainbow Grill is "atop the world." When she turns back into the room and into her life, tears stream down her face.

"I've visited my life. I've seen where I've been, what I've done, not done, and what's been done to me. I see the highs and I feel the lows. It has been a very long journey but I see it now with no shame and no regret. It was all His design . . . His plan for my life. It all had a purpose. I've come full circle. I'm here in this life *to live* and . . . to do His work. I will do both. And . . . I will never be shat upon again!"

Yes, it is twice as hard for a black woman to survive. But . . . it is not in the black woman's nature to be flushed away. Nor will she be spat upon. Those are her dividends after her years of oppression.

LENA HORNE, *Essence*, MAY 1973